divine right in legacy of 30 years war +
religious wars of 16th + _____ down
+ destruction made people
optimistic

Karl Marx

political
Enlightenment + Revolution

reaction to   utopian   reaction
    it   socialists
man is   liberals   perfectibility   strict
  an   continuation   of   1815 - 1830
criminal   of it   man   loose
strict order reform   change   1830 - 1848
+   change men   environment   Revolution
discipline then change   change men
must prevail environment   reaction strict 1848-
man won't   ↓   to loose 51 - 70
change   ↓   Revolution
    ↓   nationalists   internationalists
ultra   ↓   ↓
nationalists your tribe   all men
            is your   are brothers
trust only   brothers!
those who are
like yourself

German Avant-Garde in 30's

Brecht, Benjamin, Bloch, Kafka, Kraus
    theatre essay   essay   novel feuilleton
                              scholar
            vs
        French Avant Garde in 30s

Bataille, Surrealists, etc Leiris, Hyppolite
        issues, attitudes, concerns, methods
betw. mystical experience + dialectical materialism
        subjective self + history (real world)

ISAIAH BERLIN

Karl Marx

His Life and Environment

Fourth Edition

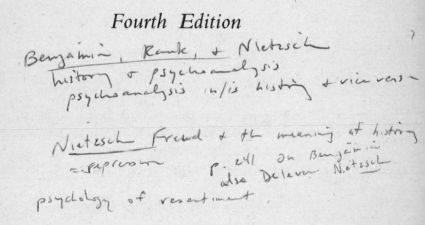

Benjamin, Rank, + Nietzsch
history + psychoanalysis
psychoanalysis in/is history + vice versa

Nietzsch Freud + the meaning of history
= repression   p. 241 On Benjamin
*   also Deleuze Nietzsch*
psychology of resentiment.

OXFORD LONDON NEW YORK

OXFORD UNIVERSITY PRESS

OXFORD UNIVERSITY PRESS
Oxford   London   Glasgow
New York   Toronto   Melbourne   Wellington
Nairobi   Dar es Salaam   Cape Town
Kuala Lumpur   Singapore   Jakarta   Hong Kong   Tokyo
Delhi   Bombay   Calcutta   Madras   Karachi

First edition published in the Home University Library, 1939

Second edition, 1948

First issued as an Oxford University Press paperback, 1959

Third edition, 1963

Fourth edition, 1978

printing, last digit: 10 9 8 7 6 5

Library of Congress Cataloging in Publication Data

Berlin, Isaiah, Sir.
    Karl Marx: his life and environment.
    Bibliography: p.
    Includes index.
    1. Marx, Karl, 1818-1883. 2. Communists—
Biography. I. Title.
HX39.5.B4   1978b   335.4'092'4 [B]   77-26943
ISBN 0-19-520052-7

Printed in the United States of America

To my parents

Contents

PREFACE

I WROTE this book almost forty years ago. My original text was more than twice its present size, but the requirements of the editors of the Home University Library were strict, and I was persuaded to shorten it by eliminating most of the discussion of philosophical, economic, and sociological issues and concentrating on intellectual biography. Since then, in particular after the social transformation of the world after the Second World War, a vast expansion of Marxist studies has taken place. Many hitherto unpublished writings by Marx saw the light; in particular the publication of the *Grundrisse*—the rough draft of *Das Kapital*—has vitally affected the interpretation of his thought. Moreover, events themselves have inevitably altered the perspective in which his work is seen; its relevance to the theory and practice of our time cannot be denied even by his most implacable critics. Such issues as the relationship of his ideas to those of preceding thinkers, especially Hegel (in the light of new interpretations of Hegel's own doctrines which have come thick and fast); the emphasis on the value and importance of his early 'humanist' writings, stimulated in part by the desire to rescue Marx from Stalinist (or, in some quarters, Plekhanov's, Kautsky's, Lenin's and even Engels's) interpretations and 'distortions'; the growing differences between the 'revisionist' and 'orthodox' expositions, principally in Paris, of the doctrines of *Das Kapital*; discussions of such themes as that of alienation—its cause and cure—especially by neo-Freudians, or of the doctrine of the unity of theory and practice by neo-Marxists of many denominations (and the sharp reaction to ideological deviations by Soviet writers and their allies)—all this has generated a hermeneutic and critical literature which by its sheer and rapidly increasing volume dwarfs earlier discussions. While some of these disputes resemble nothing so much as the controversies of his erstwhile Young Hegelian allies, whom Marx accused of wishing to exploit and adulterate the dead body of Hegelian doctrine, this ideological debate has

added a good deal to knowledge and understanding both of
Marx's own ideas and of their relation to the history of our own
times.

The fierce controversies, especially during the last twenty
years, about the meaning and validity of Marx's central doctrines
cannot have left any serious student of Marxism wholly unaffected. Consequently, if I were writing about Marx's life and ideas
now, I should inevitably have written a different book, if only
because my view of what he meant by such central concepts as the
science of society, the relation of ideas to institutions and the
forces of production, and the correct strategy for the leaders of the
proletariat at various stages of its development, have undergone
some change. This is so, even though I should not now claim to be
acquainted with the entire field of Marxist studies. When I was
preparing this book in the early 1930s I was perhaps too deeply
influenced by the classical interpretations of Engels, Plekhanov,
Mehring, on which Marxism as a movement was founded, and
also by the admirable (never reprinted) critical biography by E. H.
Carr. But when I began to revise the text, I realised that I was
engaged on writing a new, more comprehensive and ambitious
work which would go far beyond the purpose of this series. I
therefore thought it best to confine myself, in successive revi-
sions, to correcting mistakes of fact and emphasis, qualifying
over-bold generalisations, amplifying one or two points treated
in a cursory manner, and adopting relatively minor changes of
interpretation.

Marx is not the clearest of writers, nor was it his purpose to
construct a single, all-embracing system of ideas in the sense in
which this could be said to be the aim of such thinkers as Spinoza
or Hegel or Comte. Those who, like Lukács, steadfastly maintain
that what Marx wished to do (and in their view achieved) was a
radical transformation of the methods of thinking, of arriving at
the truth, rather than the replacing of one set of doctrines by
another, can find plenty of evidence for this in Marx's own words;
and since he insisted throughout his life that both the meaning
and the reality of a belief consisted in the practice which expressed
it, it is not perhaps surprising that his views on a number of
central topics, and those not the least original or influential,
are not set down systematically but must be gleaned and inferred from scattered passages in his works and, above all, from
the concrete forms of action which he advocated or initiated.

It was natural that a doctrine at once so radical and so directly allied to, indeed, identical with, revolutionary practice, should have led to a variety of interpretations and strategies. This began in his own lifetime and led to his famous and characteristic remark that he was himself anything but a Marxist. The publication of early essays by him, which tended to differ in tone and emphasis, and, to some degree, subject-matter (and, some would say, on central issues of doctrine) from his later work, vastly increased the area of disagreement among the later theorists of Marxism. And not only among theorists: it led to fierce conflicts between and within socialist and communist parties, in due course, between states and governments in our day, and has led to realignments of power which have altered the history of mankind and are likely to continue to do so. This great ferment, and the ideological positions and doctrines that are the theoretical expressions of these battles, are, however, beyond the scope of this book. The story I wish to tell is solely that of the life and views of the thinker and fighter in whose name Marxist parties were in the first place created in many countries, and the ideas on which I have concentrated are those which have historically formed the central core of Marxism as a theory and a practice. The vicissitudes of the movement and the ideas that he originated, the schisms and the heresies, and the changes of perspective which have turned notions bold and paradoxical in his day into accepted truths, while some among his pre-communist views and *obiter dicta* have grown in prominence and stimulated contemporary debate, do not, for the most part, belong to the scope of this study, although the bibliography provides guidance to the reader who wishes to pursue the further history of this, the most transforming movement of our time.

The (inevitably selective) annotated list of recommended works available in English has been brought up to date by Mr Terrell Carver, to whom my thanks are due, both by the omission of some which have been clearly superseded, and by the addition of a good many new titles to the list of books, the sheer variety of which alone is an indication of the vastly increased range both of knowledge and of ideas and novel approaches in the field of Marxist scholarship.

I should also like to express my gratitude to two friends: Professor Leszek Kolakowski for reading the text and making valuable suggestions by which I have greatly profited; and Mr G. A. Cohen for his penetrating critical comments and his encouragement, both of which I greatly needed. I should also like

to thank my friend Mr Francis Graham-Harrison for revising the
index, and the officers of the Oxford University Press for their
exemplary courtesy and patience.

Oxford, 1977   I.B.

Note to Third Edition

I HAVE taken the opportunity offered by a new edition to correct
errors of fact and of judgement, and to repair omissions in the
expositions of Marx's views, both social and philosophical, in
particular of ideas which were neglected by the first generation of
his disciples and his critics and came into prominence only after
the Russian Revolution. The most important of these is his conception of the relation between the alienation and the freedom of
men. I have also done my best to bring the bibliography up to date
(although I have had to confine myself to secondary works in
English) and should like to thank Mr C. Abramsky and Mr T. B.
Bottomore for their valuable help and advice. I should also like to
thank Professor S. N. Hampshire for re-reading the first half of
the book, and for suggesting many improvements.

Oxford, 1963   I.B.

Note to First Edition

MY thanks are due to my friends and colleagues who have been
good enough to read this book in manuscript, and have contributed valuable suggestions, by which I have greatly profited; in
particular to Mr A. J. Ayer, Mr Ian Bowen, Mr G. E. F. Chilver,
Mr S. N. Hampshire and Mr S. Rachmilewitch; I am further
greatly indebted to Mr Francis Graham-Harrison for compiling
the index; to Mrs H. A. L. Fisher and Mr David Stephens for
reading the proofs; to Messrs Methuen for permission to make
use of the passage quoted on pages 142–3; and, most of all, to the
Warden and Fellows of All Souls College for permitting me to
devote a part of the time during which I held a Fellowship of the
college to a subject outside the scope of my proper studies.

Oxford, May 1939   I.B.

1
Introduction

Things and actions are what they are, and their consequences will be what they will be: why then should we seek to be deceived?

BISHOP BUTLER

No thinker in the nineteenth century has had so direct, deliberate and powerful an influence upon mankind as Karl Marx. Both during his lifetime and after it he exercised an intellectual and moral ascendancy over his followers, the strength of which was unique even in that golden age of democratic nationalism, an age which saw the rise of great popular heroes and martyrs, romantic, almost legendary figures, whose lives and words dominated the imagination of the masses and created a new revolutionary tradition in Europe. Yet Marx could not, at any time, be called a popular figure in the ordinary sense: certainly he was in no sense a popular writer or orator. He wrote extensively, but his works were not, during his lifetime, read widely; and when, in the late seventies, they began to reach the immense public which several among them afterwards obtained, their reputation was due not so much to their intellectual authority as to the growth of the fame and notoriety of the movement with which he was identified.

Marx totally lacked the qualities of a great popular leader or agitator; he was not a publicist of genius, like the Russian democrat Alexander Herzen, nor did he possess Bakunin's spell-binding eloquence; the greater part of his working life was spent in comparative obscurity in London, at his writing-table and in the reading-room of the British Museum. He was little known to the general public, and while towards the end of his life he became the recognised and admired leader of a powerful international movement, nothing in his life or character stirred the imagination or evoked the boundless devotion, the intense, almost religious, worship, with which such men as Kossuth, Mazzini, and even Lassalle in his last years, were regarded by their followers.

His public appearances were neither frequent nor notably successful. On the few occasions on which he addressed banquets or public meetings, his speeches were overloaded with matter, and delivered with a combination of monotony and brusqueness, which commanded the respect, but not the enthusiasm, of his audience. He was by temperament a theorist and an intellectual, and instinctively avoided direct contact with the masses to the study of whose interests his entire life was devoted. To many of his followers he appeared in the role of a dogmatic and sententious German schoolmaster, prepared to repeat his theses indefinitely, with rising sharpness, until their essence became irremovably lodged in his disciples' minds. The greater part of his economic teaching was given its first expression in lectures to working men: his exposition under these circumstances was by all accounts a model of lucidity and conciseness. But he wrote slowly and painfully, as sometimes happens with rapid and fertile thinkers, scarcely able to cope with the speed of their own ideas, impatient at once to communicate a new doctrine, and to forestall every possible objection;[1] the published versions, when dealing with abstract issues, tended at times to be unbalanced and obscure in detail, although the central doctrine is never in serious doubt. He was acutely conscious of this, and once compared himself with the hero of Balzac's *Unknown Masterpiece*, who tries to paint the picture which has formed itself in his mind, touches and retouches the canvas endlessly, to produce at last a formless mass of colours, which to his eye seems to express the vision in his imagination. He belonged to a generation which cultivated the imagination more intensely and deliberately than its predecessors, and was brought up among men to whom ideas were often more real than facts, and personal relations meant more than the events of the external world; by whom indeed public life was at times understood and interpreted in terms of the rich and elaborate world of their own private experience. Marx was by nature not introspective, and took little interest in persons or states of mind or soul; the failure on the part of so many of his contemporaries to assess the importance of the revolutionary transformation of the society of their day, due to the swift advance of technology with its accompaniment of sudden increase of wealth, and, at the same time, of social

---

[1] Anyone interested in Marx's method of composition would be well advised to read the *Grundrisse* (see Guide to Further Reading, pp. 210, 212), which remained in manuscript until 1939 and contains the main doctrines both of *Das Kapital* and of earlier studies of alienation.

and cultural dislocation and confusion, merely excited his anger and contempt.

He was endowed with a powerful, active, concrete, unsentimental mind, an acute sense of injustice, and little sensibility, and was repelled as much by the rhetoric and emotionalism of the intellectuals as by the stupidity and complacency of the bourgeoisie; the first seemed to him, as often as not, aimless chatter, remote from reality and, whether sincere or false, equally irritating; the second at once hypocritical and self-deceived, blinded to the salient social features of its time by absorption in the pursuit of wealth and social status.

This sense of living in a hostile and vulgar world (intensified perhaps by his latent dislike of the fact that he was born a Jew) increased his natural harshness and aggressiveness, and produced the formidable figure of popular imagination. His greatest admirers would find it difficult to maintain that he was a responsive or tender-hearted man, or concerned about the feelings of most of those with whom he came into contact; the majority of the men he met were, in his opinion, either fools or sycophants, and towards them he behaved with open suspicion or contempt. But if his attitude in public was overbearing and offensive, in the intimate circle composed of his family and his friends, in which he felt completely secure, he was considerate and gentle; his married life was essentially not unhappy, he was warmly attached to his children, and he treated his lifelong friend and collaborator, Engels, with almost unbroken loyalty and devotion. He had little charm, his behaviour was often boorish, and he was prey to blinding hatreds, but even his enemies were fascinated by the strength and vehemence of his personality, the boldness and sweep of his views, and the breadth and brilliance of his analyses of the contemporary situation.

He remained all his life an oddly isolated figure among the revolutionaries of his time, equally unfriendly to their persons, their methods and their ends. His isolation was not, however, due merely to temperament or to the accident of time and place. However widely the majority of European democrats differed in character, aims and historical environment, they resembled each other in one fundamental attribute, which made co-operation between them possible, at least in principle. Whether or not they believed in violent revolution, the great majority of them, in the last analysis, appealed to moral standards common to all mankind. They criticised and condemned the existing condition of humanity in terms of some preconceived ideal, some system, whose desirability at least needed no demonstration, being self-evident to all men with normal moral vision; their schemes differed in the degree to which they could be realised in practice, and could accordingly be classified as less or more Utopian, but broad agreement existed between the schools of democratic thought about the ultimate ends to be pursued. They disagreed about the effectiveness of the proposed means, about the extent to which compromise with the existing powers was morally or practically advisable, about the character and value of specific social institutions, and consequently about the policy to be adopted with regard to them. But even the most violent among them—Jacobins and terrorists—and they, perhaps, more than others—believed that there was little which could not be altered by the determined will of individuals; they believed, too, that powerfully held moral ends were sufficient springs of action, themselves justified by an appeal to some universally accepted scale of values. It followed that it was proper first to ascertain what one wished the world to be; next, one had to consider in the light of this how much of the existing social fabric should be retained, how much condemned; finally, one was obliged to look for the most effective means of accomplishing the necessary transformation.

With this attitude, common to the vast majority of revolutionaries and reformers at all times, Marx came to be wholly out of sympathy. He was convinced that human history is governed by laws which cannot be altered by the mere intervention of individuals actuated by this or that ideal. He believed, indeed, that the inner experience to which men appeal to justify their ends, so far from revealing a special kind of truth called moral or religious, tends, in the case of men historically placed in certain situations, to engender myths and illusions, individual and collective. Being conditioned by the material circumstances in which they come to birth, the myths at times embody in the guise of objective truth whatever men in their misery wish to believe; under their treacherous influence men misinterpret the nature of the world in which they live, misunderstand their own position in it, and therefore miscalculate the range of their own and others' power, and the consequences both of their own and their opponents' acts. In opposition to the majority of the democratic theorists of his time, Marx believed that values could not be contemplated in isolation from facts, but necessarily depended upon the manner in which the facts were viewed. True insight into the nature and laws of the historical process will of itself, without the aid of independently known moral standards, make clear to a rational being what step it is proper for him to adopt, that is, what course would most accord with the requirements of the order to which he belongs. Consequently Marx had no new ethical or social ideal to press upon mankind; he did not plead for a change of heart; a mere change of heart was but the substitution of one set of illusions for another. He differed from the other great ideologists of his generation by making his appeal, at least in his own view, to reason, to the practical intelligence, denouncing intellectual vice or blindness, insisting that all that men need, in order to know how to save themselves from the chaos in which they are involved, is to seek to understand their actual condition; believing that a correct estimate of the precise balance of forces in the society to which men belong will itself indicate the form of life which it is rational to pursue. Marx denounces the existing order by appealing not to ideals but to history: he denounces it, as a rule, not as unjust, or unfortunate, or due to human wickedness or folly, but as being the effect of laws of social development which make it inevitable that at a certain stage of history one class, pursuing its interests with varying degrees of rationality, should dispossess and exploit another, and so lead to the repression and crippling of men. The oppressors are threatened not with deliberate retribution on the part of their victims, but with the inevitable destruction which history (in the form of activity rooted in the interests of an antagonistic social group) has in store for them, as a class that has performed its social task and is consequently doomed shortly to disappear from the stage of human events.

Yet, designed though it is to appeal to the intellect, his language is that of a herald and a prophet, speaking in the name not so much of human beings as of the universal law itself, seeking not to rescue, nor to improve, but to warn and to condemn, to reveal the truth and, above all, to refute falsehood. *Destruam et aedificabo* ('I shall destroy and I shall build'), which Proudhon placed at the head of one of his works, far more aptly describes Marx's conception of his own appointed task. By 1845 he had completed the first stage of his programme, and acquainted himself with the nature, history and laws of the evolution of the society in which he found himself. He concluded that the history of society is the history of man seeking to attain to mastery of himself and of the external world by means of his creative labour. This activity is incarnated in the struggles of opposed classes, one of which must emerge triumphant, although in a much altered form: progress is constituted by the succession of victories of one class over the other. These in the long run embody the advance of reason. Those men alone are rational who identify themselves with the progressive, i.e. ascendant class in their society, either, if need be, by deliberately abandoning their past and allying themselves with it, or, if history has already placed them there, by consciously recognising their situation and acting in the light of it.

Accordingly Marx, having identified the rising class in the struggles of his own time with the proletariat, devoted the rest of his own life to planning victory for those at whose head he had decided to place himself. This victory the process of history would in any case secure, but human courage, determination and ingenuity could bring it nearer and make the transition less painful, accompanied by less friction and less waste of human substance. His position henceforth is that of a commander, actually engaged in a campaign, who therefore does not continually call upon himself and others to show reason for engaging in a war at all, or for being on one side of it rather than the other: the state of war and one's own position in it are given; they are facts not to be questioned, but accepted and examined; one's sole business is to defeat the enemy; all other problems are academic, based on unrealised hypothetical conditions, and so beside the point. Hence the almost complete absence in Marx's later works of discussions of ultimate principles, of all attempts to justify his opposition to the bourgeoisie. The merits or defects of the enemy, or what might have been, if the enemy or the war had been other than they were, is of no interest during the battle. To introduce these irrelevant issues during the period of actual fighting is to divert the attention of one's supporters from the crucial issues with which, whether or not they recognise them, they are faced, and so to weaken their power of resistance.

All that is important during the actual war is accurate knowledge of one's own resources and of those of the adversary, and knowledge of the previous history of society, and the laws which govern it, is indispensable to this end. *Das Kapital* is an attempt to provide such an analysis. The almost complete absence from it of explicit moral argument, of appeals to conscience or to principle, and the equally striking absence of detailed prediction of what will or should happen after the victory, follow from the concentration of attention on the practical problems of action. The conceptions of unalterable, universal, natural rights, and of conscience, as belonging to every man irrespective of his position in the class struggle, are rejected as self-protecting liberal illusions. Socialism does not appeal, it demands; it speaks not of rights, but of the new form of life, liberated from constricting social structures, before whose inexorable approach the old social order has visibly begun to disintegrate. Moral, political, economic conceptions and ideals alter with the social conditions from which they spring: to regard any one of them as universal and immutable is tantamount to believing that the order to which they belong—in this case the bourgeois order—is eternal. This fallacy is held to underlie the ethical and psychological doctrines of idealistic humanitarians from the eighteenth century onwards. Hence the contempt and loathing poured by Marx upon the common assumption made by liberals and utilitarians, that since the interests of all men are ultimately, and have always been, the same, a measure of understanding, goodwill and benevolence on the part of everyone may yet make it possible to arrive at some sort of general consensus satisfactory to all. If the class war is real, these interests are totally incompatible. A denial of this fact can be due only to stupid or cynical disregard of the truth, a peculiarly vicious form of hypocrisy or self-deception repeatedly exposed by history. This fundamental difference of outlook, and no mere dissimilarity of temperament or natural gifts, is what distinguishes Marx sharply from the bourgeois radicals and Utopian socialists whom, to their own bewildered indignation, he fought and abused savagely and unremittingly for more than forty years.

He detested romanticism, emotionalism, and humanitarian appeals of every kind, and, in his anxiety to avoid any appeal to the idealistic feelings of his audience, systematically tried to remove every trace of the old democratic rhetoric from the propagandist literature of his movement. He neither offered nor invited concessions at any time, and did not enter into any dubious political alliances, since he declined all forms of compromise. The manifestos, professions of faith and programmes of action to which he appended his name contain scarcely any references to moral progress, eternal justice, the equality of man, the rights of individuals or nations, the liberty of conscience, the fight for civilisation, and other such phrases which were the stock-in-trade (and had once genuinely embodied ideals) of the democratic movements of his time; he looked upon these as so much worthless cant, indicating confusion of thought and ineffectiveness in action.[1]

The war must be fought on every front, and, since contemporary society is politically organised, a political party must be formed out of those elements which in accordance with the laws of historical development are destined to emerge as the conquering class. They must ceaselessly be taught that what seems so secure in existing society is, in reality, doomed to swift extinction, a fact which men may find it difficult to believe because of the immense protective façade of moral, religious, political and economic assumptions and beliefs, which the moribund class consciously or unconsciously creates, blinding itself and others to its own approaching fate. It requires both intellectual courage and acuteness of vision to penetrate this smoke-screen and perceive the real structure of events. The spectacle of chaos, and the imminence of the crisis in which it is bound to end, will of itself convince a clear-eyed and interested observer—for no one who is not virtually dead or dying can be a disinterested spectator of the fate of the society with which his own life is bound up—of what he must be and do in order to survive. Not a subjective scale of values revealed differently to different men, determined by the light of an inner vision, but knowledge of the facts themselves, must, according to Marx, determine rational behaviour. A society is judged to be progressive, and so worthy of support, if it is one whose institutions are capable of the further development of its productive forces without subverting its entire basis. A society is reactionary when it is inevitably moving into an impasse, unable to avoid internal chaos and ultimate collapse in spite of the most desperate efforts to survive, efforts which themselves create irrational faith in its own ultimate stability, the anodyne with which all dying orders necessarily conceal from themselves the symptoms of their true condition. Nevertheless, what history has condemned will be inevitably swept away: to say that something ought to be saved, even when that is not possible, is to deny the rational plan of the universe. To denounce the process itself—the painful conflicts through and by which mankind struggles to achieve the full realisation of its powers—was for Marx a form of childish subjectivism, due to a morbid or shallow view of life, to

[1] His remarks, in a letter to Engels, about his attitude to such expressions in the draft of the declaration of its principles which the First International Workingmen's Association submitted to him, are highly instructive in this connection.

some irrational prejudice in favour of this or that transient virtue or institution; it revealed attachment to the old world and was a symptom of incomplete emancipation from its values. It seemed to him that under the guise of earnest philanthropic feeling there throve, undetected, seeds of weakness and treachery, due to a fundamental desire to come to terms with the reaction, a secret horror of revolution based on fear of loss of comfort and privilege and, at a deep level, fear of reality itself, of the full light of day. With reality there could, however, be no compromise: and humanitarianism was but a softened, face-saving form of compromise, due to a desire to avoid the perils of an open fight and, even more, the risks and responsibilities of victory. Nothing stirred his indignation so much as cowardice: hence the furious and often brutal tone with which he refers to it, the beginning of that harsh 'materialist' style which struck an unfamiliar note in the literature of revolutionary socialism. This fashion for 'naked objectivity' took the form, particularly among Russian writers of a later generation, of searching for the sharpest, most unadorned, most shocking form of statement in which to clothe what were sometimes not very startling propositions.

Marx had, by his own account, begun to build his new instrument from almost casual beginnings: because, in the course of a controversy with the government on economic questions of purely local importance, in which he was involved in his capacity as editor of a radical newspaper, he became aware of his almost total ignorance of the history and principles of economic development. This controversy occurred in 1843. By 1848 his basic standpoint as a political and economic thinker was fully formed. With prodigious thoroughness he had constructed a complete theory of society and its evolution, which indicated with precision where and how the answers to all such questions must be sought and found. Its originality has often been questioned. It is original, not indeed in the sense in which works of art are original when they embody some hitherto unexpressed individual experience, but as scientific theories are said to be original, where they provide a new solution to a hitherto unsolved, or even unformulated problem, which they may do by modifying and combining existing views to form a new hypothesis. Marx never attempted to deny his debt to other thinkers: 'I am performing an act of historical justice, and am rendering to each man his due', he loftily declared. But he did claim to have provided for the first time a wholly adequate answer to questions which had been previously either misunderstood, or answered wrongly or insufficiently or obscurely. The characteristic for which Marx sought was not novelty but truth, and when he found it in the works of others, he endeavoured, at any rate during the early years in Paris in which the basic direction of his thought took its shape, to incorporate it in his new synthesis. What is original in the result is not any one component element, but the central hypothesis by which each is connected with the others, so that the parts are made to appear to follow from each other and to support each other in a single systematic whole.

To trace the direct source of any single doctrine advanced by Marx is, therefore, a relatively simple task which his numerous critics have been only too anxious to perform. It may well be that there is not one among his views whose embryo cannot be found in some previous or contemporary writer. Thus the doctrine of communal ownership founded upon the abolition of private property has probably, in one or other form, possessed adherents at most periods during the last two thousand years. Consequently the often debated question whether Marx derived it directly from Morelly or Mably, or Babeuf and his followers, or from some German account of French communism, is too purely academic to be of great importance. As for more specific doctrines, historical materialism of a sort is to be found fully developed in a treatise by Holbach printed almost a century before, which in its turn owes much to Spinoza; a modified form of it was restated in Marx's own day by Feuerbach. The view of human history as the history of war between social classes is to be found in Linguet and Saint-Simon, and was to a large extent adopted by such contemporary liberal French historians as Thierry and Mignet, and equally by the more conservative Guizot, as indeed Marx acknowledged. The scientific theory of the inevitability of the regular recurrence of economic crises was probably first formulated by Sismondi; that of the rise of the Fourth Estate was certainly held by the early French communists, popularised in Germany in Marx's own day by Stein and Hess. The dictatorship of the proletariat was adumbrated by Babeuf in the last decade of the eighteenth century, and was explicitly developed in the nineteenth in different fashions by Weitling and Blanqui; the present and future position and importance of workers in an industrial state was more fully worked out by Louis Blanc and the French State Socialists than Marx was prepared to admit. The labour theory of value derives from Locke, Adam Smith, Ricardo and the other classical economists; the theory of exploitation and surplus value is found in Fourier, and of its remedy by deliberate state control in the writings of early English socialists, such as Bray, Thompson and Hodgskin; the theory of the alienation of the proletarians was enunciated by Max Stirner at least one year before Marx. The influence of Hegel and German philosophy is the deepest and most ubiquitous of all; the list could easily be continued further.

There was no dearth of social theories in the eighteenth century. Some died at birth, others, when the intellectual climate was favourable, modified opinion and influenced action. Marx sifted this immense mass of material and detached from it whatever seemed to him original, true and important; and in the light of it constructed a new instrument of social analysis, the main merit of which lies not in its beauty or consistency, nor in its emotional or intellectual power—the great Utopian systems are nobler works of the speculative imagination—but in the remarkable combination of simple fundamental principles with comprehensiveness, realism and detail. The environment which it assumed actually corresponded to the personal, first-hand experience of the public to which it was addressed; its analyses, when stated in their simplest form, seemed at once novel and penetrating, and the new hypotheses which represent a peculiar synthesis of German idealism, French rationalism, and English political economy, seemed genuinely to co-ordinate and account for a mass of social phenomena hitherto thought of in comparative isolation from each other. This provided a concrete meaning for the formulas and popular slogans of the new communist movement. Above all, it enabled it to do more than stimulate general emotions of discontent and rebellion by attaching to them, as Chartism had done, a collection of specific but loosely connected political and economic ends. It directed these feelings to systematically interconnected, immediate, feasible objectives, regarded not as ultimate ends valid for all men at all times, but as objectives proper to a revolutionary party representing a specific stage of social development.

To have given clear and unified answers in familiar empirical terms to those theoretical questions which most occupied men's minds at this time, and to have deduced from them clear practical directives without creating obviously artificial links between the two, was the principal achievement of Marx's theory, and endowed it with that singular vitality which enabled it to defeat and survive its rivals in the succeeding decades. It was composed largely in Paris during the troubled years between 1843 and 1850, when, under the stress of a world crisis, economic and political tendencies normally concealed below the surface of social life increased in scope and in intensity, until they broke through the framework which was secured in normal times by established institutions, and for a brief instant revealed their real character during the luminous interlude which preceded the final clash of forces, in which all issues were obscured once more. Marx fully profited by this rare opportunity for scientific observation in the field of social theory; to him, indeed, it appeared to provide full confirmation of his hypotheses.

The system as it finally emerged was a massive structure, not to be taken by direct assault, containing within its walls resources intended to meet every known weapon in the enemy's possession. Its influence has been immense on friend and foe alike, and in particular on social scientists, historians and critics. It has altered the history of human thought in the sense that after it certain things could never again be plausibly said. No subject loses, at least in the long run, by becoming a field of battle, and the Marxist emphasis upon the primacy of economic factors in determining human behaviour led directly to an intensified study of economic history, which, although it had not been entirely neglected in the past, did not attain to its present prominent rank, until the rise of Marxism gave an impulse to exact historical scholarship in that sphere—much as in the previous generation Hegelian doctrines acted as a powerful stimulus to historical studies in general. The sociological treatment of historical and moral problems, which Comte, and after him Spencer and Taine, had discussed and mapped, became a precise and concrete study only when the attack of militant Marxism made its conclusions a burning issue, and so made the search for evidence more zealous and the attention to method more intense.

In 1849 Marx was forced to leave Paris, and came to live in England. For him London, and in particular the library of the British Museum, was 'the ideal strategic vantage-point for the student of bourgeois society', an arsenal of ammunition the importance of which its owners did not appear to grasp. He remained little affected by his surroundings, living encased in his own, largely German, world, formed by his family and a small group of intimate friends and political associates. He met few Englishmen and neither understood nor cared for them or their mode of life. He was a man unusually impervious to the influence of environment: he saw little that was not printed in newspapers or books, and remained until his death comparatively unaware of the quality of the life around him or of its social and natural background. So far as his intellectual development was concerned, he might just as well have spent his exile on Madagascar, provided that a regular supply of books, journals and government reports could have been secured: certainly the inhabitants of London could hardly have taken less notice of his existence if he had. The formative, psychologically most interesting, years of his life were over by 1851: after this he was emotionally and intellectually set and hardly changed at all. He had, while still in Paris, conceived the idea of providing a complete account and explanation of the rise and imminent fall of the capitalist system. His work upon it was begun in the spring of 1850, and continued for some twenty years, with interruptions caused by day-to-day tactical needs and the journalism by which he tried to support his household.

His pamphlets, articles and letters during his thirty years in London form a coherent commentary on contemporary political affairs in the light of his new method of analysis. They are sharp, lucid, mordant, realistic, astonishingly modern in tone, and aimed deliberately against the prevailing optimistic temper of his time.

As a revolutionary he disapproved of conspiratorial methods which he thought obsolete and ineffective, and liable to irritate public opinion without altering its foundations; instead he set himself to create an open political party dominated by the new view of society. His later years are occupied almost exclusively with the task of gathering evidence for, and disseminating, the truths which he had discovered, until they filled the entire horizon of his followers, and became consciously woven into the texture of their every thought and word and act. For a quarter of a century he concentrated his entire being upon the attainment of this purpose, and, towards the end of his life, achieved it.

The nineteenth century contains many remarkable social critics and revolutionaries no less original, no less violent, no less dogmatic than Marx, but not one so rigorously single-minded, so absorbed in making every word and every act of his life a means towards a single, immediate, practical end, to which nothing was too sacred to be sacrificed. If there is a sense in which he was born before his time, there is an equally definite sense in which he embodies one of the oldest of European traditions. His realism, his sense of history, his attacks on abstract principles, his demand that every solution must be tested by its applicability to, and emergence out of, the actual situation, his contempt for compromise or gradualism as modes of escape from the necessity of drastic action, his belief that the masses are gullible and must at all costs be rescued, if necessary by force, from the knaves and fools who impose upon them, make him the precursor of the severer generation of practical revolutionaries of the next century; but his rigid belief in the necessity of a complete break with the past, in the need for a wholly new social system as alone capable of saving the individual, who, unfettered by social constraint, will cooperate harmoniously with others, but in the meantime needs firm social direction, places him among the great authoritarian founders of new faiths, ruthless subverters and innovators who interpret the world in terms of a single, clear, passionately held principle, denouncing and destroying all that conflicts with it. His faith in his own synoptic vision of an orderly, disciplined, self-directing society, destined to arise out of the inevitable self-destruction of the irrational and chaotic world of the present, was of that boundless, absolute kind which puts an end to all questions and dissolves all difficulties; which brings with it a sense of liberation similar to that which in the sixteenth and seventeenth centuries men found in the new Protestant faith, and later in the truths of science, in the principles of the great Revolution, in the systems of the German metaphysicians. If these earlier rationalists are justly called fanatical, then in this sense Marx too was a fanatic. But his faith in reason was not blind: if he appealed to reason, he appealed no less to empirical evidence. The laws of history were indeed eternal and immutable—and to grasp this fact a quasi-metaphysical intuition was required—but what they were could be established only by the evidence of empirical facts. His intellectual system was a closed one, everything that entered was made to conform to a pre-established pattern, but it was grounded in observation and experience. He was obsessed by no fixed ideas. He betrays not a trace of the notorious symptoms which accompany pathological fanaticism, that alternation of moods of sudden exaltation with a sense of loneliness and persecution, which life in wholly private worlds often engenders in those who are detached from reality.

The main ideas of his principal work appear to have matured in his mind as early as 1847. Preliminary sketches had appeared in

1849 and again seven years later, but he was incapable of beginning to write before satisfying himself that he had mastered the entire literature of his subject. This fact, together with the difficulty of finding a publisher and the necessity of providing for his own and his family's livelihood, with its accompaniment of overwork and frequent illness, put off publication year by year. The first volume finally appeared twenty years after its conception, in 1867, and is the crowning achievement of his life. It is an attempt to give a single integrated account of the process and laws of social development, containing a complete economic theory treated historically, and, less explicitly, a theory of history and society as determined by economic factors. It is interrupted by remarkable digressions consisting of analyses and historical sketches of the condition of the proletariat and its employers, in particular during the period of transition from manufacture to large-scale industrial capitalism, introduced to illustrate the general thesis, but in fact demonstrating a new and revolutionary method of historical writing and political interpretation: and all in all it constitutes the most formidable, sustained and elaborate indictment ever delivered against an entire social order, against its rulers, its supporters, its ideologists, its willing and unwilling instruments, against all whose lives are bound up with its survival. His attack upon bourgeois society was made at a moment when it had reached the highest point of its material prosperity, in the very year in which Gladstone in a budget speech congratulated his countrymen on the 'intoxicating augmentation of their wealth and power' which recent years had witnessed, during a mood of buoyant optimism and universal confidence. In this world Marx is an isolated and bitterly hostile figure, prepared, like an early Christian, or a French enragé, to reject boldly all that it was and stood for, calling its ideals worthless and its virtues vices, condemning its institutions because they were bourgeois, that is because they belonged to a corrupt, tyrannous and irrational society which must be annihilated totally and for ever. In an age which destroyed its adversaries by methods not less efficient because they were dignified and slow, which forced Carlyle and Schopenhauer to seek escape in remote civilisations or an idealised past, and drove its arch-enemy Nietzsche to hysteria and madness, Marx alone remained secure and formidable. Like an ancient prophet performing a task imposed on him by heaven, with an inner tranquillity based on clear and certain faith in the harmonious society of the future, he bore witness to the signs of decay and ruin which he saw on every side. The old order seemed to him to be patently crumbling before his eyes; he did more than any man to hasten the process, seeking to shorten the final agony which precedes the end.

2

Childhood and Adolescence

Nimmer kann ich ruhig treiben
Was die Seele stark befasst,
Nimmer still behaglich bleiben
Und ich stürme ohne Rast.[1]

KARL MARX, *Empfindungen* (from an album of poems dedicated
to Jenny von Westphalen)

KARL HEINRICH MARX, eldest son of Heinrich and Henrietta
Marx, was born on 5 May 1818 in Trier, in the German Rhine-
land, where his father practised as a lawyer. Once the seat of a
Prince-Archbishop, it had, some fifteen years before, been
occupied by the French and was incorporated by Napoleon in the
Confederation of the Rhine. After his defeat ten years later it was
assigned by the Congress of Vienna to the rapidly expanding
Prussian kingdom.

The kings and princes of the German states whose personal
authority had recently been all but destroyed by the successive
French invasions of their territories, were at this time busily
engaged in repairing the damaged fabric of hereditary monarchy,
a process which demanded the obliteration of every trace of the
dangerous ideas which had begun to rouse even the placid
inhabitants of the German provinces from their traditional
lethargy. Napoleon's defeat and exile had finally destroyed the
illusions of those German radicals who hoped that the result of
Napoleon's centralising policy would be, if not the liberty, at any
rate the unity of Germany. The *status quo* was re-established
wherever this was possible; Germany was once more divided into
semi-feudally organised kingdoms and principalities, whose
restored rulers, resolved to compensate themselves for the years
of defeat and humiliation, set about reviving the old regime in
every detail, anxious to exorcise once and for all the spectre of

[1] Never can I pursue in quiet that which holds my soul in thrall, never
rest at peace contented, and I storm without cease.

democratic revolution whose memory was sedulously kept alive
by the more enlightened among their subjects. The king of Prussia, Frederick William III, was particularly energetic in this
respect. Helped by the squirearchy and such land-owning aristocracy as there was in Prussia, and following the example set by
Metternich in Vienna, he succeeded in arresting the normal social
development of the majority of his countrymen for many years,
and induced an atmosphere of profound and hopeless stagnation,
beside which even France and England during the reactionary
years seemed liberal and alive. This was felt most acutely by the
more progressive elements in German society—not merely by the
intellectuals, but by the bulk of the bourgeoisie and of the liberal
aristocracy of the towns, particularly in the west, which had
always preserved some contact with general European culture. It
took the form of economic, social and political legislation
designed to retain, and in some cases to restore, a multitude of
privileges, rights and restrictions, many of them dating from the
Middle Ages, sordid survivals that had long ceased to be even
picturesque; and since they were in direct conflict with the needs
of the new age, they needed and obtained an elaborate and ruinous
structure of tariffs to keep them in being. This led to a policy of
systematic discouragement of trade and industry and, since the
obsolete structure had to be preserved against popular pressure, to
the creation of a despotic officialdom, whose task it was to insulate German society from the contaminating influence of liberal
ideas and institutions.

The increased power of the police, the introduction of rigid
supervision over all departments of public and private life, pro-
voked a literature of protest which was rigorously suppressed by
the government censors. German writers and poets went into
voluntary exile, and from Paris or Switzerland conducted passionate propaganda against the regime. The general situation was
reflected particularly clearly in the condition of that section of
society which throughout the nineteenth century tended to act as
the most sensitive barometer of the direction of social change
—the small but widely scattered Jewish population.

The Jews had every reason to feel grateful to Napoleon.
Wherever he appeared he set himself to destroy the traditional
edifice of social rank and privilege, of racial, political and religious
barriers, putting in its place his newly promulgated legal code,
which claimed as the source of its authority the principles of
reason and human equality. This act, by opening to the Jews the

Napoleon & Jews

doors of trades and professions which had hitherto remained rigidly barred to them, had the effect of releasing a mass of imprisoned energy and ambition, and led to the enthusiastic—in some cases over-enthusiastic—acceptance of general European culture by a hitherto segregated community, which from that day became a new and important factor in the evolution of European society.

Some of these liberties were later withdrawn by Napoleon himself, and what was left of them was for the most part revoked by the restored German princes, with the result that many Jews who had eagerly broken away from the traditional mode of life led by their fathers, toward the prospects of a wider existence, now found that the avenue which had so suddenly been half-opened before them had as suddenly become barred again, and consequently were confronted with a difficult choice. They had either to retrace their steps and painfully re-enter the ghetto in which their families for the most part still continued to live, or else, altering their names and religion, to start new lives as German patriots and members of the Christian Church. The case of Herschel Levi was typical of a whole generation. His father, Marx Levi, his brother, and their father before them, were Rabbis in the Rhineland, who, like the great majority of their fellow Jews, had passed their entire existence within the confines of a pious, inbred, passionately self-centred community which, faced with the hostility of its Christian neighbours, had taken refuge behind a defensive wall of pride and suspicion, which had for centuries almost wholly preserved them from contact with the changing life outside. The enlightenment had, nevertheless, begun to penetrate even this artificial enclave of the Middle Ages, and Herschel, who had received a secular education, became a disciple of the French rationalists and their disciples, the German *Aufklärer*, and was early in life converted to the religion of reason and humanity. He accepted it with candour and naïvety, nor did the long years of darkness and reaction succeed in shaking his faith in God and his simple and optimistic humanitarianism. He detached himself completely from his family, changed his surname to Marx, and acquired new friends and new interests. His legal practice was moderately successful, and he began to look to a settled future as the head of a respectable German bourgeois family, when the anti-Jewish laws of 1816 suddenly cut off his means of livelihood.

He probably felt no exceptional reverence for the Established Church, but he was even less attached to the Synagogue, and, holding vaguely deist views, saw no moral or social obstacle to complete conformity with the mildly enlightened Lutheranism of his Prussian neighbours. At any rate, if he did hesitate, it was not for long. He was officially received into the Church early in 1817, a year before the birth of his eldest son, Karl. The hostility of the latter to everything connected with religion, and in particular with Judaism, may well be partly due to the peculiar and embarrassed situation in which such converts sometimes found themselves. Some escaped by becoming devout and even fanatical Christians, others by rebelling against all established religion. They suffered in proportion to their sensitiveness and intelligence. Both Heine and Disraeli were all their lives obsessed by the personal problem of their peculiar status; they neither renounced nor accepted it completely, but mocked at or defended the religion of their fathers, or alternated between these attitudes, uneasily aware of their ambiguous position, perpetually suspicious of latent contempt or condescension concealed beneath the fiction of their complete acceptance by the society in which they lived.

The elder Marx suffered from none of these complications. He was a simple, serious, well-educated man, but he was neither conspicuously intelligent nor abnormally sensitive. A disciple of Leibniz and Voltaire, Lessing and Kant, he possessed in addition a gentle, timid and accommodating temper, and ultimately became a passionate Prussian patriot and monarchist, a position which he sought to justify by pointing to the figure of Frederick the Great—a tolerant and enlightened prince who compared favourably with Napoleon, with his notorious contempt for enlightened intellectuals. After his baptism he adopted the Christian name of Heinrich, and educated his family as liberal protestants, faithful to the existing order and to the reigning King of Prussia. Anxious as he was to identify that ruler with the ideal prince depicted by his favourite philosophers, the unattractive figure of Frederick William III defeated even his loyal imagination. Indeed, the only occasion on which this tremulous and retiring man is known to have behaved with courage was a public dinner at which he made a speech on the desirability of moderate social and political reforms worthy of a wise and benevolent ruler. This swiftly drew upon him the attention of the Prussian police. Heinrich Marx at once retracted everything, and convinced everyone of his complete harmlessness. It is not improbable that this slight but humiliating *contretemps*, and in particular his father's

craven and submissive attitude, made a definite impression on his
eldest son Karl Heinrich, then sixteen years old, and left behind it
a smouldering sense of resentment, which later events fanned into
a flame.

His father had early become aware that while his other children
were in no way remarkable, in Karl he had an unusual and difficult
son; with a sharp and lucid intelligence he combined a stubborn
and domineering temper, a truculent love of independence,
exceptional emotional restraint, and, over all, a colossal, ungov-
ernable intellectual appetite. The timorous lawyer, whose life was
spent in social and personal compromise, was puzzled and
frightened by his son's intransigence, which, in his opinion, was
bound to antagonise important persons, and might, one day, lead
him into serious trouble. He anxiously begged him in his letters to
moderate his enthusiasms, to impose some sort of discipline on
himself, not to waste time on subjects likely to prove useless in
later life, to cultivate polite, civilised habits, not to neglect possible benefactors, above all not to estrange everyone by violently
refusing to adapt himself—in short to satisfy the elementary
requirements of the society in which he was to live his life. But
these letters, even at their most disapproving, remained gentle
and affectionate; in spite of growing uneasiness about his character and career, Heinrich Marx treated his son with an instinctive
delicacy, and never attempted to oppose or bully him on any
serious issue. Consequently their relations continued to be warm
and intimate until the death of the older Marx in 1838.

It seems certain that the father had a definite influence on his
son's intellectual development. The elder Marx believed with
Condorcet that man is by nature both good and rational, and that
all that is needed to ensure the triumph of these qualities is the
removal of artificial obstacles from his path. They were disappearing already, and disappearing fast, and the time was rapidly
approaching when the last citadels of reaction, the Catholic
Church and the feudal nobility, would melt away before the
irresistible march of reason. Social, political, religious, racial barriers were so many products of the deliberate obscurantism of
priests and rulers; with their disappearance a new day would
dawn for the human race, when all men would be equal, not only
politically and legally, in their formal, external relations, but
socially and personally, in their most intimate daily intercourse.

His own history seemed to him to corroborate this triumphantly. Born a Jew, a citizen of inferior legal and social status, he

had attained to equality with his more enlightened neighbours, had earned their respect as a human being, and had become assimilated into what appeared to him as their more rational and dignified mode of life. He believed that a new day was dawning in the history of human emancipation, in the light of which his children would live their lives as free-born citizens in a just and liberal state. Elements of this belief are clearly apparent in his son's social doctrine. Karl Marx did not, indeed, believe in the power of rational argument to influence action: unlike some of the thinkers of the French Enlightenment, he did not believe in continuous amelioration of the human condition; whatever could be defined as progressive in terms of the human conquest of nature had been achieved at the price of the increasing exploitation and degradation of the real producers—the working masses; there was no steady movement in the direction of ever-increasing happiness or freedom of the majority of men; the path to the ultimate, harmonious realisation of the full potentialities of men lay through increasing misery and 'alienation' of vast numbers of them; this is what Marx meant by the 'contradictory' character of human progress. There is, nevertheless, a definite sense in which he remained both a rationalist and a perfectibilian to the end of his life. He believed in the complete intelligibility of the process of social evolution; he believed that society is inevitably progressive, that its movement from stage to stage is a forward movement; each successive stage did represent development, in the sense that it brought the establishment of the rational ideal nearer than its precursors. He detested, as passionately as any eighteenth-century thinker, emotionalism, belief in supernatural causes, visionary fantasy of every kind, and systematically underestimated the influence of such non-rational forces as nationalism, and religious and racial solidarity. Although, therefore, it remains true that the Hegelian philosophy is probably the greatest single formative influence in his life, the principles of philosophical rationalism, which were planted in him by his father and his father's friends, performed a definite work of inoculation, so that when later he encountered the metaphysical systems developed by the romantic school, he was saved from that total surrender to their fascination which undid so many of his contemporaries. It was this pronounced taste, acquired early in life, for lucid argument and an empirical approach that enabled him to preserve a measure of critical independence in the face of the prevalent philosophy, and later, under the influence of Feuerbach, to alter it to his own more positivist pattern. This may perhaps account for the realistic and concrete quality of his thought, even when it is influenced by romantic ideas, as contrasted with the outlook of such leading radicals of his time as Börne, Heine, or Lassalle, whose origins and education are in many respects closely analogous to his own.

Little is known of his childhood and early years in Trier. His mother played a singularly small part in his life; Henrietta Pressburg (or Pressburger) belonged to a family of Hungarian Jews settled in Holland, where her father was a Rabbi, and was a solid and uneducated woman entirely absorbed in the cares of her large household, who did not at any time show the slightest understanding of her son's gifts or inclinations, was shocked by his radicalism, and in later years appears to have lost all interest in his existence. Of the eight children of Heinrich and Henrietta Marx, Karl was the second; apart from a mild affection as a child for his eldest sister Sophia, he showed little interest in his brothers and sisters either then or later. He was sent to the local high school, where he obtained equal praise for his industry and the high-minded and earnest tone of his essays on moral and religious topics. He was moderately proficient in mathematics and theology, but his main interests were literary and artistic: a tendency due principally to the influence of two men from whom he learned most and of whom all his life he spoke with affection and respect. The first of these was his father; the other was their neighbour, Freiherr Ludwig von Westphalen, who was on friendly terms with the amiable lawyer and his family. Westphalen was a distinguished Prussian government official, and belonged to that educated and liberal section of the German upper class whose representatives were to be found in the vanguard of every enlightened and progressive movement in their country in the first half of the nineteenth century. An open-minded, attractive and cultivated man, he belonged to the generation dominated by the great figures of Goethe, Schiller and Hölderlin, and under their influence he had wandered beyond the aesthetic frontiers so strictly established by the literary mandarins in Paris, and shared in the growing German passion for the rediscovered genius of Dante, Shakespeare, Homer and the Greek tragedians. He was attracted by the striking ability and eager receptiveness of Heinrich Marx's son, encouraged him to read, lent him books, took him for walks in the neighbouring woods and talked to him about Aeschylus, Cervantes, Shakespeare, quoting long passages to his enthusiastic listener. Karl, who reached maturity at a very early age, became a devoted reader of the new romantic literature: the taste he acquired during these impressionable years remained unaltered until his death. He was in later life fond of recalling his evenings with Westphalen, during what seemed to him to have been the happiest period of his life. He had been treated by a man much older than himself on terms of equality at a time when he was in particular need of sympathy and encouragement; when one tactless or insulting gesture might have left a lasting mark, he was received with rare courtesy and hospitality. His doctoral thesis contains a glowing dedication to Westphalen, full of gratitude and admiration. In 1837 Marx asked for the hand of his daughter in marriage and obtained his consent; an act which, owing to the great difference in their social condition, is said to have dismayed her relations. Speaking of Westphalen in later life Marx, whose judgements of men are not noted for their generosity, grew almost sentimental. Westphalen had humanised and strengthened that belief in himself and his own powers which was at all periods Marx's single most outstanding characteristic. He is one of the rare revolutionaries who were neither thwarted nor persecuted in their early life. Consequently, in spite of his abnormal sensitiveness, his *amour propre*, his vanity, his aggressiveness and his arrogance, it is a singularly unbroken, positive and self-confident figure that faces us during forty years of illness, poverty and unceasing warfare.

He left the Trier school at the age of seventeen, and, following his father's advice, in the autumn of 1835 became a student in the faculty of law in the University of Bonn. Here he seems to have been entirely happy. He announced that he proposed to attend at least seven courses of weekly lectures, among them lectures on Homer by the celebrated August Wilhelm Schlegel, lectures on mythology, on Latin poetry, on modern art. He lived the gay and dissipated life of the ordinary German student, played an active part in university societies, wrote Byronic poems, got into debt and on at least one occasion was arrested by the authorities for riotous behaviour. At the end of the summer term of 1836 he left Bonn, and in the autumn was transferred to the University of Berlin.

This event marks a sharp crisis in his life. The conditions under which he had lived hitherto had been comparatively provincial: Trier was a small and pretty town which had survived from an older order, untouched by the great social and economic revolution which was changing the contour of the civilised world. The growing industrial development of Cologne and Düsseldorf seemed infinitely remote; no urgent problems, social, intellectual, or material, had troubled the peace of the gentle and cultivated milieu of his father's friends, a placid preserve of the eighteenth century which had artificially survived into the nineteenth. By comparison with Trier or Bonn, Berlin was an immensely large and populous city, modern, ugly, pretentious and intensely serious, at once the centre of the Prussian bureaucracy and the meeting-place of the discontented radical intellectuals who formed the nucleus of the growing opposition to it. Marx retained all his life a considerable capacity for enjoyment and a strong if rather ponderous sense of fun, but no one could even at that time describe him as superficial or frivolous. He was sobered by the tense and tragic atmosphere in which he suddenly felt himself, and with his accustomed energy began at once to explore and criticise his new environment.

3

The Philosophy of the Spirit

Was Ihr den Geist der Zeiten heisst
Das ist im Grund des Herren eigner Geist
In dem die Zeiten sich bespiegeln.[1]

GOETHE

La Raison a toujours raison.[2]

1

THE dominant intellectual influence in the University of Berlin, as
indeed in every other German university at this time, was the
Hegelian philosophy. The soil for this had been prepared by
gradual revolt from the beliefs and idiom of the classical period,
which had begun in the seventeenth, and was consolidated and
reduced to a system in the eighteenth century. The greatest and
most original figure in this movement among the Germans was
Gottfried Wilhelm Leibniz, whose ideas were developed by his
followers and interpreters into a coherent and dogmatic metaphysical system which, so their popularisers claimed, was logically
demonstrated by deductive steps from simple premises, in their
turn self-evident to those who could use that infallible intellectual
intuition with which all thinking beings were endowed at birth.
This rigid intellectualism was attacked in England, where no
form of pure rationalism had ever found a congenial soil, by the
most influential philosophical writers of the age, Locke, Hume,
and, towards the end of the century, Bentham and the philosophical radicals, who agreed in denying the existence of any such
faculty as an intellectual intuition into the real nature of things.
No faculty other than the familiar physical senses could provide
that initial empirical information on which all other knowledge of
the world is ultimately founded. Since all information was conveyed by the senses, reason could not be an independent source of

[1] What you call the spirit of the age is in reality one's own spirit, in
which the age is mirrored.
[2] Reason is always right.

knowledge, and was reponsible only for arranging, classifying and fitting together such information, and drawing deductions from it, operating upon material obtained without its aid. In France the rationalist position was attacked by the materialist school in the eighteenth century, and while Voltaire and Diderot, Condillac and Helvétius, freely acknowledged their debt to the free-thinking English, they constructed an independent system, whose influence on European thought and action continues into the present day. Some did not go to the length of denying the existence of knowledge obtained otherwise than by the senses, but claimed that, though such innate knowledge itself exists and indeed reveals valuable truth, it provides no evidence for the propositions whose incontrovertible truth the older rationalists claimed to know, a fact which careful and scrupulous mental self-examination would show to any open-minded man not blinded by religious dogmatism or political and ethical prejudice. Too many abuses had been defended by appeals to authority, or to a special intuition: thus Aristotle, appealing to reason for confirmation, had maintained that men were by nature unequal, that some were naturally slaves, others free men; and so too the Bible, which taught that truth could be revealed by supernatural means, afforded texts which could be invoked to prove that man was naturally vicious and must be curbed—theses used by reactionary governments to support the existing state of political, social, even moral inequality. But experience and reason, properly understood, combined to show the precise opposite of this. Arguments could be produced to show beyond any possible doubt that man was naturally good, that reason existed equally in all sentient beings, that the cause of all oppression and suffering was human ignorance, produced partly by social and material conditions which arose in the course of natural historical development, partly through the deliberate suppression of the truth by ambitious tyrants and unscrupulous priests, most frequently by the interplay of both. These evil influences could, by the action of an enlightened and benevolent government, be exposed and thereby annihilated. Left to themselves, with no obstacles to obscure their vision and to frustrate their endeavours, men would pursue virtue and knowledge; justice and equality would take the place of authority and privilege, competition would yield to co-operation, happiness and wisdom would become universal possessions. The central tenet of this semi-empirical rationalism consisted in boundless faith in the power of reason to explain and improve the world, all previous failure to do so being explained as ultimately caused by ignorance of the laws which regulate the behaviour of nature, animate and inanimate. Misery is the complex result of ignorance, not only of nature but of the laws of social behaviour. To abolish it one measure is both necessary and sufficient: the employment of reason, and of reason alone, in the conduct of human affairs.

This task is admittedly far from easy; men have lived too long in a world of intellectual darkness to be able to move unblinkered in the sudden light of day. A process of gradual education in scientific principles is therefore required: the growth of reason and the advance of truth, while in themselves sufficient to conquer the forces of prejudice and ignorance, cannot occur until enlightened men are found ready to devote their whole lives to the task of educating the vast benighted mass of mankind. *victim* *purposeful action of one class by another*

But here a new obstacle arises: whereas the original cause of human misery, neglect of reason and intellectual indolence, was not deliberately brought about, there exists in our own day, and has existed for many centuries past, a class of men who, perceiving that their own power rests on ignorance, which blinds men to injustice, promote unreason by every invention and means in their power. By nature all men are rational, and all rational beings have equal rights before the natural tribunal of reason. But the ruling classes, the princes, the nobility, the priests, the generals, realise only too well that the spread of reason would soon open the eyes of the peoples of the world to the colossal fraud by which, in the name of such hollow figments as the sanctity of the church, the divine right of kings, the claims of national pride or the possession of power or wealth, they are forced to give up their natural claims and labour uncomplainingly for the maintenance of a small class which has no shadow of a right to exact such privilege. It is therefore in the direct personal interest of the upper class in the social hierarchy to thwart the growth of natural knowledge, wherever it threatens to expose the arbitrary character of its authority, and in its place to substitute a dogmatic code, a set of unintelligible mysteries expressed in high-sounding phrases, with which to confuse the feeble intelligences of their unhappy subjects, and to keep them in a state of blind obedience. Even though some among the ruling class may be genuinely self-deceived and come themselves to believe in their own inventions, some there must be who know that only by systematic deception, propped up by the occasional use of violence, could so corrupt and unnatural an order be preserved. It is the first duty, therefore, of an enlightened ruler to break the power of the privileged classes, and to allow natural reason, with which all men are endowed, to re-assert itself; and since reason can never be opposed to reason, all private and public conflict is ultimately due to some irrational element, to some simple failure to perceive how a harmonious adjustment of apparently opposed interests may be made.

Reason is always right. To every question there is only one true answer which with sufficient assiduity can be infallibly discovered, and this applies no less to questions of ethics or politics, of personal and social life, than to the problems of physics or mathematics. Once found, the putting of a solution into practice is a matter of mere technical skill; but the traditional enemies of progress must first be removed, and men taught the importance of acting in all questions on the advice of disinterested scientific experts whose knowledge is founded on reason and experience. Once this has been achieved, the path is clear to the millennium.

But the influence of environment is no less important than that of education. If you should wish to foretell the course of a man's life, you must consider such factors as the character of the region in which he lives, its climate, the fertility of its soil, its distance from the sea, in addition to his physical characteristics and the nature of his daily occupation. Man is an object in nature, and the human soul, like material substance, is swayed by no supernatural influences and possesses no occult properties; its entire behaviour can be adequately accounted for by means of ordinary verifiable physical hypotheses. The French materialist La Mettrie developed this empiricism to, and indeed beyond its fullest limits in a celebrated treatise, *L'Homme Machine*, which caused much scandal at the time of its publication. His views were an extreme example of opinions shared in varying degrees by the editors of the Encyclopedia, Diderot and d'Alembert, by Holbach, Helvétius and Condillac, who, whatever their other differences, were agreed that man's principal difference from the plants and lower animals lies in his possession of self-consciousness, in his awareness of certain of his own processes, in his capacity to use reason and imagination, to conceive ideal purposes and to attach moral values to any activity or characteristic in accordance with its tendency to forward or retard the ends which he desires to realise. A serious difficulty which this view involved was that of reconciling the existence of free will on the one hand, with complete deter-

mination by character and environment on the other; this was
only the old conflict between free will and divine foreknowledge
in a new form, with Nature in the place of God. Spinoza had
observed that if a stone falling through the air could think, it
might well imagine that it had freely chosen its own path, being
unaware of the external causes, such as the aim and force of the
thrower and the natural medium, which determine its fall. Similarly, it is only his ignorance of the natural causes of his behaviour
that makes man suppose himself in some fashion different from
the falling stone: omniscience would quickly dispel this vain
delusion, even though the feeling of freedom to which it gives rise
may itself persist, but without its power to deceive. So far as
extreme empiricism is concerned, this deterministic doctrine can
be made consistent with optimistic rationalism: but it carries the
very opposite implications with regard to the possibility of
reform in human affairs. For if men are made saints or criminals
solely by the movement of matter in space, the educators are as
rigorously determined to act as they do, as are those whom it is
their duty to educate. Everything occurs as it does as a result of
unalterable processes of nature; and no improvement can be
effected by the free decisions of individuals, however wise, however benevolent and powerful, since they cannot, any more than
any other entity, alter natural necessity. This celebrated crux,
stripped of its old theological dress, emerged even more sharply
in its secular form; it presented equal difficulties to both sides, but
became obscured by the larger issues at stake. Atheists, sceptics,
deists, materialists, rationalists, democrats, utilitarians, belonged
to one camp; theists, metaphysicians, supporters and apologists of
the existing order to the other. The rift between enlightenment
and clericalism was so great, and the war between them so savage,
that doctrinal difficulties within each camp passed relatively
unperceived.

It is the first of the two theses that became the fundamental
doctrine of the radical intellectuals of the next century. They
emphasised the natural or potential goodness of men unspoiled by
a bad or ignorant government, and emphasised the immense
power of rational education to rescue the masses of mankind from
their present miseries, to institute a juster and more scientific
distribution of the world's goods, and so to lead humanity to the
limits of attainable happiness. The imagination of the eighteenth
century was dominated by the phenomenal strides made by the
mathematical and physical sciences during the previous century,

and it was a natural step to apply the method which had proved so successful in the hands of Kepler and Galileo, Descartes and Newton, to the interpretation of social phenomena and to the conduct of life. If any single individual may be said to have created this movement, it is unquestionably Voltaire. If he was not its originator, he was its greatest and most celebrated protagonist for more than half a century. His books, his pamphlets, his mere existence did incomparably more to destroy the hold of absolutism and catholicism than any other single factor. Nor did his death arrest his influence. Freedom of thought was identified with his name: its battles were fought under his banner; no popular revolution from his day to ours had failed to draw some of its most effective weapons from that inexhaustible armoury, which two centuries have not rendered obsolete. But if Voltaire created the religion of man, Rousseau was the greatest of its prophets. His conception of man was different from, and ultimately subversive of, that of the radicals of his time. But he was a preacher and a propagandist of genius, and gave the movement a new eloquence and ardour, a richer, vaguer and more emotionally charged language, which profoundly affected the writers and thinkers of the nineteenth century. Indeed, he may be said to have created the new modes of thought and of feeling, a new idiom, which glorified the will at the expense of reason and observation, an idiom which was adopted as their natural vehicle of self-expression by the artistic and social rebels of the nineteenth century—that first generation of romantics who sought inspiration in the revolutionary history and literature of France and in her name raised the banner of revolt in their own backward lands.

One of the most fervent and certainly the most effective among the advocates of this doctrine in England was the idealistic Welsh manufacturer, Robert Owen. His creed was summarised in the sentence inscribed at the head of his journal, *The New Moral World*: 'Any general character, from the best to the worst, from the most ignorant to the most enlightened, may be given to any community, even the world at large, by the application of proper means, which means are to a great extent at the command and under the control of those who have influence in the affairs of men.' He had triumphantly demonstrated the truth of his theory by establishing model conditions in his own cotton mills in New Lanark, limiting working hours, and creating provision for health and a savings fund. By this means he increased the productivity of

utopianism = perfectibility of mankind

his factory and raised immensely the standard of living of his workers, and, what was even more impressive to the outside world, trebled his own fortune. New Lanark became a centre of pilgrimage for kings and statesmen, and, as the first successful experiment in peaceful co-operation between labour and capital, had a considerable influence on the history both of socialism and of the working class. His later attempts at practical reform were less successful. Owen, who died in deep old age in the middle of the nineteenth century, was the last survivor of the classical period of rationalism, and, his faith unshaken by repeated failures, believed until the end of his life in the omnipotence of education and the perfectibility of man.

The effect which the victorious advance of the new ideas had upon European culture is hardly inferior to that of the Italian Renaissance. The spirit of free inquiry into personal and social issues, of calling all things in question before the bar of reason, acquired a formal discipline and an increasingly enthusiastic acceptance in wide sections of society. Intellectual courage and, even more, intellectual disinterestedness became fashionable virtues. Voltaire and Rousseau were universally fêted and admired, Hume was magnificently received in Paris. This was the climate of opinion which formed the character of the revolutionaries of 1789, a severe and heroic generation which yields to none in the clearness and purity of its convictions, in the robust and unsentimental intelligence of its humanism—above all, in its absolute moral and intellectual integrity securely founded upon the belief that the truth must ultimately prevail because it is the truth, a belief which years of exile and persecution did not weaken. Their moral and political ideas, and their words of praise and blame, have long since become the common inheritance of democrats of all shades and hues; socialists and liberals, utilitarians and believers in natural rights, speak their language and profess their faith, not so naïvely, nor with such utter confidence, but also less eloquently, less simply and less convincingly.

II

The counter-attack came with the turn of the century. It grew on German soil, but soon spread over the whole civilised world, checking the advance of empiricism from the west, and putting in its place a less rationalistic view of nature and of the individual, which, for good or ill, has had a vital and transforming effect on our views of man and society. Germany, spiritually and materially crippled by the Thirty Years' War, was, at the end of a long and sterile period, beginning to produce once more, towards the end of the eighteenth century, an indigenous culture of its own, influenced by, but fundamentally independent of, the French models which all Europe vied in imitating. Both in philosophy and in criticism the Germans began to produce works which were in form clumsier, but more ardently felt, more vehemently expressed, and more disquieting than anything written in France outside the pages of Rousseau. The French saw in this rich disarray only a grotesque travesty of their own limpid style and exquisite symmetry. The Napoleonic Wars, which added to the Germans' wounded intellectual pride the humiliation of military defeat, made the rift still wider, and the strong patriotic reaction which began during these wars and rose to a wild flood of national feeling after Napoleon's defeat, became identified with the new, so-called romantic philosophy of Kant's successors, Fichte, Schelling and the brothers Schlegel; their philosophy thus obtained national significance and became broadened and popularised into an almost official German faith. Against the scientific empiricism of the French and English, the Germans put forward the metaphysical historicism of Herder and of Hegel. Founded on the criticism of its rivals, it offered a bold alternative, the influence of which altered the history of civilisation in Europe and left an ineffaceable impression on its imagination and modes of feeling.

The classical philosophers of the eighteenth century had asked: Given that man is neither more nor less than an object in nature, what are the laws which govern his behaviour? If it is possible to discover by empirical means under what conditions bodies fall, planets rotate, trees grow, ice turns into water and water into steam, it must be no less possible to find out under what conditions men are caused to eat, drink, sleep, love, hate, fight one another, constitute themselves into families, tribes, nations, and again into monarchies, oligarchies, democracies. Until this is discovered by a Newton or a Galileo, no true science of society can come into being.

This radical empiricism appeared to Hegel to embody a scientific dogmatism even more disastrous than the theology which it wished to displace, involving the fallacy that only methods successful in the natural sciences can be valid in every other department of experience. He was sceptical of the new method even in the case of the material world, and quite groundlessly suspected natural scientists of arbitrarily selecting the phenomena which they discussed and no less arbitrarily limiting themselves to certain kinds of reasoning alone. But if his attitude towards empiricism in the sciences was unsympathetic, he was even more intensely convinced of its ruinous consequences when applied to the subject of human history. If history were written in accordance with scientific rules, as the word was understood by Voltaire or by Hume, a monstrous distortion of the facts would result, which the greatest historians, from Thucydides to Montesquieu, indeed Hume and Voltaire themselves, when they were not theorising, but writing history, had unconsciously avoided by a sure historical intuition. He conceived of history, as it were, in two dimensions: the horizontal, in which the phenomena of different spheres of activity are seen to be broadly interconnected in some unitary pattern, which gives each period its own individual, 'organic', recognisably unique character; and the vertical dimension, in which the same cross-section of events is viewed as part of a temporal succession, as a necessary stage in a developing process, in some sense contained and generated by its predecessor in time, which is itself seen already to embody, although in a less developed state, those very tendencies and forces whose full emergence makes the later age that which it ultimately comes to be. Hence every age, if it is to be genuinely understood, must be considered in relation not to the past alone, for it contains within its womb seeds of the future, foreshadowing the contour of what is yet to come; and this relation, no historian, however scrupulous, however anxious to avoid straying beyond the bare evidence of the facts, can allow himself to ignore. Only so can he represent in correct perspective the elements which compose the period with which he is dealing, distinguishing the significant from the trivial, the central determining characteristics of an age from those accidental, adventitious elements in it which might have happened anywhere and at any time, and consequently have no deep roots in its particular past and no appreciable effects on its particular future.

The conception of growth by which the acorn is said potentially to contain the oak, and to be adequately described only in terms of such development, is a doctrine as old as Aristotle and indeed older. In the Renaissance it came to light once more and was developed to its fullest extent by Leibniz, who taught that the universe was compounded of a plurality of independent individual substances, each of which is to be conceived as composed of its own whole past and its own whole future. Nothing was accidental; no object could be described as the empiricists wished to describe it, namely as a succession of continuous or discontinuous phenomena or states, connected at best only by the external relation of mechanical causation. The only true definition of an object was in terms which explained why it necessarily developed as it did in terms of its individual history, as a growing entity, each stage of which was, in the words of Leibniz, 'chargé du passé et gros de l'avenir'. Leibniz made no detailed attempt to apply this metaphysical doctrine to historical events, and yet that seemed to Hegel to be the sphere to which it best applied. For unless some relation other than that of scientific causation be postulated, history becomes nothing but a succession of externally related events. To explain is to give rational grounds and not merely antecedents. To explain a sequence of episodes, in this sense, is to attribute them to a rationally intelligible process—the purposive activity of a being or beings—God or men. Without this the events remain unexplained, groundless, 'meaningless'. A mechanical model may enable one to predict or control the behaviour of objects, but it cannot give a rational explanation; and unexplained events in human lives do not add up to human history. Similarly, it seems impossible to account for, even to express, the individual character of a particular personality or period of history, the individual essence, that is, the purpose, embodied in a particular work of art or science, by the methods of natural science, for even though its characteristics may indeed closely resemble something that has occurred before or after it, yet its totality is in some sense unique, and exists only once; this cannot therefore be accounted for by a scientific method whose successful application depends upon the occurrence of the precise opposite, namely, that the same phenomenon, the same combination of characteristics, should repeat itself, regularly recur, again and again.

The new method was first triumphantly applied by Herder, who, perhaps under the influence of the growth of national and cultural self-consciousness in Europe, and moved by hatred of the levelling cosmopolitanism and universalism of the prevailing French philosophy, applied the concept of organic development (as it later came to be called) to the history of entire cultures and nations as well as individuals. Indeed, he represented it as more fundamental in the case of the former, since individuals can only properly be viewed as occurring at a particular stage of the development of a society, which, in the thought and action of its greatest sons, reaches its most typical conscious expression. He immersed himself in the study of national German culture, its philology and archaeology, its barbarian beginnings, its medieval history and institutions, its traditional folklore and antiquities. From this he attempted to draw a portrait of the living German spirit as a formative force responsible for the unity of its own peculiar national development, which cannot be accounted for by the crudely mechanistic relation of mere loose before-and-afterness in time, by which the uniform, monotonous cycle of caused events, the rotation of the crops or the yearly revolutions of the earth, which are not history because they are not ways of human expression, may perhaps be satisfactorily explained.

Hegel developed this theme more widely and ambitiously. He taught that the explanation offered by French materialism afforded at best a hypothesis for explaining static but not dynamic phenomena, differences but not change. Given such and such material conditions, it may be possible to predict that the men born in them will develop certain characteristics, directly attributable to physical causes and to the education given to them by previous generations, themselves affected by the same conditions. But even if this is so, how much does it really tell us? The physical conditions of Italy, for example, were much the same in the first as they were in the eighth and fifteenth centuries, and yet the ancient Romans differ widely from their Italian descendants, and the men of the Renaissance showed certain marked characteristics which Italy in decline was losing or had totally lost. It cannot therefore be these relatively invariant conditions, with which alone the natural scientists are competent to deal, that are responsible for the phenomena of historical change, for progress and reaction, glory and decline. Some dynamic factor must be postulated to account both for change as such, and for the particular and unique form and direction which it has. Such change is plainly not repetitive: each age inherits something new from its predecessors, in virtue of which it differs from every preceding period; the principle of development excludes the principle of uniform repetition which is the foundation on which Galileo and Newton built. If history possesses laws, these laws must evidently be different in kind from what has passed for the only possible pattern of scientific law so far; and since everything that is persists, and has some history, the laws of history must for that very reason be identical with the laws of being of everything that exists.

Where is this principle of historical motion to be found? It is a confession of human failure, of the defeat of reason, to declare that this dynamic principle is that notorious object of the empiricist's gibes, a mysterious and occult power which men cannot expect ever to detect. It would be strange if that which governs our normal lives were not more present to us, a more familiar experience than any other that we have. For we need only take our own lives as the microcosm and pattern of the universe. We speak familiarly enough of the character, of the temper, of the purposes, motives, aims of a man as accounting for his acts and thoughts, not as some independent thing totally distinct from them, but as the common pattern which they express; and the better we know a man, the better we may be said to understand his moral and mental activity in its relation to the external world. Hegel transferred the concept of the personal character of the individual, the aims, logic, quality of his thoughts, his choices—his whole activity and experience as it unfolds itself throughout a man's life—to the case of entire cultures and nations. He referred to it variously as the Idea or Spirit, distinguished stages in its evolution, and pronounced it to be the motive, dynamic factor in the development of specific peoples and civilisations and so of the sentient universe as a whole. Further, he taught that the error of all previous thinkers was to assume the relative independence of different spheres of activity at a given period, of the wars of an age from its art, of its philosophy from its daily life. We should not naturally make this separation in the case of individuals; in the case of those with whom we are best acquainted, we half-unconsciously correlate all their acts as different manifestations of a single stream of purposive activity; we are affected by innumerable data drawn from this or that phase of their careers, which collectively constitute our mental portrait of them. This, according to Hegel, applies no less to our concept of a culture or of a particular historical period. The historians of the past have tended to write monographs on the history of this or that city or campaign, of the acts of this or that king or commander, as if they could be represented in isolation from the other phenomena of their time. But just as the acts of an individual are the acts of the whole individual, so the cultural phenomena of an age, the particular pattern of events that constitute it, are expressions of the whole age and of its whole personality, of a particular phase of the questing human spirit, seeking to understand, to control whatever it meets: that is, in its pursuit of complete self-mastery, which is Hegel's notion of freedom. This unitary character of an age, as expressing an integral outlook, is a fact which we do indeed tacitly recognise in speaking of a phenomenon as typical of the ancient rather than the modern world, or of an age of chaos rather than of one of settled peace.

This should be recognised explicitly. In writing, for instance, the history of seventeenth-century music, and in considering the rise of a particular form of polyphony, it is at least relevant to ask whether a development of a similar pattern may not be observed in the history of science at this time; whether, for example, the discovery of the differential calculus simultaneously by Newton and Leibniz was purely accidental, or due to certain general characteristics of that particular stage of European culture, which produced a not dissimilar genius in Bach and Leibniz, in Milton and Poussin. Obsession with rigorous scientific method might lead historians, as it does natural scientists, to build walls between their fields of inquiry and treat each branch of human activity as functioning in relative isolation, like so many parallel streams which cross rarely and without effect; whereas, if the historian is fully to realise his task, to rise above the chronicler and the antiquary, he must endeavour to paint a portrait of an age in movement, to collect that which is characteristic, distinguish between its component elements, between the old and the new, the fruitful and the sterile, the dying survivals of a previous age and the heralds of the future, born before their time.

This command to look for the most vivid expression of the universal in the particular, the concrete, the differentiated, the individual, to emulate the art and the realism of the biographer and the painter rather than the photographer and the statistician, is the peculiar legacy of German historicism. If history is a science, it must not be beguiled by the false analogy of physics or mathematics, which, looking for the widest obtainable, least varying, common characteristics, deliberately ignores what specifically belongs to only one time and one place, seeking to be as general, as abstract, as formal, as possible. The historian, on the contrary, must see and describe phenomena in their fullest context, against the background of the past and the foreground of the future, as being organically related to all other phenomena which spring from the same cultural impulse.

The effect of this doctrine, at once a symptom and a cause of a change of outlook on the part of an entire generation, and now grown so familiar, is inestimably great. Our habit of attaching particular characteristics to particular periods and places and of seeing individuals or their acts as typical of nations or of times; of bestowing almost a personality of their own, active causal properties, upon certain periods or peoples, or even on widely felt social attitudes, in virtue of which acts are described as expressions of the spirit of the Renaissance or of the French Revolution, of German romanticism or of the Victorian Age, springs from this new historicism of outlook. Hegel's specifically logical doctrines and his view of the method of the natural sciences were barren and their effects were on the whole disastrous. His true importance lies in his influence in the field of social and historical studies, in the creation of new disciplines, which consist in the history and criticism of human institutions, viewed as great collective quasi-personalities, which possess a life and character of their own, and cannot be described purely in terms of the individuals who compose them. This revolution in thought has bred irrational and dangerous myths—the treatment of state, race, history, epoch, for example, as super-persons exercising influence—but its effect on humane studies has been very fruitful. It was largely due to its influence that there came into existence a new school of German historians whose work made all writers who explained events as the outcome of the character or intentions, the personal defeat or triumph of this or that king or statesman, seem naïve and unscientific.

If history is the development of the Absolute Spirit, which Hegel did not identify solely with the human spirit, since he denied any essential divorce between mind and matter, it is necessary to rewrite it as the history of the achievement of the Spirit. The horizon suddenly seemed immensely widened. Legal history ceased to be a remote and special preserve of archaeologists and antiquaries and was transformed into Historical Jurisprudence, wherein contemporary legal institutions were interpreted as an orderly evolution from Roman or earlier law, embodying the Spirit of the Law in itself, of society in its legal aspect, interwoven with political, religious, social aspects of its life.

Henceforth the history of art and the history of philosophy began to be treated as complementary and indispensable elements in the general history of culture: facts previously thought trivial or sordid were accorded sudden importance as being hitherto unexplored domains of the activity of the Spirit—the histories of trade, of dress, of fashion, of language, of folklore, of the useful arts, were seen to be essential elements in the complete, 'organic', institutional history of mankind.

There was one respect, however, in which Hegel sharply diverged from the Leibnizian conception of development as a smooth progression of an essence gradually unfolding itself from potentiality into actuality. He insisted on the reality and necessity of conflicts and wars and revolutions, of the tragic waste and destruction in the world. He declared (following Fichte) that every process is one of necessary tension between incompatible forces, each straining against the other, and by this mutual conflict advancing their own development. This struggle is sometimes concealed and sometimes open, and can be traced in all provinces of conscious activity as the clash between so many rival physical, moral and intellectual attitudes and movements, each of which claims to provide total solutions and breeds new crises by its very one-sidedness; it grows in strength and sharpness until it turns into an open conflict which culminates in a final collision, the violence of which destroys all the contenders. This is the point at which the hitherto continuous development is broken, a sudden leap takes place to a new level, whereupon the tension between a new cluster of forces begins once more. Certain among those leaps, those, namely, which occur on a sufficiently large and noticeable scale, are termed political revolutions. But, on a more trivial scale, they occur in every sphere of activity, in the arts and sciences, in the growth of physical organisms studied by biologists and in the atomic processes studied by chemists, and finally in ordinary argument between two opponents, when, in the conflict between two partial falsehoods, new truth is discovered, itself only relative, itself assaulted by a counter-truth, the destruction of each by the other leading once more to a new level in which the antagonistic elements are transfigured into a new organic whole—a process which continues without end. He called this process dialectical. The notion of struggle and of tension provides precisely that dynamic principle which is required to account for movement in history. Thought is reality become conscious of itself, and its processes are the processes of nature in their clearest form. The principle of perpetual absorption and resolution (*Aufhebung*) in an ever higher unity occurs in nature as in discursive thought, and demonstrates that its processes are not purposeless, like the mechanical movements postulated by materialism, but possess an inner logic and lead in the direction of greater and greater self-realisation. Each major transition is marked by a large-scale revolutionary leap, such as, for example, the rise of Christianity, the destruction of Rome by the barbarians, or the great French Revolutions and the new Napoleonic world. In each case the Spirit or universal idea advances a step nearer to complete consciousness of itself, humanity is carried a stage forward, but never strictly in the direction anticipated by any of the movements engaged in the preliminary conflict, that side being more deeply and more irrationally disappointed which believed most firmly in its own peculiar ability to shape the world by its own efforts.

The new methods of research and interpretation which had suddenly been revealed produced a startling, and even intoxicating, effect on enlightened German society, and to a lesser extent on its cultural dependencies, the Universities of St Petersburg and Moscow. Hegelianism became the official creed of almost every man with intellectual pretensions: the new concepts were applied in every sphere of thought and action with an uncontrolled enthusiasm which an age more sceptical of ideas may find it difficult to conceive. Academic studies were transformed: Hegelian logic, Hegelian jurisprudence, Hegelian ethics and aesthetics, Hegelian theology, Hegelian philology, Hegelian historiography, surrounded the student of the humanities wherever he turned. Berlin, where Hegel's last years were spent, was the headquarters of the movement. Patriotism and political and social reaction lifted their heads again. The advance of the doctrine that all men were brothers, that national, racial and social differences were the artificial products of defective education, was arrested by the Idealist counter-thesis, according to which such differences, for all their apparent irrationality, express the peculiar historical role of a given race or nation, and are grounded in some metaphysical necessity. They are needed for the development of the Idea, of which the nation is a partial incarnation, and they cannot be made to vanish overnight by the mere application of reason by individual reformers. Reform must spring from historically prepared soil; otherwise it is doomed to failure, condemned in advance by the forces of history which move in accordance with their own logic in their own time and at their own pace. To demand freedom from these forces and seek to rise above them is to wish to escape from one's logically necessary historical position, from the society of which one is an integral part, from the complex of relations, public and private, by which every man is made to be what he is, which are the man, are what he is; to wish an escape from this is to wish to lose one's proper nature, a self-contradictory demand, which could be made only by men who do not understand what they are demanding, men whose ideas of personal liberty are childishly subjective.

True freedom consists in self-mastery, escape from external control. This can be achieved only by discovering what one is and can become; that is, by the discovery of the laws to which, in the particular time and place in which one lives, one is necessarily subject, and by the attempt to make actual those potentialities of one's rational, that is, one's law-abiding nature, the realisation of which advances the individual and thereby the society to which he 'organically' belongs, and which expresses itself in him and in others like him. Only 'world-historical' individuals who embody the laws of history in realising their own purposes can successfully break with the past. But when a man of lesser stature, in the name of some subjective ideal, attempts to destroy a tradition instead of modifying it and, in the course of this, to oppose the laws of history, he attempts the impossible, and thereby reveals his own irrationality. Such behaviour is condemned, not only because it is necessarily doomed to failure and therefore futile: situations might occur in which it might be thought to be nobler to perish quixotically than to survive. It is condemned because it is irrational, since the laws of history which it opposes are the laws of the Spirit, which is the ultimate substance of which everything is composed, and are therefore necessarily rational; indeed, if they were not, they would not be amenable to human explanation. The Spirit approaches its perfection by gradually attaining to greater self-consciousness with every generation; and the highest point of its development is reached in those who at any time see themselves most clearly in their relation to their universe, that is, in the profoundest thinkers of every epoch. The thinkers, for Hegel and his disciples, include the artists and the philosophers, the scientists and the poets, all those sensitive and inquiring spirits who are more acutely and more profoundly conscious than the rest of their society of the stage of development which humanity has reached, of what has been gained in their time and partly by their effort.

The history of philosophy is the history of the growth of this self-awareness, in which the Spirit becomes conscious of its own activity; and the history of humanity, on this view, is itself nothing other than the story of the progress of the Spirit in the process of its growing self-awareness. All history is thus the history of thought, that is, the history of philosophy, which is identical with the philosophy of history, since that is but a name for the awareness of this awareness. The celebrated Hegelian epigram, 'the philosophy of history is the history of philosophy', is, for anyone who accepts the Hegelian metaphysic, not an obscure paradox, but a platitude, quaintly expressed—with the important and peculiar corollary that all true progress is progress of the Spirit—most conscious in men, not conscious in nature—since that is the substance of which all else is compounded. Hence the sole method by which those who have the good of society at heart can improve society is to develop in themselves and in others the power of analysing themselves and their environment, an activity later called criticism, the growth of which is identical with human progress. From this it follows that changes involving physical violence and bloodshed are due solely to the recalcitrance of brute matter, which, as Leibniz had taught, is itself but spirit, at a lower, less conscious level. The revolutions instituted by Socrates, or by Jesus, or by Newton, were therefore far more truly revolutions than events which are commonly so called, although they occurred without battles; all genuine conquest, all true victory is literally, and not in metaphor, gained always in the realm of the Spirit. Thus the French Revolution was in effect over when the philosophers had transformed men's consciousness of their world, before the guillotine began its work.

This doctrine appeared to solve at last the great problem which vexed men's minds throughout the early nineteenth century; the question to which all its leading political theories are so many different answers. The French Revolution had been made in order to secure liberty, equality and fraternity among men; it was the greatest attempt in modern history to embody a wholly new revolutionary ideology in concrete institutions by the violent and successful seizure of power on the part of the ideologues themselves: it failed, and its purpose, the establishment of human freedom and equality, seemed as remote from realisation as ever. What answer was there to those who, bitterly disillusioned, fell into cynical apathy, proclaiming the impotence of good over evil, of truth over falsehood, affirming the total inability of mankind to improve its lot by its own efforts? To this problem, with which the social thought of the period of political reaction in Europe is preoccupied, Hegel provided an impressive solution by his doctrine of the inevitable character of the historical process, which involves the predestined failure of any attempt to deflect it or hasten it by violence—a sign of fanaticism, that is, one-sided exaggeration of some one aspect of the dialectic—a view directly opposed to the rival technological hypotheses then being advanced in France by Saint-Simon and Fourier. The problem of social freedom, and of the causes of the failure to attain it, is therefore quite naturally the central subject of all Marx's early writings. His approach to the problem and his solution are in spirit profoundly influenced by Hegel. His early training and his natural instincts inclined him towards empiricism; and the modes of thought which belong to this outlook are sometimes visible below the metaphysical structure beneath which they are for the most part concealed. This emerges most clearly in his passion for exposing irrationalism and myths in every shape and guise; often in his argument he uses the methods and examples of eighteenth-century materialism; but the form in which it is expressed, and the theses it is designed to prove, are wholly Hegelian: the ascent of humanity, which by its labours transforms itself, and the external nature to which it is organically related, by subjugating all it deals with to rational control. He was converted to the new outlook in his youth, and for many years, despite his vehement attack on the idealist metaphysic, remained a convinced, consistent and admiring follower of the great philosopher.

Freud   Darwin   Marx   Copernicus   Newton
Freud   Nietzsche   Marx

4

The Young Hegelians

They [the Germans] will never rise. They would sooner die than rebel . . . perhaps even a German, when he has been driven to absolute despair, will cease to argue, but it needs a colossal amount of unspeakable oppression, insult, injustice and suffering to reduce him to that state.

MICHAEL BAKUNIN

THE years which Marx spent as a student in the University of Berlin were a period of profound depression among the radical intelligentsia of Germany. In 1840 a new king from whom much was expected had ascended the throne of Prussia. Before his accession he had spoken more than once of a natural alliance of patriotism, democratic principles, and the monarchy; he had spoken of granting a new constitution; ecstatic references began to appear in the liberal press to Don Carlos and The Crowned Romantic. These promises came to less than nothing. The new monarch was no less reactionary, but more astute and less bound by routine than his father; the methods of suppression employed by his police were more imaginative and more efficient than those in use in the days of Frederick William III; otherwise his accession made little difference. There was no sign of reform, either political or social; the July Revolution in France, which was greeted with immense enthusiasm by German radicals, had merely caused Metternich to set up a central commission to suppress dangerous thought in all German lands, a measure zealously welcomed by the Prussian landowning gentry, whose continued power paralysed every effort towards freedom. The governing class did all that was in its power to obstruct—it could not entirely suppress—the growing class of industrialists and bankers, which, even in backward and docile Prussia, began to show unmistakable signs of restiveness. Open expression in the Press or at public meetings was unthinkable: the official censorship was too efficient and ubiquitous; the Diet was packed with the King's supporters; the gathering feeling of resentment against the landlords and officials, increased by the growing sense of its own strength on the part of the middle class, finally emerged through the only available outlet of German self-expression, in a flood of words, a philosophy of opposition.

If orthodox Hegelianism was a conservative movement and the answer of wounded German traditionalism to the French attempt to impose its new principle of universal reason upon the world, the secession of its younger members represents an effort to find some progressive interpretation for the formulas of natural development, to detach the Hegelian philosophy from its preoccupation with past history and to identify it with the future, to adapt it to the new social and economic factors which were everywhere coming into being. Both camps, the right and the left, the old, and as they came to be called, the Young Hegelians, based themselves on their founder's famous dictum according to which the real is the rational and the rational is the real; and both agreed that this was to be interpreted as meaning that the true explanation of any phenomenon was equivalent to the demonstration of its logical—which to them meant historical or metaphysical (for all these were in some sense identical)—necessity, which was tantamount to its rational justification. Nothing could be both evil and necessary, for whatever is real is necessarily so, and the necessity of anything is its justification: *Die Weltgeschichte ist das Weltgericht* (World history is world justice). So much was accepted by both sides. The schism arose over the relative emphasis to be placed on the crucial terms, 'rational' and 'real'.

The conservatives, proclaiming that only the real was rational, declared that the measure of rationality was actuality, or capacity for survival—that the stage reached by social or personal institutions, as they existed at any given moment, was the sufficient measure of their excellence. So, for example, Germanic (that is western) culture, as Hegel did in fact declare, was a higher, and probably ultimate, synthesis of its predecessors, the Oriental and Graeco-Roman cultures. From which it followed (for some of the master's disciples) that the last stage being of necessity the best, the most perfect political framework yet attained by men consisted in the highest incarnation to date of western values—the modern, that is, the Prussian State. To wish to alter this State or subvert it was morally wrong, because directed against the rational will embodied in it, and in any case futile, because set against a decision already made by history. This is a form of argument adapted to its own purposes with which Marxism later familiarised the world.

The radicals, stressing the converse, protested that only the rational was real. The actual, they insisted, is often full of inconsistencies, anachronisms and blind unreason: it cannot therefore be regarded in any genuine, that is metaphysical, sense as being real. Basing themselves on numerous texts from Hegel, they pointed out that the master recognised that mere occurrence in space or time was by no means equivalent to being real: the existent might well be a tissue of chaotic institutions, each frustrating the purposes of the other, and so from the metaphysical point of view contradictory and therefore utterly illusory. Degrees of reality were measured by the extent to which the entities under examination tended to form a rational whole, which may necessitate a radical transformation of given institutions in accordance with the dictates of reason. These are best known to those who have emancipated themselves from the tyranny of the merely actual, and have revealed its inadequacy to its historic role, as deduced from a correct interpretation of the character and direction of the past and present. This critical activity directed against the social institutions of his time, on the part of the individual who lifts himself above them, is the noblest function of man; the more enlightened the critic, the more searching his criticism, the more rapid will be the actual progress towards the real. For, as Hegel had indubitably said, reality is a process, a universal effort to attain to self-consciousness, and grows more perfect in the very growth of critical self-consciousness among men. Nor was there any reason to suppose that such progress must be gradual and painless. Citing again the texts enunciated by Hegel, the radicals reminded their opponents that progress was the result of tension between opposites, which grew to a crisis and then burst into open revolution: then and only then did the leap into the next stage occur. These were the laws of development found equally in the obscurest processes of brute nature and in the affairs of men and societies.

The plain duty of the philosopher who bears the burdens of civilisation on his shoulders is, therefore, to promote revolution by the special technical skill which he alone commands, that is by intellectual warfare. It is his task to stir men from their indolence and torpor, to sweep away obstructive and useless institutions with the aid of his critical weapons much as the French philosophers had undermined the *ancien régime* by the power of ideas alone. There must be no resort either to physical violence or to the brute force of the masses: to appeal to the mob, which represents the lowest level of self-consciousness reached by the Spirit among men, is to make use of irrational means, which could only produce irrational consequences: a revolution of ideas will of itself bring about a revolution in practice: *Hinter die Abstraktion stellt sich die Praxis von selbst* (Behind the abstract theory practice materialises of its own accord). But since open political pamphleteering was forbidden, the opposition was driven into less direct methods of attack; the first battles against orthodoxy were fought in the field of Christian theology, whose professors had hitherto tolerated, if not encouraged, a philosophy which had shown every disposition to support the existing order. In 1835 David Friedrich Strauss published a critical life of Jesus in which the new critical method was used to show that some portions of the Gospels were pure invention, while others represented not facts, but semi-mythological beliefs entertained in the early Christian communities—a stage in the self-awareness of mankind. The whole subject was treated as an exercise in the critical examination of a historically important but unreliable text. His book caused an immediate storm not only in orthodox circles, but also among the Young Hegelians, whose most prominent representative, Bruno Bauer, then a lecturer in theology in the University of Berlin, published several attacks upon it from the point of view of an even extremer Hegelian atheism, wholly denying the historical existence of Jesus, and attempting to explain the Gospels as works of pure fiction, as the literary expression of the 'ideology' prevalent in its time, as the highest point reached at this period by the development of the Absolute Idea. The Prussian authorities were not in general interested in sectarian controversies among philosophers, but in this quarrel both sides appeared to hold views subversive of religious, and so, in all likelihood, of political orthodoxy. Hegelianism, which had previously been left in peace as a harmless, and even a loyal and patriotic philosophical movement, was suddenly accused of demagogic tendencies. Hegel's greatest opponent, Schelling, by then a pious and bitterly reactionary old romantic, was brought to Berlin in order to refute these doctrines publicly, but his lectures failed to produce the desired result. The censorship was tightened, and the Young Hegelians found themselves driven into a position in which they were given the choice of capitulating completely or of moving farther to the political left than the majority wished to go. The only arena where the issue should be still raised was the universities, where a curtailed, but nevertheless genuine, academic freedom continued to survive. The University of Berlin was the chief seat of Hegelianism, and it was not long before Marx became immersed in its philosophical politics.

He began his academic career as a student of the faculty of law by attending Savigny's lectures on jurisprudence and those of Gans on criminal law. Savigny, the founder and the greatest theorist of the Historical School of Jurisprudence and a convinced and rabid anti-liberal, was the most distinguished defender of Prussian absolutism in the nineteenth century. He was not a Hegelian, but agreed with the school in rejecting equally the theory of unalterable natural rights and utilitarianism, and interpreted law and institutional structures historically, as a continuous orderly, traditional development springing from, and justified by, the ideals and character of a given nation in its historical surroundings.

Marx attended Savigny's lectures regularly for two terms, and the immense erudition and power of close historical argument for which the latter was notable was probably Marx's first contact with the new method of historical research, which demanded minute knowledge of facts as a basis for broad general theses. Savigny's chief professional opponent was the professor of criminal law, Eduard Gans, whose effect on Marx was more considerable. Gans was one of Hegel's favourite disciples: he was by birth a Jew, a friend of Heine, and like him a humanitarian radical who did not share his teacher's low opinion of the French Enlightenment. His lectures, models, it seems, both of eloquence and of courage, were widely attended; his free criticism in the light of reason of legal institutions and of methods of legislation, with no trace of mysticism about the past, affected Marx profoundly, and inspired him with a conception of the proper purpose and method of theoretical criticism which he never completely lost.

Under the influence of Gans he saw in jurisprudence the natural field for the application and verification of every type of philosophy of history. Hegelianism at first repelled his naturally positivist intelligence. In a long and intimate letter to his father he described his efforts to construct a rival system; after sleepless nights and disordered days spent in wrestling with the adversary, he fell ill and left Berlin to recuperate. He returned with a sense of failure and frustration, equally unable to work or to rest. His father wrote him a long paternal letter, begging him not to waste his time on barren metaphysical speculation when he had his career to think of. His words fell on deaf ears. Marx resolutely plunged into an exhaustive study of Hegel's work, read night and day, and after three weeks announced his complete conversion. He sealed it by becoming a member of the *Doktorklub* (Graduates' Club), an association of free-thinking university intellectuals, who met in beer cellars, wrote mildly seditious verse, professed violent hatred of the King, the Church, the bourgeoisie, and above all argued endlessly on points of Hegelian theology. Here he met, and was soon on terms of intimacy with, the leading members of this bohemian group, the brothers Bruno, Edgar and Egbert Bauer, Köppen, one of the earliest students of Tibetan lamaism and the author of a history of the French Terror, Max Stirner, who preached an ultra-individualism of his own, and other free spirits (as they called themselves).

He abandoned his legal studies, and became entirely absorbed in philosophy. No other subject seemed to him to possess sufficient contemporary significance. He planned to become a lecturer in philosophy in one of the universities, and, together with Bauer, to launch a violent atheistic campaign which should put an end to the timorous, half-hearted toying with dangerous doctrines to which the milder radicals confined themselves. It was to take the form of an elaborate hoax, appearing as an anonymous diatribe against Hegel by a pious Lutheran charging him with atheism and subversion of public order and morality, and armed with copious quotations from the original text. This joint work actually appeared and caused some stir; a few reviewers were genuinely taken in, but the authors were discovered, and the episode ended by Bauer's removal from his academic post. As for Marx, he frequented social and literary salons, met the celebrated Bettina von Arnim, the friend of Beethoven and Goethe, who was attracted by his audacity and wit, wrote a conventional philosophical dialogue, and composed a fragment of a Byronic tragedy and several volumes of bad verse which he dedicated to Jenny von Westphalen, to whom he had in the meantime become secretly engaged. His father, frightened by this intellectual dissipation, wrote letter after letter full of anxious and affectionate advice, begging him to think of the future and prepare himself to be a lawyer or a civil servant. His son sent soothing answers, and went on with his previous mode of life.

He was now twenty-four years of age, an amateur philosopher of no fixed occupation, respected in advanced circles for his erudition and for his powers as an ironical and bitter controversialist. He soon began to be increasingly irritated by the prevailing literary and philosophical style of his friends and allies, an extraordinary compound of pedantry and arrogance, full of obscure paradoxes and laboured epigrams, embedded in elaborate, alliterative, punning prose which can never have been intended to be fully understood. Marx was to some extent infected by it himself, particularly in his early polemical pieces; yet his prose is compact and luminous in comparison with the mass of neo-Hegelian patter which at this time was let loose upon the German public. Some years later he wrote a description of the condition of German philosophy at this time: 'According to the reports of our ideologists', he wrote, 'Germany has, during the last decade, undergone a revolution of unexampled proportions . . . a revolution in comparison with which the French Revolution was mere child's play. With unbelievable rapidity one empire was supplanted by another, one mighty hero was struck down by another still bolder and more powerful in the universal chaos. During three years, from 1842 to 1845, Germany went through a cataclysm more violent in character than anything which had happened in any previous century. All this, if it is true, took place only in the region of pure thought. For we are dealing with a remarkable phenomenon—the decomposition of the Absolute Spirit.

'When the last spark of life disappeared from its body, its various constituents disintegrated and entered into new combinations and formed new substances. Dealers in philosophy, who had previously made a living by exploiting the Absolute Spirit, now threw themselves avidly on the new combinations. Each busily began to dispose of his share of it. Plainly this could not be done without competition. At first it possessed a solidly commercial, respectable character; but later when the German market became glutted, and the world market, in spite of all efforts, proved incapable of assimilating further goods, the whole business—as usual in Germany—was spoilt by mass production, lowering of quality, adulteration of raw material, forged labels, fictitious deals, financial chicanery, and a credit structure which lacked all real basis. Competition turned into an embittered struggle, which is now represented to us in glowing colours as a revolution of cosmic significance, rich in epoch-making achievements and results.'

father dies

This was written in 1846; in 1841 Marx might perhaps have continued to live in this fantastic world, himself taking part in the inflation and mass production of words and concepts, if his circumstances had not suffered a sudden catastrophic change: his father, on whom he financially depended, died, leaving a barely sufficient competence to his widow and youngest children. At the same time, the Prussian Minister of Education finally decided to condemn the Hegelian Left officially, and expelled Bauer from his post. This effectively closed the possibility of an academic career to Marx who was heavily compromised in the Bauer affair, and it forced him to look for another occupation. He did not have long to wait. Among his warmest admirers was a certain Moses Hess, a Jewish publicist from Cologne, a sincere and enthusiastic radical, who was even then far in advance even of the Hegelian Left. He had visited Paris and had there met the leading French socialist and communist writers of the day, to whose views he became a passionate convert. Hess, who was a curious blend of ardent traditional Judaism with idealistic humanitarianism and Hegelian ideas, preached the primacy of economic over political factors and the impossibility of emancipating mankind without previously liberating the wage-earning proletariat. Its continued slavery, he declared, made all the efforts of intellectuals to establish a new moral world unavailing, since justice cannot exist in a society which tolerates economic inequality and exploitation. The institution of private property was the source of all evil; men could be freed only by the abolition of both private and national property, which must involve the removal of national frontiers, and the reconstitution of a new international society on a rational, collectivist, economic basis. His meeting with Marx overwhelmed him: in a letter to a fellow radical he declared: 'He is the greatest, perhaps the one genuine philosopher now alive and will soon . . . draw the eyes of all Germany . . . Dr Marx—that is my idol's name—is still very young (about twenty-four at most) and will give medieval religion and politics their *coup de grâce*. He combines the deepest philosophical seriousness with the most biting wit. Imagine Rousseau, Voltaire, Holbach, Lessing, Heine and Hegel fused into one person—I say fused, not thrown together in a heap—and you have Dr Marx.'

Marx thought Hess's enthusiasm endearing but ridiculous, and adopted a patronising tone which Hess was at first too amiable to resent. Hess was a disseminator of ideas, a fervent missionary rather than an original thinker, and converted more than one of

end to academic career

Engels

his contemporaries to communism, among them a young radical named Friedrich Engels who had not at this time met Marx. Both learnt from association with him far more than either was ready to admit; in later years they tended to treat Hess, who remained a dedicated Marxist (but added subsequently a fervent belief in Zionism, and, in any case, was not a man of action), as a harmless but tedious fool. At this time, however, Marx found him a useful ally, since Hess, who was a tireless agitator, had managed to persuade a group of liberal industrialists in the Rhineland to finance the publication of a radical journal which should contain articles on political and economic subjects directed against the economically reactionary policy of the Berlin government, and in general sympathy with the needs of the rising bourgeois class. It was issued at Cologne and was called the *Rheinische Zeitung.*

Marx was invited, and he eagerly consented, to contribute regular articles to this journal; ten months later he became its chief editor. It was his first experience of practical politics: he conducted his paper with immense vigour and intolerance: his dictatorial nature asserted itself early in the venture, and his subordinates were only too glad to let him do entirely as he pleased, and write as much of the paper as he wished. From a mildly liberal paper it rapidly became a vehemently radical one, more violently hostile to the Government than any other German newspaper. It published long and scurrilous attacks on the Prussian censorship, on the Federal Diet, on the landowning class in general; its circulation rose, its fame grew throughout Germany, and the Government was at last forced to take notice of the surprising behaviour of the Rhineland bourgeoisie. The shareholders were, indeed, scarcely less surprised than the authorities, but as the number of subscribers was steadily increasing, and the economic policy pursued by the paper was scrupulously liberal, advocating free trade and the economic unification of Germany, they did not protest. The Prussian authorities, anxious not to irritate the newly annexed western provinces, also refrained from interference. Emboldened by this toleration, Marx intensified the attack and added to the discussion of general political and economic subjects two particular issues over which there was much bitter feeling in the province: the first was the distressed condition of the Moselle vine-growing peasantry; the second, the harsh law punishing thefts by the poor of decayed timber in the neighbouring forests. Marx used both these as texts for a particularly violent indictment of the government of landlords. The government, after cautiously exploring feeling in the district, decided to apply its power of censorship, and did so with increasing severity. Marx used all his ingenuity to circumvent the censors, who were mostly men of limited intelligence, and he managed to publish a quantity of thinly veiled democratic and republican propaganda, which more than once led to reprimands by the censor and his replacement by another and stricter official. The year 1842 was spent in this elaborate game, which might have continued indefinitely if Marx had not inadvertently overstepped the limit. The Russian Government throughout the nineteenth century represented the greatest embodiment of obscurantism, barbarism and oppression in Europe, the inexhaustible reservoir whence the reactionaries of other nations were able to draw strength, and consequently became the bugbear of western liberals of all shades of opinion. It was at this time the dominant partner in the Russo-Prussian alliance, and as such was fiercely attacked by Marx in successive editorial articles: a war against the Russians seemed to him both then and later the best blow that could be struck on behalf of European liberty. The Emperor Nicholas I himself happened to come upon a copy of one of these philippics, and expressed angry surprise to the Prussian Ambassador. A severe note was sent by the Russian Chancellor upbraiding the King of Prussia for the inefficiency of his censors. The Prussian Government, anxious to appease its powerful neighbour, took immediate steps; the *Rheinische Zeitung* was suppressed without warning in April 1843, and Marx was free once more. One year had sufficed to turn him into a brilliant political journalist of notorious views, with a fully developed taste for baiting illiberal governments, a taste which his later career was to give him full opportunity of satisfying.

Meanwhile he had been working with restless energy: he had taught himself French by reading the works of the Paris socialists, Fourier, Proudhon, Dézamy, Cabet and Leroux. He read recent French and German history and Machiavelli's *Prince*. For a month he was absorbed in the histories of ancient and modern art in order to gather evidence to demonstrate the basically revolutionary and disruptive character of Hegel's fundamental categories; like the young Russian radicals of this period he looked upon them as being, in Herzen's phrase, 'the algebra of revolution'. 'Too frightened to apply them openly', wrote Herzen, 'in the storm-tossed ocean of politics, the old philosopher set them afloat in the tranquil inland lake of aesthetic theory.' Marx's view of their proper interpretation had lately been affected, however, by a book which had appeared during that year—the *Preliminary Theses on the Reformation of Philosophy*, by Ludwig Feuerbach.

Feuerbach is one of those interesting authors, not infrequently met with in the history of thought, who, without being thinkers of the first order, nevertheless provide men of greater gifts with the sudden spark which sets on fire long-accumulated fuel. He defended empirical positions at a time when Marx was reacting violently against the subtleties of the decadent idealism in which he had been immersed during the past five years. Feuerbach's simpler style seemed suddenly to open a window into the real world. The neo-Hegelian scholasticism of the Bauers and their disciples suddenly seemed to him like a heavy nightmare which had but lately lifted, and the last memories of which he was determined to shake off.

Hegel had asserted that the thoughts and acts of men who belonged to the same period of a given culture were determined by the working in them of an identical spirit which manifested itself in all the phenomena of the period. Feuerbach vehemently rejected this. 'What', he inquired in effect, 'is the spirit of an age or a culture other than a compendious name for the totality of the phenomena which compose it?' To say, therefore, that the phenomena were determined to be what they were by it, was to assert that they were determined by the totality of them-selves—an empty tautology. Nor was the case improved, he went on to point out, by substituting for this totality the concept of a pattern, for patterns cannot cause events; a pattern was a form, an attribute of events, which could themselves be caused only by other events. The Greek genius, the Roman character, the spirit of the Renaissance, the spirit of the French Revolution, what were these but abstractions, labels to describe compendiously a given complex of qualities and historical events, general terms invented by men for their own convenience, but in no sense real objective inhabitants of the world, capable of effecting this or that alter-ation in human affairs? The older view according to which it is the decision and action of individuals that is responsible for change was fundamentally less absurd: for individuals at least exist and act in a sense in which general notions and common names do not. Hegel had rightly stressed the inadequacy of this view, because it failed to give an explanation of how the total result emerged from the interplay of a colossal number of indi-vidual lives and acts, and he showed genius in looking for some single common force responsible for giving a definite direction to these wills, some general law in virtue of which history can be made a systematic account of the progress of whole societies. But in the end he failed to be rational, and ended in an obscure mysticism; for the Hegelian Idea, if it was not a tautological re-formation of what it was intended to explain, was but a disguised name for the personal God of Christianity, and so lifted the subject beyond the confines of rational discussion.

Feuerbach's next step was to declare that the motive force of history was not spiritual, but the sum of the material conditions which at any given time determine the men who live in them to think and act as they do. Their material distress caused them, however, to seek solace in an immaterial ideal world of their own, albeit unconscious, invention, where as a reward for the unhappiness of their lives on earth, they would enjoy eternal bliss hereafter. All that they lack on earth—justice, harmony, order, goodness, unity, permanence—they transform into transcendent attributes of a transcendent world, which alone they call real, and which they turn into an object of worship. If this illusion was to be exposed, it must be analysed in terms of the material maladjustments which psychologically give rise to it. Like Holbach and the author of *L'Homme Machine*, Feuerbach's hatred of transcendentalism often led him to seek for the crudest and simplest explanation in purely physical terms. *Der Mensch ist was er isst* (Man is what he eats) is his own Hegelian caricature of his doctrine: human history is the history of the decisive influence of physical environment on men in society; therefore knowledge of physical laws alone can make man master of these forces by enabling him to adapt his life consciously to them.

His materialism, and in particular his theory that all 'ideologies' whether religious or secular are often an attempt to provide ideal compensation for real miseries, and hence at once disclose and obscure their existence, made a profound impression both on Marx and on Engels, as it later did on Lenin, who read Feuerbach during his Siberian exile. Feuerbach's best-known work, the *Essence of Christianity* of 1841 (translated into English by George Eliot), which Marx had read, as well as the earlier *Criticism of the Philosophy of Hegel*, are profoundly felt, passionately polemical treatises, at times simple-minded and showing little sense of history, but well organised and cogent; after the absurdities of the unbridled Hegelianism of the thirties, their very simplicity, honesty and courage must have seemed refreshingly sane. Marx, who was still a radical and an idealist at this period, was roused by it from his dogmatism. The Hegelian Idea had turned out to be a meaningless expression: Hegel now seemed to him to have built a specious edifice of words about words, and one which it was the duty of his generation, armed with the valuable Hegelian method, to replace by symbols denoting real objects in time and space, in their observable empirical relations to each other. He still believed in the efficacy of the appeal to reason and was opposed to violent revolution. He was a dissident idealist, but an idealist still: a year previously he had obtained a doctor's degree in the University of Jena, with a characteristically Young Hegelian thesis on the contrast between the views of Democritus and Epicurus, in which he defends theses which he attributed to the latter in terms not much less nebulous than much of what he later himself condemned as typical idealist verbiage.

In April 1843, he married Jenny von Westphalen, against the wishes of the greater part of her family. This hostility only served to increase the passionate loyalty of the serious and profoundly romantic young woman: her existence had been transformed by the revelation to her of a new world by her husband, and she dedicated her whole being to his life and his work. She loved, admired and trusted him, and was, emotionally and intellectually, entirely dominated by him. He leaned on her unhesitatingly in all times of crisis and disaster, remained all his life proud of her beauty, her birth and her intelligence. The poet Heine, who knew them well in Paris, paid eloquent tribute to her charm and wit. In later years, when they were reduced to penury, she displayed great moral heroism in preserving intact the framework of a family and a household, which alone enabled her husband to continue his work.

Together they decided to emigrate to France. He knew that he had an original contribution to make to the agitating questions of the day, and that in Germany it was impossible to speak openly on any serious topic. Nothing held him back: his father was dead, for his family he cared nothing. He had no fixed source of income in Germany. His old associates of Berlin now seemed to him to be a collection of intellectual mountebanks who wished to cover the poverty and confusion of their thought by violent language and scandalous private lives. All his life he detested two phenomena with peculiar passion: disorderly life and histrionic display. It seemed to him that bohemianism and deliberate flouting of conventions was but inverted philistinism, emphasising and paying homage to the very same false values by exaggerated protest against them, and exhibiting therefore the same fundamental vulgarity. Köppen he still respected, but he lost all personal touch with him, and formed a new and tepid friendship with Arnold Ruge, a gifted Saxon journalist who edited a radical periodical to which Marx had contributed. Ruge was a pompous and irritable man, a discontented Hegelian, a radical who after 1848 gradually became transformed into a reactionary nationalist. As a writer he had a wider outlook and surer taste than many of his fellow radicals in Germany, and appreciated the gifts of greater men, such as Marx and Bakunin, with whom he came into contact. He saw no possibility of continuing his journal on German soil in the teeth of the censor and the Saxon police, and decided to establish it in Paris. He invited Marx to assist him in editing a new journal to be called *Deutsch-Französische Jahrbücher*; Marx accepted the offer with alacrity. 'The atmosphere here is really too intolerable and asphyxiating', he wrote to Ruge in the summer of 1843. 'It is not easy to cringe even for the sake of liberty, armed with pins instead of a sword: I am tired of this hypocrisy and stupidity, of the boorishness of officials, I am tired of having to bow and scrape and invent safe and harmless phrases. In Germany there is nothing I can do . . . in Germany one can only be false to oneself.' Marx left Prussian territory in November 1843, and two days later arrived in Paris. His reputation had to some extent preceded him: at that date he was principally thought of as a liberal journalist with a mordant pen, who was forced to leave Germany because he had too violently advocated democratic reform. Two years later he was known to the police of many lands as an uncompromising revolutionary communist, an opponent of reformist liberalism, the notorious leader of a subversive movement with international ramifications. The years 1843–5 are the most decisive in his life: in Paris he underwent his final intellectual transformation. At the end of it he had arrived at a clear position personally and politically: the remainder of his life was devoted to its development and practical realisation.

5
Paris

The time will come when the sun will shine only upon a world of free men who recognise no master except their reason, when tyrants and slaves, priests, and their stupid or hypocritical tools, will no longer exist except in history or on the stage.

CONDORCET

THE social, political and artistic ferment of Paris in the middle of the nineteenth century is a phenomenon without parallel in European history. A remarkable concourse of poets, painters, musicians, writers, reformers and theorists had gathered in the French capital, which, under the comparatively tolerant monarchy of Louis-Philippe, gave asylum to exiles and revolutionaries of many lands. Paris had long been notable for wide intellectual hospitality; the thirties and forties were years of profound political reaction in the rest of Europe, and artists and thinkers in growing numbers flocked to the circle of light from the surrounding darkness, finding that in Paris they were neither, as in Berlin, bullied into conformity by the native civilisation, nor yet, as in London, left coldly to themselves, clustering in small isolated groups, but rather were welcomed freely and even enthusiastically, and given free entry into the artistic and social *salons* which had survived the years of monarchist restoration. The intellectual atmosphere in which these men talked and wrote was excited and idealistic. A common mood of passionate protest against the old order, against kings and tyrants, against the Church and the army, above all against the uncomprehending philistine masses, slaves and oppressors, enemies to life and the rights of the free human personality, produced an exhilarating sense of emotional solidarity, which bound together this tumultuous and widely heterogeneous society. The emotions were intensely cultivated, individual feelings and beliefs were expressed in ardent phrases, revolutionary and humanitarian slogans were repeated with fervour by men who were prepared to stake their lives upon them; it was a decade during which a richer international traffic in ideas, theories, personal sentiments, was carried on than during any previous period; there were alive at this time, congregated in the same place, attracting, repelling and transforming each other, men of gifts more varied, more striking and more articulate than at any time since the Renaissance. Every year brought new exiles from the territories of the Emperor and the Tsar. Italian, Polish, Hungarian, Russian, German colonies throve in the atmosphere of universal sympathy and admiration. Their members formed international communities, wrote pamphlets, addressed assemblies, entered conspiracies, but above all talked and argued ceaselessly in private houses, in the streets, in cafés, at public banquets; the mood was exalted and optimistic.

The revolutionary writers and radical politicians were at the height of their hopes and power, their ideals not yet killed, nor the revolutionary phrases tarnished by the débâcle of 1848. Such international solidarity for the cause of freedom had never before been achieved in any place: poets and musicians, historians and social theorists felt that they wrote not for themselves or a particular public but for humanity. In 1830 a victory had been achieved over the forces of reaction. They continued to live on its fruits; the suppressed Blanquist conspiracy of 1839 had been ignored by the majority of romantic liberals as an obscure *émeute*, yet it was no isolated outbreak: for this seething and nervous artistic activity took place against a background of hectic financial and industrial progress accompanied by ruthless corruption, in which vast sudden fortunes were made and lost again in colossal bankruptcies. A government of disillusioned realists was controlled by the new ruling class of great financiers and railway magnates, large industrialists who moved in a maze of intrigue and bribery, in which shady speculators and sordid adventurers controlled the economic destiny of France. The frequent riots of the industrial workers in the south indicate a state of turbulent unrest due as much to the unscrupulous behaviour of particular employers of labour as to the industrial revolution which was transforming the country more rapidly and more brutally, although on a far smaller scale, than in England. Acute social discontent, together with the universal recognition of the weakness and dishonesty of the Government, added to the general sense of crisis and transition, which made anything seem attainable to one who was sufficiently gifted, unscrupulous and energetic; it fed the imagination, and produced full-blooded, ambitious opportunists of the type to be found in the pages of Balzac, and in Stendhal's unfinished novel, *Lucien Leuwen*, while the laxity of the censorship, and the tolerance exercised by the July monarchy, permitted that sharp and violent form of political journalism, sometimes rising to noble eloquence, which, at a time when printed words had a greater power to move, stirred the intellect and the passions, and served still further to intensify the already electric atmosphere. The memoirs and letters left by writers, painters, musicians—Musset, Heine, Tocqueville, Delacroix, Wagner, Berlioz, Gautier, Herzen, Turgenev, Victor Hugo, George Sand, Liszt—convey something of the enchantment which surrounds those years marked by the acute and conscious sensibility and heightened vitality of a society rich in genius, by a preoccupation with self-analysis, morbid and self-dramatising, but proud of its novelty and strength, by a sudden freedom from ancient fetters, a new sense of spaciousness, of room in which to move and to create. By 1851 this mood was dead; but a great legend had been created, which has survived to our own day, and has made Paris a symbol of revolutionary progress in its own and other's eyes.

Marx had not, however, come to Paris in quest of novel experience. He was a man of unemotional, even frigid nature, upon whom environment produced little effect, and who rather imposed his own unvarying form on any situation in which he found himself: he distrusted all enthusiasm, and in particular one which fed on gallant phrases. Unlike his compatriot, the poet Heine, or the Russian revolutionaries Herzen and Bakunin, he did not experience that sense of emancipation expressed by them when in ecstatic letters they proclaimed that they had found in this centre all that was most admirable in European civilisation. He chose Paris rather than Brussels, or a town in Switzerland, for the more practical and specific reason that it seemed to him the most convenient place from which to issue the *Deutsch-Französische Jahrbücher*, which was intended as much for the non-German as for the German public. Moreover, he still wished to find an answer to the question to which he had found no satisfactory solution either in the Encylopedists, or in Hegel, or in Feuerbach, or in the mass of political and historical literature which he consumed so rapidly and impatiently in 1843. What ultimately was responsible for the failure of the French Revolution? What fault of theory or of practice made the Directoire, the Empire, and finally the return of the Bourbons possible? What errors must be avoided by those who half a century later still sought to discover the means of founding a free and just society? Are there no laws which govern social change, knowledge of which might have saved the great revolution? The more extreme among the Encyclopedists had doubtless grossly over-simplified human nature by representing it as capable of being made overnight wholly rational and wholly good by enlightened education. As for the Hegelian answer that the time was not ripe, that the revolution had failed because the Absolute Idea had not then reached the appropriate stage, because the ideals which the revolutionaries sought to achieve were too abstract and unhistorical, this, in its turn, seemed to suffer from the same faults inasmuch as no criterion of appropriateness was given, save the occurrence of the stage itself; nor did the substitution for the orthodox solutions of such new formulas as human self-realisation, or embodied reason, or critical criticism, appear to make it any more concrete, or indeed to add anything significant. Furthermore, no stage of the Absolute Idea was held to embody a 'free and just society' as Marx and the radicals understood the phrase.

Faced with the question, Marx acted with characteristic thoroughness: he studied the facts, and read the historical records of the revolution itself; he also plunged headlong into the colossal mass of the polemical literature written in France upon this and kindred questions, and accomplished both tasks within a year. His leisure, since his schooldays, had been mainly spent in reading, but the extent of his appetite in Paris surpassed all limits. As in the days of his conversion to Hegelianism, he read in a kind of frenzy, filling his notebooks with extracts and abstracts and lengthy comments on which he largely drew in his later writings. By the end of 1844 he had made himself familiar with the political and the economic doctrines of the leading French and English thinkers, examined them in the light of his own still semi-orthodox Hegelianism, and finally established his own position by sharply defining his attitude towards these two irreconcilable tendencies. He read principally the economists, beginning with Quesnay and Adam Smith, and ending with Sismondi, Ricardo, Say, Proudhon and their followers. Their lucid, cool, unsentimental style contrasted favourably with the confused emotionalism and rhetoric of the Germans; the combination of practical shrewdness and emphasis on empirical investigation with bold and ingenious general hypotheses, attracted Marx and strengthened his natural tendency to avoid all forms of romanticism and to accept only such naturalistic explanations of phenomena as could be supported by the evidence of critical observation. The influence of French socialist writers and English economists had begun to dispel the all-enveloping mist of Hegelianism.

He compared the general condition of France with that of his native land and was impressed by its infinitely higher level of intelligence and capacity for political thought: 'in France every class is tinged with political idealism', he wrote in 1843, 'and feels itself a representative of general social needs . . . whereas in Germany, where practical life is unintelligent, and intelligence unpractical, men are driven to protest only by the material necessity, the actual chains themselves . . . but revolutionary energy and self-confidence are not sufficient by themselves to enable a class to be the liberator of society—it must identify another class with the principle of oppression . . . as in France the nobility and priesthood were identified. This dramatic tension is absent in German society . . . there is only one class whose wrongs are not specific but those of the whole of society—the proletariat.' He declares that the Germans are the most backward of western peoples. The past of England and of France is faithfully mirrored in the German present: the real emancipation of the Germans, who stand to more advanced peoples as the proletariat to other classes, will necessarily entail the emancipation of the whole of European society from political and economic oppression.

But if he was impressed by the political realism of those writers, he was no less shocked by their lack of historical sense. This alone, it seemed to him, made possible their easy and shallow eclecticism, the remarkable unconcern with which they introduced modifications and additions into their systems with no apparent intellectual discomfort. Such tolerance seemed to him to show a lack either of seriousness or of integrity. His own view was at all times clear-cut and violent, and was deduced from premises which permitted of no vagueness in the conclusions; such intellectual elasticity, it seemed to him, could be due only to insufficient grasp of the rigorous framework of the historical process. The assumption made by the classical economists that the contemporary categories of political economy held good of all times and all places struck him as particularly absurd. As Engels later put it, 'the economists of the day speak as if Richard Coeur de Lion, had he only known a little economics, might have saved six centuries of bungling, by setting up free trade, instead of wasting his time on the crusades', as if all previous economic systems were so many blundering approximations to capitalism, by the standards of which they must be classified and assessed. Such inability to grasp the fact that every period can be analysed only in terms of concepts and categories peculiar to itself, and determined by its own socio-economic structure, is responsible for Utopian socialism, for those elaborate schemes which turn out to be so many idealised versions of bourgeois or feudal society, with the 'bad' aspects left out; whereas the question to ask is not what one would wish to happen, but what history will permit to happen, which tendencies in the present are destined to develop and which to perish; one must build solely in accordance with the results of this scientific method of investigation.

Nevertheless, Marx found the moral taste of these writers sympathetic. They too distrusted innate intuitions and appeals to sentiment which transcend logic and empirical observation: they too saw in this the last defence of reaction and irrationalism; they too were passionately anti-clerical and anti-authoritarian. Many of them held oddly outmoded views about the natural harmony of all human interests, or believed in the capacity of the individual freed from the interference of states and monarchs to secure his own and others' happiness. Such views his Hegelian education had made wholly unacceptable; but in the last resort these men were the enemies of his enemies, ranged on the side of progress, fighters for the advance of reason.

II

If Marx derived from Hegel his view of the historical structure—that is, of the formal relations between the elements of which human history consists—he obtained his knowledge of the elements themselves from Saint-Simon and his disciples, as well as the new liberal historians, Guizot, Thierry and Mignet. Saint-Simon was a thinker of bold and original views: he was the first writer to assert that the development of economic relationships is the determining factor in history—and to have done this in his day in itself constitutes a sufficient claim to immortality—and further to analyse the historical process as a continuous conflict between economic *classes*, between those who, at any given period, are the possessors of the main economic resources of the community, and those who lack this advantage and come to depend upon the former for their subsistence. According to Saint-Simon, the ruling class is seldom sufficiently able or disinterested to make wholly rational use of its resources, or to institute an order in which those most capable of doing so apply and increase the resources of the community, and seldom flexible enough to adapt itself, and the institutions which it controls, to the new social conditions which its own activity brings about. It therefore tends to pursue a short-sighted and egoistic policy, to form a close caste, accumulate the available wealth in a few hands, and by means of the prestige and power thus obtained, to reduce the dispossessed majority to social and economic slavery. The unwilling subjects naturally grow restive and devote their lives to the overthrow of the tyrannical minority; this, when the conjunction of circumstances favours them, they eventually succeed in doing. But they grow corrupted by the long years of servitude, and become incapable of conceiving ideals higher than those of their masters, so that when they acquire power they use it no less irrationally and unjustly than their own former oppressors; in their turn they create a new oppressed class, and so at a new level the struggle continues. Human history is the history of such conflicts: due ultimately—as Adam Smith and the eighteenth-century French philosophers would have said—to the blindness of both masters and subjects to the coincidence of the best interests of both under a rational distribution of economic resources. Instead of this the ruling classes attempt to arrest all social change, lead idle and wasteful lives, obstructing economic progress in the form of technical invention, which, if only it were properly developed, would, by creating unlimited plenty and distributing it scientifically, swiftly ensure the eternal happiness and prosperity of mankind. Saint-Simon, who was a better historian than his encyclopedist predecessors, took a genuinely evolutionary view of human society, and estimated past epochs, not in terms of their remoteness from the civilisation of the present, but in terms of the adequacy of their institutions to the social and economic needs of their own day; with the result that his account of, for example, the Middle Ages is far more penetrating and sympathetic than that of the majority of his liberal contemporaries. He saw human progress as the inventive, creative activity of men in society, whereby they transform and enlarge their own nature and its needs and the means of satisfying them, both spiritual and material; human nature is not, as the eighteenth century had assumed, a fixed entity, but a process of growth, the direction of which is determined by its own failures and successes. Hence he noted that a social order which responded to genuine needs in its own day might tend to hamper the movements of a later time, becoming a straitjacket, the nature of which is concealed by the classes protected by its existence. The army and the Church, organic and progressive elements in the medieval hierarchy, are now obsolete survivals, whose functions are performed in modern society by the banker, the industrialist, and the scientist; with the consequence that priests, soldiers, *rentiers*, can survive only as idlers and social parasites, wasting the substance and holding up the advance of the new classes; they must therefore be eliminated. In their place industrious and skilful experts, chosen for their executive ability, must be placed at the head of society: financiers, engineers, organisers of large, rigorously centralised, industrial and agricultural enterprises, must govern. The Saint-Simonians taught that the laws of inheritance which lead to undeserved inequalities of wealth must be abolished; but on no account must this be extended to private property in general: every man has a right to the fruit of his own personal labour. Like the makers of the Revolution, and Fourier and Proudhon after them, Saint-Simon and his disciples firmly believed that the ownership of property furnished at the same time the sole incentive to energetic labour and the foundation of private and public morality. Bankers, company promoters, industrialists, inventors, mathematicians, scientists, engineers, thinkers, artists, poets, must be adequately rewarded by the state in proportion to their efficiency; once the economic life of the society is rationalised by the experts, the natural virtue of progressive human nature, the natural harmony of the interests of all, will guarantee universal justice, security, contentment and equality of opportunity for all men alike.

Saint-Simon lived at a time when the last relics of feudalism in Western Europe were finally disappearing before the advance of the bourgeois entrepreneur and his new mechanical devices. He had endless faith in the immense possibilities of technical invention and in its naturally beneficent effect on human society: he saw in the rising middle class able and energetic men animated by a sense of justice and disinterested altruism, hampered by the blind hostility of the landowning aristocracy and the Church, which trembled for their own privileges and possessions, and so became enemies to all justice and to all scientific and moral progress.

The belief was not so naïve then as it may now seem to be. As Marx was himself later to repeat, in the actual moment of struggle for social emergence the vanguard of the rising class in a nation naturally identifies its own cause with the whole mass of the oppressed, and feels, and to a certain degree is, the disinterested champion of a new ideal, fighting at the furthest outposts of the progressive front. Saint-Simon was the most eloquent prophet of the rising bourgeoisie in its most generous and idealistic mood. He naturally set the highest value on industry, initiative, inventiveness, and the capacity for large-scale planning; but he also sharply formulated the theory of the class struggle, little knowing to what application this portion of his doctrine would one day be put. He was himself a landed nobleman of the eighteenth century, ruined by the Revolution, who had chosen to identify himself with the advancing power, and so to explain and justify the supersession of his own class.

His most celebrated ideological rival, Charles Fourier, was a commercial traveller who lived in Paris during those first decades of the new century, when the financiers and industrialists, upon whom Saint-Simon had placed all his hopes, so far from effecting social reconciliation, proceeded to sharpen class antagonism by the creation of strongly centralised monopolist concerns. By obtaining control of credit, and employing labour on an unprecedented scale, they created the possibility of mass production and mass distribution of goods, and so competed on unequal terms with the smaller traders and artisans, whom they systematically drove out of the open market, and whose children they absorbed into their factories and mines. The social effect of the Industrial Revolution in France was to create a rift and a state of permanent bitterness between the *grande* and the *petite bourgeoisie*. Fourier, a typical representative of the ruined class, inveighs bitterly against the illusion that capitalists are the predestined saviours of society. His older contemporary, the Swiss economist Sismondi, had defended, with an immense mass of historical evidence, at a period when it required something akin to genius to have perceived it, the view that, whereas all previous class struggles occurred as a result of the scarcity of goods in the world, the discovery of new mechanical means of production would flood the world with excessive plenty, and would shortly, unless checked, lead to a class war before which previous conflicts would pale into insignificance. The necessity of marketing the ever-growing produce would lead to a continual competition between the rival capitalists, who would be forced systematically to lower wages and increase the working hours of the employees in order to secure even temporary advantage over a slower rival, which in turn would lead to a series of acute economic crises,

ending in social and political chaos, due to the internecine wars
between groups of capitalists. Such artificial poverty, growing in
direct proportion with the increase of goods, above all the monstrous trampling on those very fundamental human rights to
guarantee which the great revolution was made, could only be
prevented by state intervention, which must curtail the right of
accumulating capital and of the means of production. But
whereas Sismondi was an early New Dealer, or prophet of the
welfare state, who believed in the possibility of a centrally organised, rationally and humanely conducted society, and confined
himself to general recommendations, Fourier distrusted all central authority, and declared that bureaucratic tyranny is bound to
develop if the government units are too large; he proposed that
the earth should be divided into small groups which he called
phalansteries, each self-governing and federated into larger and
larger units; all machinery, land, buildings, natural resources
should be owned in common. His vision, an odd blend of eccen-
tricity and genius, at its most apocalyptic moments remains
elaborate and precise: a great central electric plant will by its
power do all the mechanical labour of the phalanstery; profits
should be divided between labour, capital and talent in the strict
proportion 5 : 3 : 2; and its members, with no more than a few
hours of daily work, will thus be free to occupy themselves with
developing their intellectual, moral and artistic faculties to an
extent hitherto unprecedented in history.

The exposition is at times interrupted by bursts of pure fantasy,
such as the prophecy of the emergence in the immediate future of
a new race of beasts, not dissimilar in appearance to existing
species, but more powerful and more numerous—'anti-lions',
'anti-bears', 'anti-tigers', as friendly and attached to man as their
present ancestors are hostile and destructive, and doing much of
his work with the skill, intelligence and foresight wanting in mere
machines. The thesis is at its best at its most destructive. In the
remorseless exactness of its analysis of the self-destructive effects
both of centralisation and of free competition; in the intense
quality of its indignation and its sense of genuine horror at the
wholesale disregard for the life and liberty of the individual by the
monstrous regime of financiers and their hirelings, the judges, the
soldiers, the administrators, Fourier's indictment is the prototype
of all later attacks on the doctrine of the unchecked *laissez-faire*, of
the great denunciations of Marx and Carlyle, of Daumier's car-
toons and Büchner's plays, no less than of the left- and right-wing

protests against the substitution of new forms of privilege for old, and against the enslavement of the individual by the very machinery designed to set him free.

The Revolution of 1830, which expelled Charles X and brought Louis-Philippe to the throne of France, revived public interest in social questions once more. During the decade which followed, an endless succession of books and pamphlets poured from the presses, attacking the evils of the existing system, and suggesting every kind of remedy, from the mildly liberal proposals of Lamartine or Crémieux to the more radical semisocialist demands of Marrast or Ledru Rollin and the developed State socialism of Louis Blanc, and ending with the drastic programmes of Barbès and Blanqui, who in their journal *L'Homme Libre* advocated a violent revolution and the abolition of private property. Fourier's disciple Considérant proclaimed the imminent collapse of the existing system of property relations; and well-known socialist writers of the time, Pecqueur, Louis Blanc, Dézamy, and the most independent and original figure among them, Proudhon, published their best known attacks on the capitalist order between 1839 and 1842, and were in their turn followed by a host of minor figures who diluted and popularised their doctrines. In 1834 the Catholic priest Lamennais published his Christian socialist *Words of a Believer*, and in 1840 appeared the *Bible of Freedom* by the Abbé Constant, fresh evidence that even in the Church there were men unable to resist the great popular appeal of the new revolutionary theories.

The sensational success of Louis Blanc's *Ten Years*, a brilliant and bitter analysis of the years 1830–40, indicated the trend of opinion. Literary and philosophical communism began to come into fashion: Cabet wrote a highly popular communist *Utopia* called *Voyage to Icaria*. Pierre Leroux preached a mystical egalitarianism to the novelist George Sand, and Heine discussed it with sympathy in his celebrated vignettes of social and literary life in Paris during the July monarchy.

The subsequent fate of these movements is of small importance. The Saint-Simonians, after some years of desultory existence, disappeared as a movement: some of them became highly prosperous railway magnates and *rentiers*, fulfilling at least one aspect of their master's prophecy. The more idealistic Fourierists founded communist settlements in the United States, some of which, like the Oneida community, lasted for some decades and attracted leading American thinkers and writers; in the sixties they had considerable influence through their newspaper, the New York *Tribune*.

Marx familiarised himself with these theories, and his own doctrines owe much to them. Saint-Simon's vision of vast new productive possibilities, and of their revolutionary effect on society, spoke (and speaks still) to those who see that only bold industrialisation holds out the prospects of rapid advance towards power and the expansion and realisation to the fullest degree of human capacities in all spheres. Fourier spoke to those who, on the contrary, saw the unbridled drive towards production, heedless of distribution, as breaking natural human relations, turning men into commodities, mocking justice, twisting men's faculties into channels in which they are blocked or turned against men's most natural needs, creating a hideous, mutually destructive field of jungle warfare, curbed only by ruthless centralisation, which equally crushed its victims and which the frenzied expansion of productive enterprises seemed to make inescapable. Marx accepted both theses; he attempted to show that men were progressing—through seas of mud and blood—to a society in which men's most optimistic prophecies of unchecked productivity were conjoined with social control which saved men from waste, oppression, frustration, atomisation. To show this and give concrete evidence for it, he tested the social theories of the French thinkers as best he could, by acquiring knowledge of the details of recent social history from all available sources, from books, from newspapers, by meeting writers and journalists, and by spending his evenings among the small revolutionary groups composed of German journeymen which, under the influence of communist agitators, met to discuss the affairs of their scattered organisation and more vaguely the possibility of a revolution in their native country. In conversation with these artisans he discovered something of the needs and hopes of a class, of which a somewhat abstract portrait had been drawn in the works of Saint-Simon and his epigoni. Marx had given little thought to the precise parts which the *petite bourgeoisie* and the proletariat were to play in the advance of reason and the improvement of society. There was in addition the unstable, *déclassé* element, composed of marginal figures, members of odd trades, Bohemians, unemployed soldiers, actors, intellectuals, neither masters nor slaves, independent and yet precariously situated on the very edge of the subsistence level, whose existence had hardly been recognised by social historians, still less accounted for or analysed. His interest in the economic writings of the socialists who formed the left wing of the French party of reform turned his attention to these questions. Ruge had commissioned him to write an essay for his periodical, on Hegel's *Philosophy of Right*. He wrote it together with an essay on the Jewish question, early in 1844. The essay on the Jews was intended as an answer to Bruno Bauer's articles on this topic. Bauer had declared that the Jews, lagging historically one stage behind the Christians, must be baptised before they could reasonably claim full civil emancipation. Marx in his reply declared that Jews were no longer a religious or racial entity, but a purely economic one, forced into usury and other unattractive professions by the treatment they received from their neighbours, an excrescence of the capitalist system; they could, therefore, be emancipated only with the emancipation of the rest of European society; to baptise them would be but to substitute one set of chains for another; to give them solely political liberties would play into the hands of those liberals who see in these all that any human being can hope, and indeed ought, to possess. Despite brilliant moments, it is a superficial analysis, but it shows Marx in a typical mood: he was determined that the sarcasms and insults, to which some of the notable Jews of his generation, Heine, Lassalle, Disraeli, were all their lives a target, should, so far as he could effect it, never be used to plague him. Consequently he decided to kill the Jewish problem once and for all so far as he was concerned, declaring it to be an unreal subject, invented as a screen for other more pressing questions: a problem which offered no special difficulty, but arose from the general social chaos which demanded to be put in order. He was baptised a Lutheran, and was married to a Gentile; he had once been of assistance to the Jewish community in Cologne; during the greater part of his life he held himself aloof from anything remotely connected with his race, showing open hostility to all its institutions.

The critique of Hegel is more important: the doctrine which it expounds is unlike anything he had published before. In it he had begun, as he himself declared, to settle his account with the idealist philosophy. It was the beginning of a lengthy, laborious, and thorough process which, when it reached its culminating point four years later, proved to have created the foundations of a new movement and a new outlook, and to have grown into a dogmatic faith and a plan of action, which dominates the political consciousness of Europe to this day.

III

If what Marx required was a complete plan of action, based on the study of history and observation of the contemporary scene, he must have found himself singularly out of sympathy with the reformers and prophets who gathered in the *salons* and cafés of Paris at the time of his arrival. They were, indeed, more intelligent, more politically influential and more responsible than the café philosophers of Berlin, but to him they seemed either gifted visionaries like Robert Owen, reformist liberals like Ledru Rollin, or, like Mazzini, both at once, unprepared, in the last resort, to do anything for the working class; or else they were sentimental *petit bourgeois* idealists in disguise, sheep in wolves' clothing, like Proudhon or Louis Blanc, whose ideals might indeed be at least partially attainable, but whose gradualist, unrevolutionary tactics showed them to be radically mistaken in their estimates of the enemy's strength, and who were, consequently, to be fought all the more assiduously as the internal, often quite unconscious, enemies of the revolution. Nevertheless, he learnt much from them which he did not acknowledge, notably from Louis Blanc, whose book on the organisation of labour influenced him in his view of the evolution and correct analysis of industrial society.

He was attracted far more strongly to the party, which, to distinguish itself from the moderates who came to be called socialists, adopted the name of communists. Neither was a party in the modern sense of the word: both consisted of loosely associated groups and individuals. But whereas the former consisted predominantly of intellectuals, the latter was almost entirely composed of factory workers and small artisans, the majority of whom were simple and self-educated men, exasperated by their wrongs and easily converted to the necessity of a revolutionary conspiracy to abolish privilege and private property, a doctrine preached by Babeuf's disciple Philippe Buonarroti, and inherited by the lifelong conspirator, the Jacobin–communist Blanqui, who was implicated in the abortive rising of 1839. Marx was impressed in particular by Auguste Blanqui's organising capacity and by the boldness and violence of his convictions; but he thought him lacking in ideas, and excessively vague as to the steps to be taken after the successful result of the *coup d'état*. He found a similarly irresponsible attitude among the other advocates of violence, the most notable of whom, the itinerant German tailor Weitling and the Russian exile Bakunin, he knew well at this time. Only one among the communists whom he met in Paris seemed to him to display a genuine understanding of the situation. This was a certain Friedrich Engels, a well-to-do young German radical, the son of a cotton manufacturer in Barmen. They met in Paris over the publication of economic articles by Engels in Marx's journal. The meeting proved decisive for both. It was the beginning of a remarkable career of friendship and collaboration which lasted during the remainder of their lives.

Engels began life as a radical poet and journalist and ended it, after the death of Marx, as the acknowledged leader of international socialism, which, in his own lifetime, had grown into a world movement. He was a man of solid and robust, but hardly creative, mind; a man of exceptional integrity and strength of character, of many varied gifts, but in particular endowed with a remarkable capacity for the rapid assimilation of knowledge. He possessed a shrewd and lucid intellect and a sense of reality, which few, if any, among his radical contemporaries could claim; himself little capable of original discovery, he had an exceptional talent for sifting, assessing and perceiving the practical applicability of the discoveries of others. His knack of writing rapidly and clearly, his unbounded loyalty and patience, made him an ideal ally and collaborator for the inhibited and difficult Marx, whose own writing was often clumsy, overcharged and obscure. In his own lifetime Engels desired no better fate than to live in the light of Marx's teaching, perceiving in him a spring of original genius which gave life and scope to his own peculiar gifts; with him he identified himself and his work, to be rewarded by sharing in his master's immortality. Before they met he had, beginning as a disciple of Hess, independently arrived at a position not unlike that of Marx, and in later years he understood his friend's new, only half articulated, ideas sometimes more clearly than he understood them himself, and clothed them (at times at the cost of drastic simplification) in language more attractive and intelligible to the masses than Marx's often tortuous style. Most important of all, he possessed a quality essential for permanent intercourse with a man of Marx's temperament, a total uncompetitiveness in relation to him, absence of all desire to resist the impact of that powerful personality, to preserve and retain a protected position of his own; on the contrary, he was only too eager to receive his whole intellectual sustenance from Marx unquestioningly, like a devoted pupil, and he repaid him by his sanity, his enthusiasm, his vitality, his gaiety, and finally, in the most literal sense, by supplying him with means of livelihood at moments of desperate poverty. Marx, who, like many dedicated intellectuals, was himself haunted by a perpetual feeling of insecurity, and was morbidly thin-skinned and jealously suspicious of the least signs of antagonism to his person or his doctrines, required at least one person who understood his outlook, in whom he could confide completely, on whom he could lean as heavily and as often as he wished. In Engels he found a devoted friend and intellectual ally, whose very pedestrianism restored his sense of perspective and his belief in himself and his purpose. Throughout the greater part of his life his actions were performed with the knowledge that this massive and dependable man was always at hand to support the burden in every contingency. For this he paid him with an affection, and a sense of pride in his qualities, which he gave to no one else beside his wife and children.

They met in the autumn of 1844 after Engels had sent him for publication in his periodical a sketch of a critique of the doctrines of the liberal economists. Marx had hitherto vaguely counted Engels among the Berlin intellectuals, an impression which their only previous meeting had failed to dispel. He now wrote to him at once: the result was a meeting in Paris in the course of which the similarity of their views on the fundamental issues became clear to both. Engels, who had been travelling in England and had published a vivid description of the condition of the English working class, disliked social humanitarianism of the school of Sismondi even more acutely than Marx. He provided that for which Marx had long been looking, a rich supply of concrete information about the actual state of affairs in a progressive industrial community, to act as the material evidence for the broad historical thesis which was rapidly crystallising in Marx's mind. Engels, on the other hand, found that Marx gave him what he had been lacking, a solid framework within which to fit his facts, so as to make of them a weapon against the prevalent abstractions upon which, in his opinion, no serious revolutionary philosophy could be based. The effect which the meeting with Marx had upon him must have resembled that which it had made earlier on the more impressionable Hess. It heightened his vitality, clarified his hitherto undeveloped political ideas, provided him with a sense of definite orientation, an ordered view of society within which he could work with the assurance of the concrete, attainable character of the revolutionary goal. This, after aimless wandering in the intricate maze of the young Hegelian movement, must have resembled the beginning of a new life, and, indeed, such for him it proved to be. Their immense correspondence, which lasted for forty years, was, from the very beginning, at once familiar and business-like in tone; neither was greatly given to introspection; both were entirely occupied with the movement which they were engaged in creating and which became for them the most solid reality of their lives. Upon this firm and reliable foundation was built a unique friendship, free from all trace of possessiveness, patronage or jealousy. Neither ever referred to it without a certain shyness and embarrassment; Engels was conscious of receiving far more than he gave, living in a mental universe created and furnished by Marx out of his own inner resources. When Marx died, he looked upon himself as its appointed guardian, jealously protecting it against all attempts at reform by the reckless and impatient younger generation of socialists.

The two years which Marx passed in Paris were the first and last occasion in his life on which he met, and was on terms of friendly intercourse with, men who were his equals, if not always in intelligence, at any rate in the originality of their personalities and their lives. After the débâcle of 1848, which broke the spirit of all but the strongest characters amongst the radicals, decimated them by death, imprisonment and transportation, and left the majority listless or disillusioned, he withdrew into an attitude of aggressive isolation, preserving contact only with men who had proved their personal loyalty to the cause with which he was identified. Henceforth Engels was his chief of staff; the rest he treated openly as rivals or subordinates.

The portrait of him that emerges from the memoirs of those who were his friends at this time, Ruge, Freiligrath, Heine, Annenkov, is that of a bold and energetic figure, a vehement, eager, contemptuous controversialist, applying to everything his cumbrous and heavy Hegelian weapons, but, in spite of the clumsiness of the mechanism, revealing an acute and powerful intellect, the quality of which even those who were most hostile to him—and there were few prominent radicals whom he had failed to wound and humiliate in some fashion—in later years came to acknowledge.

He met and formed a warm friendship with the poet Heine, by whom he may have been influenced, and in whom, despite his anti-democratic views, he saw a more genuinely revolutionary poet than Herwegh or Freiligrath, both, at this time, idolised by the radical youth of Germany. He was also on good terms with the circle of Russian liberals, some among them genuine rebels, others cultivated aristocratic dilettanti, connoisseurs of curious men and situations. One of these, a shrewd and agreeable man of letters, Paul Annenkov, for whom Marx conceived a liking, has left a brief description of him at this time: 'Marx belonged to the type of men who are all energy, force of will and unshakeable conviction. With a thick black mop of hair on his head, with hairy hands and a crookedly buttoned frock coat, he had the air of a man used to commanding the respect of others. His movements were clumsy but self-assured. His manners defied the accepted conventions of social intercourse and were haughty and almost contemptuous. His voice was disagreeably harsh, and he spoke of men and things in the tone of one who would tolerate no contradiction, and which seemed to express his own firm conviction in his mission to sway men's minds and dictate the laws of their being.' Another, and far more remarkable member of this circle was the celebrated Michael Bakunin, upon whom his meeting with Marx in Paris at this time had a more lasting effect. Bakunin had left Russia at approximately the same time as Marx had left Germany and for much the same reason. He was at this time an ardent 'critical' left-wing Hegelian, a passionate enemy of Tsarism and all absolutist government. He had a generous, extravagant, wildly impulsive character, a rich, chaotic, unbridled imagination, a passion for the violent, the immense, the sublime, a hatred of all discipline and institutionalism, total lack of all sense of personal property, and, above all, a savage and overwhelming desire to annihilate the narrow society of his time, in which, like Gulliver in Lilliput, the human individual was suffocating for want of room to realise his faculties to their fullest and noblest extent. His friend and compatriot Alexander Herzen, who at once admired him and was intensely irritated by him, said of him in his memoirs:

'Bakunin was capable of becoming anything—an agitator, a tribune, a preacher, the head of a party, of a sect, a heresy. Put him where you like, so long as it always is the most extreme point of a movement, and he will fascinate the masses and sway the destinies of peoples . . . but in Russia this Columbus without America and without a ship, having served, greatly against his will, a year or two in the artillery, and after that another year or so in the Moscow Hegelians, longed desperately to tear himself away from a land where every form of thought was prosecuted as evil-mindedness, and independence of judgement or speech was looked upon as an insult to public morality.'

He was a marvellous mob orator, consumed with a genuine hatred of injustice and a burning sense of his mission to rouse mankind to some act of magnificent collective heroism which would set it free for ever; and he exercised a personal fascination over men, blinding them to his irresponsibility, his mendacity, his fundamental frivolity, by the overwhelming revolutionary enthusiasm which he communicated. He was not an original thinker, and easily absorbed the views of others; but he was an inspired teacher, and, although his entire creed amounted to not much more than a passionate egalitarian belief in the need for destruction of all authority and the freeing of the oppressed, mingled with a short-lived Panslavism, he built on this alone a movement which lived on long after his death.

Bakunin differed from Marx as poetry differs from prose; the political connection between them rested on inadequate foundations and was very short-lived. Their main bond was a common hatred of every form of reformism; but this hatred sprang from dissimilar roots. Gradualism to Marx was always a disguised attempt on the part of the ruling class to deflect their enemies' energy into ineffective and harmless channels: a policy which the clearer heads among them knew to be a deliberate stratagem, while the rest were themselves deceived by it, as much taken in as the radical reformers, whose fear of violence was itself a form of unconscious sabotage of their professed ends. Bakunin detested reform because he held that all frontiers limiting personal liberty were intrinsically evil, and all destructive violence, when aimed against authority, was good in itself, inasmuch as it was a fundamental form of creative self-expression. On this ground he was passionately opposed to the aim accepted by both Marx and the reformists—the replacement of the *status quo* by a centralised socialism—since, according to him, this was a new form of tyranny at once meaner and more absolute than the personal and class despotism it was intended to supplant. This attitude had as its emotional basis a temperamental dislike of ordered forms of life in normal civilised society, a discipline taken for granted in the ideas of western democrats, which to a man of his luxuriant imagination, chaotic habits and hatred of all restraints and barriers, seemed colourless, petty, oppressive and vulgar. An alliance built on an almost complete absence of common aims could not last: the orderly, rigid, unimpressionable Marx came to regard

Bakunin as half charlatan, half madman, and his views as absurd and barbarian. He saw in Bakunin's doctrine a development of the wild individualism for which he had already condemned Stirner: but whereas Stirner was an obscure instructor in a High School for girls, a politically ineffective intellectual, neither capable nor ambitious of stirring the masses, Bakunin was a resolute man of action, an adroit and fearless agitator, a magnificent orator, a dangerous megalomaniac consumed by a fanatical desire to dominate men, at least intellectually, fully equal to that which possessed Marx himself.

Bakunin recorded his view of Marx many years later in one of his political tracts. 'M. Marx', he wrote, 'is by origin a Jew. He unites in himself all the qualities and defects of that gifted race. Nervous, some say, to the point of cowardice, he is immensely malicious, vain, quarrelsome, as intolerant and autocratic as Jehovah, the God of his fathers, and like Him, insanely vindictive.

'There is no lie, no calumny, which he is not capable of using against anyone who has incurred his jealousy or his hatred; he will not stop at the basest intrigue if, in his opinion, it will serve to increase his position, his influence and his power.

'Such are his vices, but he also has many virtues. He is very clever, and widely learned. In about 1840 he was the life and soul of a very remarkable circle of radical Hegelians—Germans whose consistent cynicism left far behind even the most rabid Russian nihilists. Very few men have read so much and, it may be added, have read so intelligently, as M. Marx . . .

'Like M. Louis Blanc, he is a fanatical authoritarian—triply so, as a Jew, a German and a Hegelian—but where the former, in place of argument, uses declamatory rhetoric, the latter, as behoves a learned and ponderous German, has embellished this principle with all the tricks and fancies of the Hegelian dialectic, and with all the wealth of his many-sided learning.'

Their mutual hatred became more and more evident as time went on: outwardly friendly relations continued uneasily for some years, saved from complete rupture by the reluctant and apprehensive respect which each had for the formidable qualities of the other. When the conflict ultimately did break out, it all but destroyed the work of both, and did incalculable damage to the cause of European socialism.

If Marx treated Bakunin as an equal, he did not conceal his contempt for the other famous agitator, Wilhelm Weitling, whom he met at this time. A tailor by profession, a wandering preacher by calling, this earnest and fearless German visionary was the last and most eloquent descendant of the men who raised peasant revolts in the late Middle Ages, and whose modern representatives, for the most part artisans and journeymen, congregated in secret societies dedicated to the cause of revolution; there were branches in many industrial towns in Germany and abroad, scattered centres of political disaffection round which there accumulated many victims and casualties of the social process, men violently embittered by their wrongs and confused as to their cause and remedy, but united by a common sense of grievance and a common desire to eradicate the system which had destroyed their lives. In his books, *A Poor Sinner's Gospel* and *Guarantees of Harmony and Freedom*, Weitling advocated a class war of the poor against the rich, with open terrorism as its chief weapon; and, in particular, the formation of shock troops out of the most deeply wronged and, therefore, the most abandoned and fearless elements in society—the outlaws and criminals—who would fight desperately to avenge themselves on the class which had dispossessed them, for a new and uncompetitive world in which they would begin new lives. Weitling's belief in the solidarity of the workers of all lands, his personal stoicism, the years which he spent in various prisons and, above all, the fervent evangelical zeal of his writings, attracted to him many devoted followers among his fellow artisans, and made him, for a brief period, a figure of European magnitude. Marx, who cared nothing for sincerity when it was misdirected, and particularly disliked itinerant prophets and the vague emotionalism with which they inevitably infected serious revolutionary work, nevertheless conceded Weitling's importance. His conception of an open declaration of war against the ruling class by desperate men who had nothing to lose and everything to gain by the total destruction of existing society,[1] the personal experience which lay behind his denunciations and moved his audiences, his emphasis on the economic realities, and attempt to penetrate the deceptive façade of political parties and their official programmes, above all his practical achievement in creating the nucleus of an international communist party, impressed Marx profoundly. Weit-

[1] The thesis that only the ruined and the outcasts can be relied on to carry through the revolution to its conclusion, since others will inevitably stop short when their own interests are threatened, influenced Bakunin decisively, and through him the conception of a ruthless revolutionary élite familiar in our own day.

ling's detailed doctrines, however, he treated with open contempt, and, justly believing him to be muddled, hysterical, and a source of confusion in the party, set himself to expose his ignorance publicly and lower his prestige in every possible fashion. An account has been preserved of a meeting in Brussels in 1846 in the course of which Marx demanded to be told Weitling's concrete proposals to the working class. When the latter faltered, and murmured something about the uselessness of criticism carried on in the study, far from the suffering world, Marx struck the table and shouted, 'Ignorance has never yet helped anyone', after which the gathering rapidly came to an end. They never met again.

His relation to Proudhon was altogether more complicated. While still in Cologne he had read the book which first made Proudhon's name famous, *What is Property?*, and praised the brilliance of its style and the courage of its author. In 1843 everything appealed to him which revealed a revolutionary spark, anything which sounded clear and resolute and openly advocated the overthrow of the existing system. Soon, however, he became convinced that Proudhon's approach to social problems, for all his declared admiration for Hegel, was ultimately not historical but moral, that his praise and condemnation was directly based on his own absolute ethical standards, and that he ignored altogether the historical importance of institutions and systems. From this moment he conceived him as merely another French philistine moralist, a conscious or unconscious defender of the social ideals of *petit-bourgeois* victims of industrialism, and lost all respect for his person and his doctrines.

At the time of Marx's arrival in Paris, Proudhon was at the height of his reputation. Of peasant stock from Besançon, by profession a typesetter, he was a man of narrow, obstinate, fearless, puritanical character, a typical representative of the French lower middle class which, after playing an active part in the final overthrow of the Bourbons, found it had merely succeeded in changing masters, and that the new government of bankers and large industrialists, from whom Saint-Simon had taught them to expect so much, had merely increased the tempo of their destruction.

The two forces which Proudhon conceived as fatal to social justice and the brotherhood of man were the tendency towards the accumulation of capital, which led to the continual increase of inequalities of wealth, and the tendency directly connected with it, which openly united political authority with economic control, and so was designed to secure a growth of a despotic plutocracy under the guise of free liberal institutions. The state became, according to him, an instrument designed to dispossess the majority for the benefit of a small minority, a legalised form of robbery, which systematically deprived the individual of his natural right to property by giving to the rich sole control of social legislation and financial credit, while the *petite bourgeoisie* was helplessly expropriated. Proudhon's best-known book, which opens with the statement that all property is theft, had misled many as to his mature views. Early in life he held that all property was misappropriation; later, however, he taught that a minimum of property was required by every man in order to maintain his personal independence, his moral and social dignity: a system under which this minimum was lost, under whose laws a man could, by a commercial transaction, barter it away, and so, in effect, sell himself into economic slavery to others, was a system that legalised and encouraged theft, theft of the individual's elementary rights, without which he had no means of pursuing his proper ends. The principal cause of this process Proudhon perceived in the unchecked economic struggle between individuals, groups, social orders, which necessarily leads to the domination of the ablest and best organised, and of those least restrained by a sense of moral or social duty, over the mass of the community. This represents the triumph of unscrupulous force allied to tactical skill over reason and justice; but for Proudhon, who was not a determinist, there was no historical reason why this situation should continue indefinitely. Competition, the favourite panacea of enlightened thinkers of the previous century, which appeared to nineteenth-century liberals and rationalists in an almost sacred light, as the fullest and richest expression of the individual's strenuous rational activity, his triumph over the blind forces of nature and over his own undisciplined appetites, was to Proudhon the greatest of all evils, the perversion of all the faculties towards the unnatural promotion of an acquisitive and, therefore, unjust society, in which the advantage of each depended on, even consisted in, his ability to outwit, defeat or exterminate the others. The evil was identical with that attacked earlier by Rousseau, Fourier and Sismondi, but it was differently expressed and differently accounted for. Fourier was heir to both the thought and the style of the eighteenth century, and interpreted the calamities of his time as the results of the suppression of reason by deliberate conspiracy on the part of those who feared its application, the priests, the well born, the bureaucrats, the rich. Proudhon did not accept this simple view; he was to some extent affected by the historicism of his age: he knew no German, but had had Hegelianism poured into him by Bakunin and later by German exiles. Proudhon's attempt to adapt the new theory to his own doctrine, with its stress on justice and human rights, led to results which to Marx seemed a crude caricature of Hegelianism.

The method, indeed, by which everything was described in the form of two antithetical conceptions, which made every statement seem at once realistic and paradoxical, suited Proudhon's talent for coining sharp and arresting phrases, his love of epigram, his desire to move, to startle and to provoke. Everything is contradictory; property is theft; to be a citizen is to be deprived of rights; capitalism is at once the despotism of the stronger over the weaker, and of the lesser over the greater; to accumulate wealth is to rob; to abolish it is to undermine the foundations of morality. Proudhon's remedy for this is the suppression of competition and the introduction in its place of a 'mutualist' co-operative system under which limited private property should be permitted, and indeed enforced, but not the accumulation of capital. Whereas competition evokes the worst and most brutal qualities in men, co-operation, besides promoting greater efficiency, moralises and civilises them by revealing the true end of communal life. The state may be endowed with certain centralising functions, but its activity must be severely controlled by the association of trades, professions, occupations, and again of consumers and producers, under which society would be organised. Organise society into a single, decentralised economic whole on non-competitive 'mutualist' lines, and the antinomies will be resolved, the good remain, the evil disappear. Poverty, unemployment, the frustration of men forced into uncongenial tasks as a result of the class maladjustments of an unplanned society, will disappear, and men's better natures will find it possible to assert themselves; for there is no lack of idealism in human nature, but under the existing economic order it is rendered ineffectual or, through misdirection, dangerous. But, for Proudhon, it is useless to preach to the rich; their generous instincts became atrophied long ago. The enlightened prince dreamt of by the encyclopedists, and at times by Saint-Simon and Fourier too, will not be born, being himself a social contradiction. Only the real victims of the system, the small farmers, the small bourgeoisie and the urban proletariat can be appealed to. They alone can alter their own condition, since, being at once the most numerous and the most indispensable members of society, they alone have the power to transform it. To them consequently Proudhon addressed himself. He warned the workers against organising themselves politically, since by imitating the ruling class they will inevitably place themselves at its mercy. The enemy, being more experienced in political tactics, will, by bullying, or by financial or social bribes, succeed in luring over the weaker or less astute among the revolutionary leaders, and so render the movement impotent. In any case, even if the rebels were victorious, they would, by acquiring control over, and so preserving, the political forms of authoritarian government, give a new lease of life to the very contradiction from which they seek to escape. The workers and small bourgeoisie must therefore seek, by purely economic pressure, to impose their own pattern on the rest of society; this process should be gradual and peaceful. Again and again Proudhon declared that the workers must on no account have recourse to coercion; not even strikes were to be permitted, since this would infringe upon the individual worker's right to the free disposal of his labour.

Proudhon had the unwisdom to submit his book, *Philosophie de la misère* (Philosophy of Poverty), to Marx for criticism. Marx read it in two days and pronounced it fallacious and superficial, but written attractively and with sufficient eloquence and sincerity to mislead the masses. 'To leave error unrefuted', he declared in a similar situation many years later, 'is to encourage intellectual immorality.' For ten workers who might go further, ninety may stop with Proudhon and remain in darkness. He therefore determined to destroy it, and with it Proudhon's reputation as a serious thinker, once and for all.

In 1847 in answer to *Philosophie de la misère* there appeared *Misère de la philosophie* (Poverty of Philosophy), containing the bitterest attack delivered by one thinker upon another since the celebrated polemics of the Renaissance. Marx took immense trouble to demonstrate that Proudhon was totally incapable of abstract thought, a fact which he vainly attempted to conceal by a use of pseudo-Hegelian terminology. Marx accused Proudhon of radically misunderstanding the Hegelian categories by naïvely interpreting the dialectical conflict as a simple struggle between good and evil, which leads to the fallacy that all that is needed is to remove the evil, and the good will remain. This is the very height of superficiality: to call this or that side of the dialectical conflict good or bad is a sign of unhistorical subjectivism out of place in serious social analysis. Both aspects are equally indispensable for the development of human society. Genuine progress is constituted not by the triumph of one side and the defeat of the other, but by the duel itself which necessarily involves the destruction of both. In so far as Proudhon continually expresses his sympathy for this or that element in the social struggle, he remains, however sincerely he may think himself convinced of the necessity and value of the struggle itself, hopelessly idealist, that is, committed to evaluating objective reality in terms of his own *petit-bourgeois* desires and preferences disguised as eternal values—itself an absurdity—without reference to the stage of evolution which the class war has reached. This is followed by a laborious refutation of Proudhon's economic theory, which Marx declared to rest on a fallacious conception of the mechanism of exchange: Proudhon had misunderstood Ricardo no less profoundly than he had misunderstood Hegel, and confused the proposition that human labour determines economic value, with the proposition that it ought to do so. This leads in its turn to a total misrepresentation of the relation of money to other commodities, which vitiates his entire account of the contemporary economic organisation of capitalist society. The fiercest attack is directed against Proudhon's crypto-individualism, against his obvious hatred of any tendency to collective organisation, his nostalgic faith in the sturdy yeoman farmer and his morality, his belief in the indestructible value of the institution of private property, in the sanctity of marriage and of the family, in the absolute moral and legal authority of its head over his wife and children; which was indeed the basis of his own life and was responsible for his deep-seated fear of any form of violent revolution, of anything likely to destroy the fundamental forms of life on a small farm, in which his ancestors were born and bred, and to which, in spite of his brave revolutionary phrases, he remained immovably loyal. In effect Marx accused Proudhon of wishing to remedy the immediate wrongs of the existing system without destroying the system itself, because, like all Frenchmen of his class, he was emotionally attached to it; of not believing, in spite of his veneer of Hegelianism, that the historical process is either inevitable or irreversible, nor that it advances by revolutionary leaps, nor yet that the present evils are themselves as strictly necessitated by the laws of history as the stage which will one day supersede them. For it is only on the assumption that such evils are accidental blemishes that it is plausible to urge their removal by courageous legislation which need not involve the destruction of the social forms of which they are the historical product. In a rhetorical passage Marx exclaims: 'It is not enough to desire the collapse of these forms, one must know in obedience to what laws they came into being, in order to know how to act within the framework of these laws, since to act against them, whether deliberately or not, in blind ignorance of the causes and character, would be a futile and suicidal act and would, by creating chaos, defeat and demoralise the revolutionary class, and so prolong the existing agony.' This is the criticism which he used against all Utopians who claimed to have a new message for the working class.

Marx was convinced that Proudhon was constitutionally incapable of grasping the truth; that, despite an undoubted gift for telling phrases, he was a fundamentally stupid man; the fact that he was brave and fanatically honest, and attracted a growing body of devoted followers, only made him and his fantasies more dangerous; hence this attempt to annihilate his doctrine and his influence with one tremendous blow. His brutality overreached itself, however, and created indignant sympathy for its victim. Proudhon's system survived this and many subsequent Marxist onslaughts, and its influence increased in the following years.

Proudhon was not primarily an orginal thinker. He had a gift for absorbing and crystallising the radical ideas current in his time: he wrote well, sometimes with brilliance, and his eloquence was felt to be genuine by the masses for whom he wrote, springing from wants and ambitions which he had in common with them. The tradition of political non-participation, industrial action, and decentralised federalism, of which he was the most eloquent advocate, survives powerfully amongst French radicals and socialists, and found support in the individualist tendency, most pronounced in Latin countries, the vast majority of whose inhabitants were small farmers, artisans, professional men, living at a distance from the industrial life of great cities. Proudhonism is the direct ancestor of modern syndicalism. It was affected by Bakunin's anarchism and, half a century later, by the doctrine that, since economic categories were the most fundamental, therefore the units out of which the anti-capitalist force must be constituted should contain men connected not by common convictions—a mere intellectual superstructure—but by the actual occupations which they pursue, since this is the essential factor which determines their acts. Wielding as its most formidable weapon the threat of disorganising social life by suspending all vital services by a general strike, it became the most powerful left-wing doctrine in many parts of France, Italy and Spain, wherever, indeed, industrialism had not gone too far, and an agrarian craftsmen's individualist tradition still survived. Marx, who had an infallible sense of the general direction and political flavour of a movement or a doctrine whatever its ostensible appearance, at once recognised the individualistic, and therefore for him reactionary substratum of this attitude: and consequently attacked it no less violently than avowed liberalism. The *Poverty of Philosophy* is now, like the specific views which it attacked, largely out of date. But it represents a definite stage in its author's mental development: one of the elements in his lifelong attempt to synthesise his economic, social and political views into the unified body of doctrine, capable of application to every aspect of the social situation, which came to be known as the Materialist Conception of History.

6

Historical Materialism

A certain person once took it into his head that people drown in water only because they are obsessed by the *notion* of weight. If only, he thought, they could rid themselves of this idea, by calling it, for instance, superstitious or religious, they would thereby be saved from all danger of drowning. All his life he fought against the illusion of weight, concerning whose deleterious consequences statistics continually provided him with fresh evidence. This figure is the prototype of the German revolutionary philosophers of our day.

KARL MARX, The German Ideology

No full or systematic exposition of historical materialism was ever published by Marx himself. It occurs in a fragmentary form in his early work written during the years 1843–8, it is briefly expounded in 1859, and is taken for granted in his later thought. He did not regard it as a new philosophical system so much as a practical method of social and historical analysis, and a basis for political strategy. Later in life he complained of the use made of it by some of his followers, who appeared to think that it would save them the labour of historical study by providing a kind of algebraic 'table' from which, given enough factual data, automatic answers to all historical questions could be mechanically read off. In a letter which, towards the end of his life, he wrote to a Russian correspondent, he gave as an example of dissimilar development, despite analogous social conditions, the history of the Roman plebs and of the European industrial proletariat. 'When one studies these forms of evolution separately,' he wrote, 'and then compares them, one can easily find the clue to this phenomenon; but one will never get there by using as one's master key a general historico-philosophical theory which explains everything because it explains nothing, the supreme virtue of which consists in being super-historical.'

The theory matured gradually in his mind. It is possible to trace its growth in the *Critique of Hegel's Philosophy of Right* and *On the Jewish Question*; in these the proletariat is for the first time identified as the agent destined to change society in the direction adumbrated by philosophy, which because it is as yet philosophy divorced from action, is itself a symptom and an expression of impotence. It is further developed in *The Holy Family*, an amalgam of polemical outbursts against the 'critical critics', that is, the young Hegelians—principally the brothers Bauer and Stirner—interspersed with fragments on the philosophy of history, social criticism of literature, and other oddities; it is most fully stated in a volume, over six hundred pages in length, which he composed with Engels in 1846, entitled *The German Ideology*, but never published. This verbose, ill-organised and ponderous work, which deals with authors and views long dead and justly forgotten, contains in its lengthy introduction the most sustained, imaginative and impressive exposition of Marx's theory of history. Like the terse and brilliant *Theses on Feuerbach*, which belong to the same period, and the *Economic and Philosophical Manuscripts* of 1844, with their new application of Hegel's concept of alienation, the greater part of *The German Ideology* did not see the light until some years after the author's death (the *Theses* in 1888, the rest only in the present century). It is philosophically far more interesting than any other work by Marx, and represents a submerged, but a most crucial and original stage of his thought, the total ignorance or neglect of which by his immediate followers (including the makers of the Russian Revolution) led to an exclusive emphasis on the historical and economic aspects, and defective understanding of the sociological and philosophical content, of his ideas. This fact is responsible for the clear, half-positivist, half-Darwinian interpretation of Marx's thought, which we owe mainly to Kautsky, Plekhanov, and above all to Engels—a tradition that has decisively influenced both the theory and the practice of the movement which goes by Marx's name.

The framework of the new theory is undeviatingly Hegelian. It recognises that the history of humanity is a single, non-repetitive process, which obeys discoverable laws. Each moment of this process is new in the sense that it possesses new characteristics, or new combinations of known characteristics; but unique and unrepeatable though it is, it nevertheless follows from the immediately preceding state in obedience to the same laws, as this last state from its own predecessor. But whereas according to Hegel the single substance in the succession of whose states history consists, is the eternal, self-developing, universal Spirit, the internal conflict of whose elements is made concrete, in, for example, religious conflicts or the wars of national states, each being an embodiment of the self-realising Idea which it requires a supersensible intuition to perceive, Marx, following Feuerbach, denounces this as a piece of mystification on which no knowledge could be founded. For if the world were a metaphysical substance of this type, its behaviour could not be tested by the only reliable method in our power, namely, empirical observation; and a theory of it could not, therefore, be confirmed by the methods of any science. The Hegelian can, of course, without fear of refutation, attribute anything he wishes to the unobservable activity of an impalpable world-substance, much as the believing Christian or theist attributes it to the activity of God, but only at the cost of explaining nothing, of declaring the answer to be a mystery impenetrable to normal human faculties. It is only such translation of ordinary questions into less intelligible language that makes the resultant obscurity look like a genuine answer. To explain the knowable in terms of the unknowable is to take away with one hand what one affects to give with the other. Whatever value such procedure may have, it cannot be regarded as equivalent to a scientific explanation, that is, to the ordering by means of a comparatively small number of interrelated laws of the great variety of distinct, *prima facie* unconnected, phenomena. So much for orthodox Hegelianism.

But the solutions of the 'critical' schools of Bauer, Ruge, Stirner, even Feuerbach, are in principle no better. After having so mercilessly unmasked the defects of their master, they thereupon themselves, in his view, proceeded to fall into worse illusions: for Bauer's 'spirit of self-criticising criticism', Ruge's 'progressive human spirit', the 'individual self' and 'its inalienable possessions' apostrophised by Stirner, and even the human being of flesh and blood whose evolution Feuerbach traces, are all generalised abstractions no less empty, no more capable of being appealed to as something beyond the phenomena—as their cause—than the equally insubstantial but far more magnificent and imaginative edifice—shadowy, but rich and comprehensive, not reduced to some single bleak abstraction—offered by orthodox Hegelianism.

The only possible region in which to look for the principles of historical dynamics must be one that is open to scientific, that is, normal empirical, inspection. Marx maintains that since the phenomena to be explained are those of social life, the explanation must in some sense reside in the nature of the social environment which forms the context in which men spend their lives, in that network of private and public relationships of which the individuals form the terms, of which they are, as it were, the focal points, the meeting-places of the diverse strands whose totality Hegel called civil society. Hegel had shown his genius in perceiving that its growth was not a smooth progression, arrested by occasional setbacks, as those latter-day *philosophes* Saint-Simon and his disciple Comte taught, but the product of continual tension between opposing forces which guarantee its unceasing forward movement: that the appearance of regular action and reaction is an illusion caused by the fact that now the first, now the second of the conflicting tendencies makes itself most violently felt. In fact progress is discontinuous, for the tension, when it reaches the critical point, precipitates a cataclysm; the increase in quantity of intensity becomes a change of quality; rival forces working below the surface grow and accumulate and burst into the open; the impact of their encounter transforms the medium in which it occurs; as Engels was later to say, ice becomes water and water steam; slaves become serfs and serfs free men; all evolution in nature and society alike ends in creative revolution. In nature these forces are physical, chemical, biological: in society they are specifically economic and social.

What are the forces between which social conflict arises? Hegel had supposed that in the modern world they were embodied in nations which represented the development of a specific culture or incarnation of the Idea, or World Spirit. Marx, following Saint-Simon and Fourier, and not unaffected perhaps by Sismondi's theory of crises, replied that these forces were predominantly socio-economic. 'I was led', he wrote twelve years later, 'to the conclusion that legal relations, as well as forms of state, could neither be understood by themselves, nor explained by the so-called general progress of the human mind, but that they are rooted in the material conditions of life which Hegel calls . . . civil society. The anatomy of civil society is to be sought in political economy.' The conflict is always a clash between economically determined classes, a class being defined as a group of persons in a society, whose lives are determined by their position in the productive arrangements which determine the structure of that society. The status of an individual is determined by the part which he plays in the process of social production, and this in its turn directly depends upon the character of the productive forces and their degree of development at any given stage. Men act as they do in virtue of the economic relationships in which they stand to the other members of their society, whether they are aware of them or not. The most powerful of these relationships is based, as Saint-Simon had taught, on ownership of the means of subsistence: the most pressing of all needs is the need for survival.

The central Hegelian conception remains at the basis of Marx's thought, although it is transposed into semi-empirical terms. History is not the succession of the effects on men of external environment or of their own unalterable constitutions, or even the interplay between these factors, as earlier materialists had supposed. Its essence is the struggle of men to realise their full human potentialities; and, since they are members of the natural kingdom (for there is nothing that transcends it), man's effort to realise himself fully is a striving to escape from being the plaything of forces that seem at once mysterious, arbitrary and irresistible, that is, to attain to the mastery of them and of himself, which is freedom. Man attains this subjugation of his world not by increase in knowledge obtained by contemplation (as Aristotle had supposed), but by activity, by labour, the conscious moulding by men of their environment and of each other—the first and most essential form of the unity of will and thought and deed, of theory and practice. Labour transforms man's world, and himself too, in the course of its activity. Some needs are more basic than others—bare survival comes before more sophisticated wants. But man differs from the animals, with whom he shares essential physical needs, in possessing the gift of invention: thereby he alters his own nature and its needs, and escapes from the repetitive cycles of the animals, who remain unaltered and therefore have no history. The history of society is the history of the inventive labours that alter man, alter his desires, habits, outlook, relationships both to other men and to physical nature, with which man is in perpetual physical and technological metabolism. Among man's inventions—conscious or unconscious—is the division of labour, which arises in primitive society, and vastly increases his productivity, creating wealth beyond his immediate needs. This accumulation in its turn creates the possibility of leisure, and so of culture; but thereby also of the use of this accumulation—of these hoarded necessities of life—as a means of withholding benefits from others, and so of bullying them, of forcing them to work for the accumulators of wealth, of coercing, exploiting and thereby of dividing men into classes—into controllers and controlled. This last is perhaps the most far-reaching of all the unintended results of invention, technical advance and the resultant accumulation of goods. History is the interaction between the lives of the actors, the men engaged in the struggle for attaining self-direction, and the consequences of their activities. Such consequences may be intended or unintended; their effect upon men or their natural environment may be foreseen or not; they may occur in the material sphere, or that of thought or feeling, or at unconscious levels of the lives of men; they may affect only individuals, or take the form of social institutions or movements; but the complex web can only be understood and controlled if the central dynamic factor responsible for the direction of the process is grasped. Hegel, who was the first to see the matter in so illuminating and profound a fashion, found it in the Spirit seeking to understand itself in the institutions —abstract or concrete—which it has itself, at various levels of consciousness, created. Marx accepted this cosmic scheme, but charged Hegel and his disciples with giving a mythical account of the ultimate forces at work—a myth which is itself one of the unintended results of the process of externalising the work of human personality—that is, of giving the appearance of independent, external objects or forces to what are, in fact, products of human labour. Hegel had spoken of the march of the Objective Spirit. Marx identified the chief factor with human beings seeking intelligible human ends—no single goal such as pleasure, or knowledge, or security, or salvation beyond the grave, but the harmonious realisation of all human powers in accordance with the principles of reason. In the course of this quest men transform themselves, so that the predicaments and the values which determine and explain the conduct of one group or generation or civilisation to others who seek to understand it, themselves, in the course of their partial realisation and inevitable partial frustration, alter the predicaments and values of their successors. This constant self-transformation, which is the heart of all work and all creation, renders absurd the very notion of fixed timeless principles, unalterable universal goals, and an eternal human predicament. The character of the age with which he was dealing was, in Marx's view, determined by the phenomenon of class war; the behaviour and outlook of individuals and societies was decisively determined by this factor; this was the central historical truth about a culture which rests on accumulation, and on the battles for the control of this accumulation, by those who strive to realise their powers, often in useless or self-destructive ways. But precisely because it was a historical predicament, it was not eternal. It had been different in the past; and it would not last for ever. Indeed the symptoms of its approaching doom were all too visible for those who had eyes to see. The only permanent factor in the history of man was man himself, intelligible only in terms of the struggle which he had not chosen—the struggle which was part of his essence (this is the metaphysical moment in Marx), the struggle to master nature and organise his productive powers in a rational pattern in which inner and outer harmony consisted. Work in the cosmic vision of Marx is what cosmic love had been for Dante—that which makes men and their relationships what they are, given the relatively invariant factors of the external world into which they are born; its distortion by the division of labour and the class war leads to degradation, dehumanisation, perverted human relationships and conscious and unconscious falsification of vision to maintain this order and conceal the real state of affairs. When this has been understood, and action, which is the concrete expression of such understanding, takes place, labour, instead of dividing and enslaving men, unites and liberates them: gives full expression to their creative capacities in the only form in which men's nature is wholly itself, wholly free—common endeavour, social co-operation in a common, rationally understood and accepted activity. Yet Marx's attitude towards this most central of all the concepts of his system remained curiously uncertain: sometimes he speaks of labour as identical with that free creation which is the fullest expression of untrammelled human nature, the essence of happiness, emancipation, frictionless rational harmony within and between men. At other times he contrasts labour with leisure; and promises that with the abolition of the class war labour will be reduced to a minimum, but not wholly eliminated; it will not be the labour of exploited slaves but of free men building their own socialised lives in accordance with self-imposed rules freely adopted, but some forms of it will still be, so he tells us towards the end of the third volume of *Das Kapital*, in 'the realm of necessity'; the true 'realm of freedom' begins beyond this frontier, but it can, nevertheless, flourish only on 'the realm of necessity as its base'. The need for this minimum of toil is an inescapable fact of physical nature, which it is mere Utopianism to hope to conjure away. There is no final reconciliation between these views. The apparent incompatibility between these prophecies, one probably inspired by Fourier's dream of total fulfilment, the other much more sober, is one of the sources of argument about the relationship of the 'young' to the 'mature' Marx. The same ambivalence affects his combination of evolutionary determinism and libertarian belief in free choice; both are present in his thought, a 'dialectical' contradiction that remained to plague his followers, and divide them, especially in Eastern Europe, where it vitally affected their revolutionary practice.

Feuerbach had correctly perceived that men eat before they reason. The satisfaction of this need can be fully guaranteed only by the control of the means of material production, that is of human strength and skill, of natural resources, of land and water, tools, machine, slaves. There is a natural scarcity of these in the beginning, hence those who secure them are able to control the lives and actions of those who lack them—until they, in their turn, lose possession of them to their subjects, who, grown powerful and cunning in their service, oust them and enslave them, only to be ousted and expropriated by others in their turn. Immense institutions, social, political, cultural, have been created to conserve their possessions in the hands of their present owners, not indeed by deliberate policy, but arising unconsciously out of the general attitude to life of those who govern a given society. But whereas Hegel had supposed that what gave its specific character to any given society was its national character, the nation (in the large sense of an entire civilisation) being for him the embodiment of a given stage in the development of the World Spirit, for Marx it was the system of economic relations which governed the society in question. In a celebrated passage, written a decade after he had arrived at this position, he summarised this view as follows:

'In the social production of their life which men carry on, they enter into definite relations that are indispensable and independent of their will; these relations of production correspond to a definite stage of development of their material powers of production. The totality of these relations of production is due to the economic structure of society—the real foundation on which legal and political superstructures arise, and to which definite forms of social consciousness correspond. The mode of production of material life conditions the general character of the social, political and spiritual processes of life. It is not the consciousness of men that determines their being, but, on the contrary, their social being that determines their consciousness. At a certain stage of their development, the material forces of production in society come into conflict with the existing relations of production, or—what is but a legal expression for the same thing—with the property relations within which they had been at work before. From forms of development of the forces of production, these relations turn into fetters. Then comes an epoch of social revolution. With the change of economic foundation the entire, immense superstructure is sooner or later transformed. But in considering such transformations the distinction should always be made between the material transformation of the economic conditions of production, which can be determined with the precision of natural science, and the legal, political, religious, aesthetic or philosophical in short the ideological—forms in which men become conscious of the conflict and fight it out.

'Just as our opinion of an individual is not based on what he thinks of himself, so we cannot judge an entire revolutionary epoch by the conscious way in which it sees itself: on the contrary, this consciousness must be explained as the product of the contradictions of material life, of the conflict between the social forces of production and the relations of production. No social order ever disappears before all the productive forces for which there is room in it have developed, and the new higher relations of production never appear before the material conditions of their existence have matured in the womb of the old society. Therefore mankind sets itself only such problems as it can solve, since on closer examination it will always be found that the problem itself only arises when the material conditions necessary for its solution already exist or are at least in the process of formation.'[1]

Bourgeois society is the last form which these antagonisms take. After its disappearance the conflict will disappear for ever. The prehistoric period will be completed, the history of the free human individual will at last begin.

The single operative cause which makes one people different from another, one set of institutions and beliefs opposed to another is, so Marx now came to believe, the economic environ-

[1] Preface to *A Contribution to the Critique of Political Economy*, 1859, quoted in the translation of T. B. Bottomore, slightly emended by the author, from *Karl Marx, Selected Writings in Sociology and Social Philosophy*, London, 1956, pp. 51–2.

ment in which it is set, the relationship of the ruling class of possessors to those whom they exploit, arising from the specific quality of the tension which persists between them. The fundamental springs of action in the life of men, he believed, all the more powerful for not being recognised by them, are their relationships to the alignment of classes in the economic struggle: the factor, knowledge of which would enable anyone to predict successfully men's basic line of behaviour, is their actual social position—whether they are outside or inside the ruling class, whether their welfare depends on its success or failure, whether they are placed in a position to which the preservation of the existing order is or is not essential. Once this is known, men's particular personal motives and emotions become comparatively irrelevant to the investigation: they may be egoistic or altruistic, generous or mean, clever or stupid, ambitious or modest. Their natural qualities will be harnessed by their circumstances to operate in a given direction, whatever their natural tendency. Indeed, it is misleading to speak of a 'natural tendency' or an unalterable 'human nature'. Tendencies may be classified either in accordance with the subjective feeling which they engender (and this is, for purposes of scientific prediction, unimportant), or in accordance with their actual aims, which are socially conditioned. Men behave before they start to reflect on the reasons for, or the justification of, their behaviour; the majority of the members of a community will act in a similar fashion, whatever the subjective motives for which they will appear to themselves to be acting as they do. This is obscured by the fact that in the attempt to convince themselves that their acts are determined by reason or by moral or religious beliefs, men have tended to construct elaborate rationalisations of their behaviour. Nor are these rationalisations wholly powerless to affect action, for, growing into great institutions like moral codes or religious organisations, they often linger on long after the social pressures, to explain away which they arose, have disappeared. Thus these great organised illusions themselves become part of the objective social situation, part of the external world which modifies the behaviour of individuals, functioning in the same way as the invariant factors, climate, soil, physical organism, function in their interplay with social institutions.

Marx's immediate successors tended to minimise Hegel's influence upon him; but his vision of the world crumbles and yields only isolated insights if, in the effort to represent him as he conceived himself, as the rigorous, severely factual social scientist, the great unifying, necessary pattern in terms of which he thought, is left out or whittled down.

Like Hegel, Marx treats history as a phenomenology. In Hegel the Phenomenology of the human Spirit is an attempt to show, often with great insight and ingenuity, an objective order in the development of human consciousness and in the succession of civilisations that are its concrete embodiment. Influenced by a notion prominent in the Renaissance, but reaching back to an earlier mystical cosmogony, Hegel looked upon the development of mankind as being similar to that of an individual human being. Just as in the case of a man a particular capacity, or outlook, or way of dealing with reality cannot come into being until and unless other capacities have first become developed—that is, indeed, the essence of the notion of growth or education in the case of individuals—so races, nations, churches, cultures, succeed each other in a fixed order, determined by the growth of the collective faculties of mankind expressed in arts, sciences, civilisation as a whole. Pascal had perhaps meant something of this kind when he spoke of humanity as a single, centuries old, being, growing from generation to generation. For Hegel all change is due to the movement of the dialectic, which works by a constant logical criticism, that is, struggle against, and final self-destruction of, ways of thought and constructions of reason and feeling which, in their day, had embodied the highest point reached by the ceaseless growth (which for Hegel is the logical self-realisation) of the human spirit; but which, embodied in rules or institutions, and erroneously taken as final and absolute by a given society or outlook, thereby become obstacles to progress, dying survivals of a logically 'transcended' stage, which by their very one-sidedness breed logical antinomies and contradictions by which they are exposed and destroyed. Marx translated this vision of history as a battlefield of incarnate ideas into social terms, of the struggle between classes. For him alienation (for that is what Hegel, following Rousseau and Luther and an earlier Christian tradition, called the perpetual self-divorce of men from unity with nature, with each other, with God, which the struggle of thesis against antithesis entailed) is intrinsic to the social process, indeed it is the heart of history itself. Alienation occurs when the results of men's acts contradict their true purposes, when their official values, or the parts they play, misrepresent their real motives and needs and goals. This is the case, for example, when something that men have made to respond to human needs—say, a system of laws, or the rules of musical composition—acquires an independent status of its own, and is seen by men, not as something created by them to satisfy a common social want (which may have disappeared long ago), but as an objective law or institution, possessing eternal, impersonal authority in its own right, like the unalterable laws of Nature as conceived by scientists and ordinary men, like God and His Commandments for a believer. For Marx the capitalist system is precisely this kind of entity, a vast instrument brought into being by intelligible material demands—a progressive improvement and broadening of life in its own day, that generates its own intellectual, moral, religious beliefs, values and forms of life. Whether those who hold them know it or not, such beliefs and values merely uphold the power of the class whose interests the capitalist system embodies; nevertheless, they come to be viewed by all sections of society as being objectively and eternally valid for all mankind. Thus, for example, industry and the capitalist mode of exchange are not timelessly valid institutions, but were generated by the mounting resistance by peasants and artisans to dependence on the blind forces of nature. They have had their moment; and the values these institutions generated will change or vanish with them.

Production is a social activity. Any form of co-operative work or division of labour, whatever its origin, creates common purposes and common interests, not analysable as the mere sum of the individual aims or interests of the human beings involved. If, as in capitalist society, the product of the total social labour of a society is appropriated by one section of that society for its own exclusive benefit, as a result of an inexorable historical development, which Engels, more explicitly (and much more mechanistically) than Marx, attempts to describe, this goes against 'natural' human needs—against what men, whose essence as human beings is to be social, require, in order to develop freely and fully. According to Marx, those who accumulate in their hands the means of production, and thereby also its fruits in the form of capital, forcibly deprive the majority of the producers—the workers—of what they create, and so split society into exploiter and exploited; the interests of these classes are opposed; the well-being of each class depends on its ability to get the better of its adversary in a continuous war, a war that determines all the institutions of that society. In the course of the struggle technological skills develop, the culture of the class-divided society becomes more complex, its products grow richer, and the needs which its material progress breeds, more varied and more artificial—that is, more 'unnatural'. Unnatural, because both the warring classes became 'alienated', by the conflict which has replaced co-operation for common ends, from the integrated common life and creation that, according to this theory, is demanded by the social nature of man. The monopoly of the means of production held by a particular group of men enables it to bind its will on the others and to force them to perform tasks alien to their own needs. Thereby the unity of society is destroyed, and the lives of both classes become distorted. The majority—that is the propertyless proletarians—now work for the benefit, and according to the ideas, of others: the fruit of their labour as well as its instruments are taken from them; their mode of existence, their ideas and ideals correspond not to their own real predicament—that of human beings artificially prevented from living as their natures demand (namely as members of a unified society, capable of understanding the reasons for doing what they do, and of enjoying the fruits of their own united, free and rational activity)—but to the aims of their oppressors. Hence their lives rest on a lie. Their masters, in their turn, whether consciously or not, cannot help seeking to justify their own parasitic existence as being both natural and desirable. In the course of this, they generate ideas, values, laws, habits of life, institutions (a complex which Marx sometimes calls 'ideology'), the whole purpose of which is to prop up, explain away, defend, their own privileged, unnatural, and therefore unjustified, status and power. Such ideologies—national, religious, economic and so on, are forms of collective self-deception; the victims of the ruling class—the proletarians and peasants—imbibe it as part of their normal education, of the general outlook of the unnatural society, and so come to look upon it, and accept it, as objective, just, necessary, a part of the natural order which pseudo-sciences are then created to explain. This, as Rousseau had taught, serves to deepen still further human error, conflict and frustration.

The symptom of alienation is the attribution of ultimate authority, either to some impersonal power—say the laws of supply and demand—from which the rationality of capitalism is represented as being logically deducible, or to imaginary persons or forces—divinities, churches, the mystical person of the king or priest, or disguised forms of other oppressive myths, whereby men, torn from a 'natural' mode of life (which alone makes it possible for entire societies to perceive the truth and live harmoniously), seek to explain their unnatural condition to themselves. If men are ever to liberate themselves, they must be taught to see through these myths. The most oppressive of all, in Marx's demonology, is bourgeois economic science, which represents the movement of commodities or of money—indeed the process of production, consumption and distribution—as an impersonal process, similar to those of nature, an unalterable pattern of objective forces before which men can only bow, and which it would be insane to attempt to resist. Deterministic as he was, Marx nevertheless resolved to show that the conception of any given economic or social structure as a part of an unchangeable world order was an illusion brought about by man's alienation from the form of life natural to him—a typical 'mystification', the effects of purely human activities masquerading as laws of nature; it would be removed ('unmasked') only by other, equally human activities—the application of 'demystifying' reason and science; but this is not sufficient; such delusions are bound to persist so long as the relations of production—that is, the social and economic structure by which they are generated—are as they are; these can be altered only by the weapon of revolution. These liberating activities may themselves be determined by objective laws, but what these laws determine is the activity of human thought and will (particularly of men taken in the mass), and not merely the movement of material bodies, obeying their own inexorable patterns that are independent of human decisions and actions. If, as Marx believed, human choices can affect the course of events, then, even if these choices are themselves ultimately determined and scientifically predictable, such a situation is one in which Hegelians and Marxists think it legitimate to call men free, since such choices are not, like the rest of nature, mechanically determined.

The laws of history are not mechanical: history has been made by men, even if not 'out of whole cloth' but conditioned by the social situation in which they found themselves. What, according to Marx, is the relation of these laws to human freedom, whether individual or collective? It is clear that his conception of social advance, which he identifies with the progressive conquest of freedom, consists in increasing control of nature by conscious, concerted, rationally planned, and therefore harmonious, social activity. 'Darwin did not know what a bitter satire about humanity, and his own countrymen in particular, he was writing when he showed that free competition, the struggle for existence which the economists hold up as the highest achievement of history, was the normal condition of the animal kingdom. Only a conscious organisation of social production, in which production and distribution are planned, can lift human society above the rest of the animal kingdom, as production in general has already done for men in certain respects.' Or again, '. . . the socialisation of men, which previously faced them as a fact imposed by nature and history, will then be achieved by their own free act . . . this will be mankind's leap from the realm of necessity into that of freedom.' What kind of freedom? Marx in general speaks of the development of society as an objective process. In the Introduction to *Das Kapital* the succession of economic forms is described as 'a process of natural history'. In 1873 Marx, in the epilogue to the second edition of *Das Kapital*, quotes a passage from the Russian reviewer of the original edition who said 'Marx regards social movement as a process of natural history governed by laws that are not only independent of men's will, consciousness and intentions, but on the contrary, determine their will, consciousness and intentions.' Marx declares that this is the correct interpretation of his purpose—namely, the discovery of the laws that govern social development.

It is passages such as this that have inspired the rigorously deterministic interpretation of Marx's conception of human history and the laws that determine it, with 'iron necessity'. At most the process can be slowed down or accelerated, but 'even when a society has traced the natural laws that govern its movement, it can neither leap over nor decree the abolition of its natural phases of development', it can only 'shorten . . . the birth pangs'. That is why 'the industrially more developed country shows the less developed merely the picture of its own future'. This is clearly what Engels meant when, in his speech at Marx's grave, he said that his great achievement was his discovery of 'the law of development of human history', where the contradictions that develop between productive forces and productive relations lead to an unalterable sequence of economic relationships that determine social and political and, ultimately, all other aspects of collective life. But the notion of 'the free development' of men— that state of human association in which the development of each is a condition for the free development of all (of which the *Communist Manifesto* speaks)—is not *prima facie* a clear one. If men are themselves only the product of objective conditions, not only economic but environmental—geographical, climatic, biological, physiological and so on—of the fact that these forces work 'through' them and not merely 'upon' them (according to the laws of which Marx had become aware by the kind of investigation that *Das Kapital* was intended to be), and if the application of this knowledge can at most only 'shorten . . . the birth pangs' which precede the classless society but is impotent to alter the process itself, then the concept of human freedom, whether in its social or individual aspects, is clearly in need of explanation. It is one thing to say that unless men understand the laws that govern their lives they will fall foul of them and remain victims of forces they do not understand; and another to say that everything that they are and do is subject to these laws, and that freedom is merely the perception of their necessity and itself a factor in the unalterable process in which human choice, whether individual or social, is subject to causes that fully determine it, and is, in principle, wholly predictable by a sufficiently informed external observer. Marx's own utterances can be quoted in support of either of these alternatives. Attempts to interpret these apparently contradictory views, whether for the purpose of sharpening or reconciling them, has generated a large and ever-growing literature of its own, particularly in our day.

Because the historical function of capitalism, and its relation to the interests of a specific class, are not understood, it comes not to enrich but to crush and distort the lives of millions of workers, and indeed of their oppressors too, like everything that is not rationally grasped and therefore blindly worshipped as a fetish. Money for instance, which played a progressive role in the days of liberation from barter, has now become an absolute object of pursuit and worship for its own sake, brutalising and destroying man whom it was invented to liberate. Men are divorced from the products of their own toil and from the instruments with which they produce: these acquire a life and status of their own, and in the name of their survival or improvement, living human beings are oppressed and treated like cattle or saleable commodities. This is true of all institutions, churches, economic systems, forms of government, moral codes, which, through being systematically (and, at certain stages of the class struggle, necessarily) misunderstood, become more powerful than their inventors, monsters worshipped by their makers—the blind, unhappy Frankensteins whose lives they frustrate and twist. At the same time, merely to see through or criticise this predicament, which the young Hegelians thought sufficient, will not destroy it. To be effective, the weapons with which one fights, among them ideas, must be those called for by the historical situation—neither those that served a previous period, nor those for which the historical process has not yet called. Men must ask themselves, first and foremost, what stage the class war—which is the dialectic at work—has reached, and then act accordingly. This is to be 'concrete' and not timeless, or idealistic or 'abstract'. Alienation—the substitution of imaginary relations between, or worship of, inanimate objects or ideas for real relations between, or respect for, persons—will come to an end only when the final class—the proletariat—defeats the bourgeoisie. Then the ideas which this victory will generate will automatically be those expressive of, and beneficial to, a classless society; that is, all mankind. Neither institutions nor ideas which rest on falsifying the character of any section of the human race, and so leading to (or expressive of) their opposition, will survive. Capitalism, under which the labour power of human beings is bought and sold, and the workers are treated merely as sources of labour, is plainly a system which distorts the truth about what men are and can be, and seeks to subordinate history to a class interest, and is therefore due to be superseded by the gathering power of its indignant victims which its own victories call into existence. All frustration, for Marx, is the product of alienation—the barriers and distortions that are created by the inevitable war of classes, and shut out this or that body of men from the harmonious co-operation with one another for which their nature craves.

In *The German Ideology* the claims of the neo-Hegelians are examined one by one, and 'awarded' their due. The brothers Bruno, Edgar and Egbert Bauer are dealt with briefly and savagely here as in the published, though little read, *The Holy Family*. They are represented as three sordid peddlers of inferior metaphysical wares, who believe that the mere existence of a fastidious critical *élite*, raised by its intellectual gifts above the philistine mob, will itself effect the emancipation of such sections of humanity as are worthy of it. This belief in the power of a frigid detachment from the social and economic struggle to effect a transformation of society, is regarded as academicism run mad, an ostrich-like attitude which will be swept away, like the rest of the world to which it belongs, by the real revolution which could not, it was clear, now be long in coming. Stirner is treated at greater length. Under the title of St Max he is pursued through seven hundred pages of heavy-handed mockery and insult. Stirner believed that all programmes, ideals, theories as well as political, social and economic orders are so many artificially built prisons for the mind and the spirit, means of curbing the will, of concealing from the individual the existence of his own infinite creative powers, and that all systems must therefore be destroyed, not because they are evil, but because they are systems, submission to which is a new form of idolatry; only when this has been achieved would man, released from his unnatural fetters, become truly master of himself and attain to his full stature as a human being. This doctrine, which had a great influence on Nietzsche and probably on Bakunin (perhaps because it anticipated Marx's own economic theory of alienation too precisely), is treated as a pathological phenomenon, the agonised cry of a persecuted neurotic, belonging to the province of medicine rather than to that of political theory.

Feuerbach is more gently treated. He is held to have written more soberly, and to have made an honest, if crude, attempt to expose the mystifications of idealism. In the eleven *Theses on Feuerbach* which he composed during the same period, Marx declared that while earlier materialist thinkers had correctly perceived that men are largely the product of circumstances and education, they had not gone on to see that circumstances are themselves altered by the activity of men, and that the educators themselves are children of their age. This doctrine (Marx is principally thinking of Robert Owen) artificially divides society into two parts: the masses, which, being helplessly exposed to every influence, must be freed; and the teachers, who contrive somehow to remain immune from the effect of their environment. But the relation of mind and matter, of men and nature, is reciprocal; otherwise history becomes reduced to physics. Feuerbach is praised for showing that in religion men delude themselves by inventing an imaginary world to redress the balance of misery in real life—it is a form of escape, a golden dream, or, in a phrase made celebrated by Marx, the opium of the people; the criticism of religion must therefore be anthropological in character, and take the form of exposing and analysing its secular origins. But Feuerbach is accused of leaving the major task untouched: he sees that religion is an anodyne unconsciously generated by the unhappy to soften the pain caused by the contradictions of the material world, but then fails to see that these contradictions must, in that case, be removed: otherwise they will continue to breed comforting and fatal delusions: the revolution which alone can do so must occur not in the superstructure—the world of thought—but in its material substratum, the real world of men and things. Philosophy has hitherto treated ideas and beliefs as possessing an intrinsic validity of their own; this has never been true; the real content of a belief is the action in which it is expressed. The real convictions and principles of a man or a society are expressed in their acts, not their words. Belief and act are one; if acts do not themselves express avowed beliefs, the beliefs are lies—'ideologies', conscious or not, to cover the opposite of what they profess. Theory and practice are, or should be, one and the same. 'Philosophers have previously offered various interpretations of the world. Our business is to change it.'

The so-called 'True Socialists', Grün and Hess, fare no better. It is true that they wrote about the actual situation; but, placing ideals before interests in order of importance, they are equally far removed from a clear view of the facts. They believed correctly that the political inequality, and the general emotional *malaise* of their generation, were both traceable to economic contradictions which could only be removed by the total abolition of private property. But they also believed that the technological advance which made this possible was not an end but a means; that action could be justified only by appeal to moral ideals; that the use of force, however noble the purpose for which it was employed, defeated its own end, since it brutalised both parties in the struggle, and made them both incapable of true freedom after the struggle was over. If men were to be freed, it must be by peaceful and civilised means alone, to be effected as rapidly and painlessly as possible, before industrialisation had spread so widely as to make a bloody class war inevitable. Indeed, unless this was done, only violence would be left, and this would, in the end, defeat itself; for a society set up by the sword, even if justice initially were on its side, could not fail to develop into a tyranny of the victorious class—even though it be that of the workers—over the rest, and this would be incompatible with that human equality which true socialism seeks to create. The 'True Socialists' opposed the doctrine of the necessity of open class war on the ground that it blinded the workers to those rights and ideals for the sake of which they fought. Only by treating men as equal from the beginning, by dealing with them as human beings, that is, by renouncing force, and appealing to the sense of human solidarity, of equal justice and the generous sentiments of mankind, could a lasting harmony of interests be obtained. Above all, the burden of the proletariat must not be removed by being shifted on to the shoulders of some other class. Marx and his party, they maintained, merely desired to reverse the roles of the existing classes, to deprive the bourgeoisie of its power only to ruin and enslave it. But this, besides being morally unacceptable, would leave the class war itself in existence and so would fail to reconcile the existing contradiction in the only way possible, by fusing conflicting interests into one common ideal.

Marx looked upon all this as so much idiocy or cant. The whole argument, he wearily points out, rests on the premiss that men, even capitalists, are amenable to a rational argument, and under suitable conditions will voluntarily give up the power which they have acquired by birth or wealth or ability, for the sake of a moral principle, to create a juster world. To Marx this was the oldest, most familiar, most outworn of all the rationalist fallacies. He had met it in its worst form in the belief of his own father and his contemporaries that in the end reason and moral goodness were bound to triumph, a theory which was utterly discredited by events during the dark aftermath of the French Revolution. To preach it now, as if one were still living in the eighteenth century, was to be guilty either of boundless stupidity, or of a cowardly escape into mere words, or else of deliberate Utopianism, when what was needed was a scientific examination of the actual situation. Marx was careful to point out that he did not himself fall into the opposite error: he did not simply contradict this thesis about human nature, and say that whereas these theorists assumed man to be fundamentally generous and just, he found him rapacious, self-seeking and incapable of disinterested action. That would have been an hypothesis as subjective and unhistorical as that of his opponents. Each was vitiated by the fallacy that men's acts were in the end determined by their moral character, which could be described in comparative isolation from their environment. Marx, true to the method, if not to the conclusions, of Hegel, maintained that a man's purposes were made what they were by the social, that is economic, situation in which he was in fact placed whether he knew it or not. Whatever his opinions, a man's actions were inevitably guided by his real interests, by the requirements of his material situation; the conscious aims of at any rate the bulk of mankind did not clash with their real interests, that is, of the class to which they belonged, although they some-times appeared disguised as so many independent, objective, disinterested ends, political, moral, aesthetic, emotional and the like. Most individuals concealed their own dependence on their environment and situation, particularly on their class affiliation, so effectively even from themselves, that they quite sincerely believed that a change of heart would result in a radically different mode of life. This was the profoundest error made by modern thinkers. It arose partly as a result of Protestant individualism, which, arising as the 'ideological' counterpart of the growth of freedom of trade and production, taught men to believe that the individual held the means for his happiness in his own hands, that faith and energy were sufficient to secure it, that every man had it in his power to attain to spiritual or material well-being, that for his weakness and misery he ultimately had only himself to blame. Marx maintained, against this, that liberty of action, the range of real possibilities between which men could choose, was determined by the precise position which the agent occupied on the social map. All notions of right and wrong, justice and injustice, altruism and egoism, were beside the point, as referring exclusively to the mental states, which, while in themselves quite genuine, were never more than symptoms of the actual condition of their owner. Acts—particularly the objective behaviour of a group, whatever the subjective motives of its members—these alone counted. Sometimes, when the patient was himself acquainted with the science of pathology, he could accurately diagnose his own condition; this is indeed what was meant by genuine insight on the part of a social philosopher. But more frequently the symptom would pose as the only true reality, occupying the whole attention of the sufferer. Since the symptoms in this case were mental states, it was this that bred the otherwise inexplicable fallacy that reality was mental or spiritual in character, or that history could be altered by the isolated decisions of unfettered human wills. Principles and causes, unless allied to real interests which caused action, were so many empty phrases; to lead men in their name, was to feed them on air, reduce them to a state in which their very failure to apprehend their true situation would involve them in chaos and destruction.

To alter the world, one must first understand the material with which one deals. The bourgeoisie which wishes not to alter it, but to preserve the *status quo*, acts and thinks in terms of concepts, which, being products of a given stage in its development, themselves serve, whatever they pretend to be, as instruments of its temporary preservation. The proletariat, in whose interest it is to alter it, blindly accepts the entire intellectual paraphernalia of middle-class thought, born of middle-class needs and conditions, although there is an utter divergence of interest between the two classes. Phrases about justice or liberty represent something more or less definite when they are uttered by the middle-class liberal, namely his attitude, however deluded, to his own mode of life, his actual or desired relation to members of other social classes. But they are empty sounds when repeated by the 'alienated' proletarian, since they describe nothing real in his life, and only betray his muddled state of mind, the result of the hypnotic power of phrases, which, by confusing issues, not only fail to promote, but hinder and sometimes paralyse his power to act. Mutualists, True Socialists, mystical Anarchists, however pure their motives, are thus even more dangerous enemies of the proletariat than the bourgeoisie: for the latter is at least an open enemy whose words and deeds the workers can be taught to distrust. But these others, who proclaim their solidarity with the workers, and assume that there always exist universal interests of mankind as such, common to all men—that men have interests independent of, or transcending, their class affiliation—spread error and darkness in the proletarian camp itself, and thus weaken it for the coming struggle. The workers must be made to understand that the modern industrial system like the feudal system before it, like every other social system, is class dominated; so long as the ruling class requires it for its continuance as a class, it remains an iron despotism imposed by the capitalist system of production and distribution, from which no individual, whether he be master or slave, can escape. All visionary dreams of human liberty, of a time when men will be able to develop their natural gifts to their fullest extent, living and creating spontaneously, no longer dependent on others for the freedom to do or think as they will, remain an unattainable Utopia so long as the fight for control of the means of production continues. It is no longer a struggle strictly for the means of subsistence, for modern inventions and discoveries have abolished natural scarcity: it is now an artificial scarcity, created by the very struggle for securing new instruments itself, a process which necessarily leads to the centralisation of power by the creation of monopolies at one end of the social scale, and the increase of penury and degradation at the other. The war between economically determined groups alone divides men from each other, blinds them to the real facts of their situation, makes them slaves to customs and rules which they dare not question, because they would crumble at the touch of historical explanation; only one remedy—the disappearance of the class struggle—can achieve the abolition of this widening gulf. But the essence of a class is to compete with other classes. Hence this end can be achieved not by creating equality between classes—a Utopian conception—but by the total abolition of classes themselves.

For Marx, no less than for earlier rationalists, man is potentially wise, creative and free. If his character has deteriorated beyond recognition, that is due to the long and brutalising war in which he and his ancestors have lived ever since society ceased to be that primitive communism out of which, according to the current anthropology, it has developed. Until this state is reached again, embodying, however, all the conquests, technological and spiritual, which mankind has won in the course of its long wandering in the desert, neither peace nor freedom can be obtained. The French Revolution was an attempt to bring this about by altering political forms only—which was no more than the bourgeoisie required, since it already possessed the economic reality: and, therefore, all it succeeded in doing (as indeed was its appointed historical task at the stage of development at which it occurred) was to establish the bourgeoisie in a dominant position by finally destroying the corrupt remnant of an obsolete feudal regime. This task could not but be continued by Napoleon, whom no one could suspect of wishing consciously to liberate humanity; whatever his personal motive for acting as he did, the demands of his historical environment inevitably made him an instrument of social change; by his agency, as Hegel had indeed perceived, Europe advanced yet another step towards the realisation of its destiny.

The gradual freeing of mankind has pursued a definite, irreversible direction: every new epoch is inaugurated by the liberation of a hitherto oppressed class; nor can a class, once it has been destroyed, ever return. History does not move backwards, or in cyclical movements: all its conquests are final and irrevocable. Most previous ideal constitutions were worthless because they ignored actual laws of historical development, and substituted in their place the subjective caprice or imagination of the thinker. A knowledge of these laws is essential to effective political action. The ancient world gave way to the medieval, slavery to feudalism, and feudalism to the industrial bourgeoisie. These transitions were not peaceful, but sprang from wars and revolutions, for no established order gives way to its successor without a struggle.

And now only one stratum remains submerged below the level of the rest, one class alone remains enslaved, the landless, propertyless proletariat, created by the advance of technology, perpetually assisting classes above itself to shake off the yoke of the common oppressor, always, after the common cause has been won, condemned to be oppressed by its own former allies, the new victorious class, by masters who were themselves but lately slaves. The proletariat is on the lowest possible rung of the social scale: there is no class below it; by securing its own emancipation the proletariat will therefore emancipate mankind. It has, unlike other classes, no specific claim, no interests of its own which it does not share with all men as such: for it has been stripped of everything but its bare humanity; its very destitution causes it to represent human beings as such—what it is entitled to is the minimum to which all men are entitled. Its fight is thus not a fight for the natural rights of a particular section of society: for natural rights are but the ideal formulation of the bourgeois attitude to the sanctity of private property; the only real rights are those conferred by history, the right to act the part which is historically imposed upon one's class. The bourgeoisie, in this sense, has a full right to fight its final battle against the masses, but its task is hopeless: it will necessarily be defeated, as the feudal nobility was defeated in its day. As for the masses, they fight for freedom not because they choose, but because they must, or rather they choose because they must: to fight is the condition of their survival; the future belongs to them, and in fighting for it, they, like every rising class, fight against a foe doomed to decay, and thereby for the whole of mankind. But whereas all other victories placed in power a class itself doomed to ultimate disappearance, this conflict will be followed by no other, being destined to end the condition of all such struggles, by abolishing classes as such; by dissolving the state itself, hitherto the instrument of a single class, into a free, because classless, society. The proletariat must be made to understand that no real compromise with the enemy is possible: that, while it may conclude temporary alliances with him in order to defeat some common adversary, it must ultimately turn against him. In backward countries, where the bourgeoisie itself is still fighting for power, the proletariat must throw in its lot with it, asking itself not what the ideals of the bourgeoisie may be, but what it is *compelled* to do in the particular situation; and must adapt its tactics to this. And while history is determined—and the victory will, therefore, be won by the rising class whether any given individual wills it or not—how rapidly this will occur, how effectively or painlessly, how far in accordance with the conscious popular will, depends on human initiative, on the degree of understanding of their task by the masses and the courage and efficiency of their leaders.

To make this clear, and to educate the masses for their destiny is, therefore, according to Marx, the whole duty of a contemporary philosopher. But, it has often been asked, how can a precept, a command to do this or that, be deduced from the truth of a theory of history? Historical materialism may account for what does in fact occur, but cannot, precisely because it is concerned solely with what is, provide the answer to questions of value, that is, tell us what ought to be. Marx does not explicitly draw this distinction, which has been brought to the forefront of philosophical attention by Hume and Kant, but it seems clear that for him (he follows Hegel on this) judgements of fact cannot be sharply distinguished from those of value: all one's judgements are conditioned by practical activity in a given social milieu which, in its turn, are functions of the stage reached by one's class in its historical evolution: one's views as to what one believes to exist and what one wishes to do with it, modify each other. If ethical judgements claim objective validity, they must be definable in terms of empirical activities and be verifiable by reference to them. He does not recognise the existence of a non-empirical, purely contemplative or specifically moral intuition or moral reason. The only sense in which it is possible to show that something is good or bad, right or wrong, is by demonstrating that it accords or discords with the historical process—the collective progressive activity of men—that it assists it or thwarts it, will survive or will inevitably perish. All causes permanently lost or doomed to fail, in the complex but historically determined ascent of mankind, are, by that very fact, made bad and wrong, and indeed this is what constitutes the meaning of such terms. But this is a dangerous empirical criterion, since causes which may appear lost may, in fact, have suffered only a temporary setback, and will in the end prevail.

His view of truth in general derives directly from this position. He is sometimes accused of maintaining that, since a man is wholly determined to think as he does by his social environment, even if some of his statements are objectively true, he cannot know it, being conditioned to think them true by material causes, not by their truth. Marx's statements on this subject are vague to a degree; but in general it may be said that he would have accepted the normal interpretation of what is meant by saying that a theory or a proposition of natural science or of ordinary sense experience is true or false. But he was scarcely interested in this, the most common, type of truth discussed by modern philosophers. He was concerned with the reasons for which social, moral, historical verdicts are thought true or false, where arguments between opponents can not so easily be settled by direct appeal to empirical facts accessible to both. He might have agreed that the bare proposition that Napoleon died in exile would have been accepted as equally true by a bourgeois and a socialist historian. But he would have gone on to say that no true historian confines himself to a list of events and dates: that the plausibility of his account of the past, its claim to be more than a bare chronicle, depends, at the very least, upon his choice of fundamental concepts, his power of emphasis and arrangement, that the very process of selection of material betrays an inclination to stress this or that event or act as important or trivial, adverse or favourable to human progress, good or bad. And in this tendency the social origin and environment and class affiliation and interests of the historian tell only too clearly.

This attitude seems to underlie his Hegelian view of rationality as entailing knowledge of the laws of necessity. Marx scarcely ever embarks on any kind of philosophical analysis; the general line of his theories of knowledge, of morals, of politics has to be inferred from scattered observations and from what he takes for granted, accepts without question. His use of such notions as freedom or rationality, his ethical terminology, seem to rest on some such view as the following (for which chapter and verse cannot be quoted, but which his orthodox disciples, Plekhanov, Kautsky, Lenin, Trotsky, no less than more independent followers like Lukács and Gramsci, embody in their thought): if you know in what direction the world process is working, you can either identify yourself with it or not; if you do not, if you fight it, you thereby compass your own certain destruction, being necessarily defeated by the forward advance of history. To choose to do so deliberately is to behave irrationally. Only a wholly rational being is wholly free to choose between alternatives: where one of these irresistibly leads to his own destruction, he cannot choose it freely, because to say that an act is free, as Marx employs the term, is to deny that it is contrary to reason. The bourgeoisie as a class is indeed fated to disappear, but individual members of it may follow reason and save themselves (as Marx might have claimed to have done himself) by leaving it before it finally founders. True freedom is unattainable until society has been made rational, that is, has overcome the contradictions which breed illusions and distort the understanding of both masters and slaves. But men can work for the free world by discovering the true state of the balance of forces, and acting accordingly; the path to freedom thus entails knowledge of historical necessity. Marx's use of words like 'right', or 'free', or 'rational', whenever he does not slip insensibly into ordinary usage, owes its eccentric air to the fact that it derives from his metaphysical views; and therefore diverges widely from that of common speech, which is largely intended to record and communicate something scarcely of interest to him—the subjective experience of class-perverted individuals, their states of mind or of body as revealed by the senses or in self-consciousness.

Such in outline is the theory of history and society which constitutes the often 'implicit' metaphysical basis of communism. It is a wide and comprehensive doctrine which derives its structure and basic concepts from Hegel and the Young Hegelians, and its dynamic principles from Saint-Simon, its belief in the primacy of matter from Feuerbach, and its view of the proletariat from the French communist tradition. Nevertheless it is wholly original; the combination of elements does not in this case lead to syncretism, but forms a bold and coherent system, with the wide range and the massive architectonic quality that is at once the greatest pride and the fatal defect of all forms of Hegelian thought. But it is not guilty of Hegel's reckless and contemptuous attitude towards the results of the scientific research of his time; on the contrary, it attempts to follow the direction indicated by the empirical sciences, and to incorporate their general results. Marx's practice did not always conform to this theoretical ideal, and that of his followers sometimes did so even less: while not actually distorted, the facts are sometimes made to undergo peculiar transformations in the process of being fitted into the intricate dialectical pattern. It is by no means a wholly empirical theory, since it does not confine itself to the description of the phenomena and the formulation of hypotheses concerning their structure and behaviour; the Marxist doctrine of movement in dialectical collisions is not a hypothesis liable to be made less or more probable by the evidence of facts, but a pattern, uncovered by a non-empirical, historical method, the validity of which is not questioned. To deny this would be tantamount, according to Marx, to a return to 'vulgar' materialism, which, ignoring the crucial discoveries of Hegel and indeed Kant, recognises only those connections as real for which there is the corrigible evidence of the physical senses.

In the sharpness and the clarity with which this theory formulates its questions, in the rigour of the method by which it proposes to search for the answers, in the combination of attention to detail and power of wide comprehensive generalisation, it is without parallel. Even if all its specific conclusions were proved false, its importance in creating a wholly new attitude to social and historical questions, and so opening new avenues of human knowledge, would be unimpaired. The scientific study of historically evolving economic relations, and of their bearing on other aspects of the lives of communities and individuals, began with the application of Marxist canons of interpretation. Previous thinkers—for example, Vico, Hegel, Saint-Simon—drew up general schemata, but their direct results, as embodied, for instance, in the gigantic systems of Comte or Spencer, are at once too abstract and too vague, and are remembered in our day only by historians of ideas. The true father of modern economic history, and, indeed, of modern sociology, in so far as any one man may claim that title, is Karl Marx. If to have turned into truisms what had previously been paradoxes is a mark of genius, Marx was richly endowed with it. His achievements in this sphere are necessarily ignored in proportion as their effects have become part of the permanent background of civilised thought.

7
1848

Gegen Demokraten Helfen nur Soldaten.[1]
Prussian Song

Liberty, Equality, Fraternity . . . when what this republic really
means is Infantry, Cavalry, Artillery. . . .
KARL MARX, *The Eighteenth Brumaire of Louis Bonaparte*

MARX was expelled from Paris at the beginning of 1845 by the
Guizot government as a result of representations from Prussia,
which had demanded the suppression of the socialist *Vorwärts* in
which offensive comments had appeared concerning the character of the reigning Prussian king. The order of expulsion was
originally intended to apply to the entire group, including Heine,
Bakunin, Ruge and several other lesser foreign exiles. Ruge, being
a Saxon citizen, was left unmolested; the French government
itself did not venture to press the order against Heine, a figure of
European fame, then at the height of his powers and influence.
Bakunin and Marx were duly expelled in spite of vigorous protests in the radical press. Bakunin went to Switzerland; Marx,
with his wife and one-year-old daughter Jenny, to Brussels where
shortly afterwards he was joined by Engels who had returned
from England for this purpose. In Brussels he lost no time in
establishing contact with the various German communist workers' organisations which contained members of the dissolved
League of the Just, an international society of proletarian
revolutionaries with a vague, but violent, programme, influenced
by Weitling; it had branches in various European cities. He
entered into relations with Belgian socialists and radicals, carried
on an active correspondence with members of similar bodies in
other countries, and established regular machinery for the
exchange of political information, but the chief sphere of his

[1] Against democrats, only soldiers help.

activity lay among the German workmen in Brussels itself. To these he attempted by means of lectures, and of articles in their organ, the *Deutsche Brüsseler Zeitung*, to explain their proper part in the coming revolution, which he, like the majority of European radicals, believed to be imminent.

As soon as he concluded that the establishment of communism could only be achieved by a rising of the proletariat, his entire existence turned into an attempt to organise and discipline it for its task. His personal history, which up to this point can be regarded as a series of episodes in the life of an individual, now becomes inseparable from the general history of socialism in Europe; an account of one is necessarily to some degree an account of the other. Attempts to distinguish the part which Marx played in directing the movement from the movement itself obscure the history of both. The task of preparing the workers for the revolution was for him a scientific task, a routine occupation, something to be performed as solidly and efficiently as possible, and not a direct means of personal self-expression. The external circumstances of his life are therefore as monotonous as those of any other educated expert, as those of Darwin or Pasteur, and offer a sharp contrast to the restless, emotionally involved lives of the other revolutionaries of his time.

The middle decades of the nineteenth century form a period in which an enormous premium was placed on sensibility. What had begun by being the isolated experience of exceptional individuals, of Rousseau and Chateaubriand, Schiller and Jean Paul, Byron and Shelley, by insensible degrees became an element in the general attitude of a part of European society. For the first time a whole generation became fascinated by the personal experience of men and women, as opposed to the external world composed of the interplay of the lives of whole groups or societies. This tendency obtained public expression in the lives and doctrines of the great democratic revolutionaries, and in the passionate adoration with which they were regarded by their followers: Mazzini, Kossuth, Garibaldi, Bakunin, Lassalle, were admired not only as heroic fighters for freedom, but for their romantic, poetical properties as individuals. Their achievements were looked upon as the expression of profound inner experience, the intensity of which gave their words and gestures a moving personal quality wholly different from the austerely impersonal heroism of the men of 1789, a quality which constitutes the distinguishing characteristic, the peculiar temper and outlook of the age. Karl Marx belonged in spirit to an earlier or a later generation. He lacked psychological insight, and poverty and hard work did not increase his emotional receptiveness; this extreme blindness to the experience and character of persons outside his immediate range made his intercourse with the outside world seem singularly boorish; he had had a brief sentimental period as a student in Berlin: this was now over and done with. He looked upon moral or emotional suffering, and spiritual crises, as so much bourgeois self-indulgence, unpardonable in time of war. Like Lenin after him, he seemed to have nothing but contempt for those who, during the heat of the battle, while the enemy gained one position after another, were preoccupied with the state of their own souls.

He set to work to create an international revolutionary organisation. He received the warmest response in London, from a society called the German Workers' Educational Association, headed by a small group of exiled artisans, whose revolutionary temper was beyond suspicion: the type-setter Schapper, the watch-maker Moll, and the cobbler Bauer were his first reliable political allies. They had affiliated their society to a federation called the Communist League which succeeded the dissolved League of the Just. He met them in the course of a journey to England with Engels, and found them men after his own heart, determined, capable and energetic. They looked on him with considerable suspicion as a journalist and an intellectual; and their relations for some years preserved a severely impersonal and business-like character. It was an association for immediate practical ends, and this he approved. Under his guidance the Communist League grew fast and began to embrace groups of radical workers, scattered for the most part in the industrial areas in Germany, with a sprinkling of army officers and professional men. Engels wrote glowing reports of the increase in their numbers and their revolutionary zeal in his own native province. For the first time Marx found himself in the position which he had long desired, the organiser and leader of an active and expanding revolutionary party. Bakunin, who had in his turn arrived in Brussels, and was on equally good terms with the foreign radicals and members of the local aristocracy, complained that Marx preferred the society of artisans and workmen to that of intelligent people, and was spoiling good and simple men by filling their heads with abstract theories and obscure economic doctrines, which they did not begin to understand, and which only made them intolerably conceited. He saw no point in lecturing to, and organising small groups of ill-educated and hopelessly limited German artisans, who understood little of what was so elaborately expounded to them; drab, underfed creatures who could not conceivably turn the scale in any decisive conflict. Marx's attack on Proudhon still further estranged them; Proudhon was an intimate friend and, in Hegelian matters, a disciple of Bakunin; and the attack was aimed no less at Bakunin's own habit of indulging in vague and exuberant eloquence in place of detailed political analysis.

The events of 1848 altered the view of both on the technique of the coming revolution, but in precisely opposed directions. Bakunin in later years turned to secret terrorist groups, Marx to the foundation of an open, official, revolutionary party proceeding by recognised political methods. He set himself to destroy the tendency to rhetoric and vagueness among the Germans, nor was he wholly unsuccessful, as may be seen in the efficient and disciplined behaviour of the members of his organisation in Germany during the two revolutionary years and after.

In 1847 the London centre of the Communist League showed its confidence in Marx and Engels by commissioning them to compose a document containing a definitive statement of its beliefs and aims. Marx eagerly embraced this opportunity for an explicit summary of the new doctrine which had lately assumed its final shape in his head. He delivered it into their hands early in 1848. It was published a few weeks before the outbreak of the Paris revolution under the title of the *Manifesto of the Communist Party*.

Engels wrote the first draft in the form of questions and answers, but since this was not thought sufficiently forcible, Marx completely rewrote it. According to Engels the result was an original work which owed hardly anything to his own hand; but he was excessively modest wherever their collaboration was concerned, and the draft shows how great a share he had in its composition. The result is the greatest of all socialist pamphlets. No other modern political movement or cause can claim to have produced anything comparable with it in eloquence or power. It is a document of prodigious dramatic force; in form it is an edifice of bold and arresting historical generalisations, mounting to a denunciation of the existing order in the name of the avenging forces of the future, much of it written in prose which has the lyrical quality of a great revolutionary hymn, whose effect, powerful even now, was probably greater at the time. It opens

with a menacing phrase which reveals its tone and its intention: 'A
spectre is wandering over Europe today—the spectre of communism. All the forces of Europe have united to exorcise it: the
Pope and the Tsar, Metternich and Guizot, French radicals and
German policemen . . . it is recognised as a real force by all the
European powers.' It proceeds as a succession of interconnected
theses which are developed and brilliantly embroidered, and ends
with a famous and magnificent invocation addressed to the
workers of the world.

The first of these theses is contained in the opening sentence of
the first section: 'The history of all previous society is the history
of class struggles.' At all periods within recorded memory mankind has been divided into exploiter and exploited, master and
slave, patrician and plebeian, and in our day proletarian and
capitalist. The immense development of discovery and invention
has transformed the economic system of modern human society:
guilds have given way to local manufacture, and this in its turn to
great industrial enterprises. Each stage in this expansion is
accompanied by political and cultural forms peculiar to itself. The
structure of the modern state reflects the domination of the
bourgeoisie—it is in effect a committee for managing the affairs of
the bourgeois class as a whole. The bourgeoisie fulfilled a highly
revolutionary role in its day; it overthrew the feudal order and in
so doing destroyed the old, picturesque, patriarchal relations
which connected a man to his 'natural masters' and left only one
real relation between them—the cash nexus, naked self-interest. It
has turned personal dignity into a negotiable commodity, to be
bought and sold; in place of ancient liberties, secured by writs and
charters, it has created freedom of trade; for exploitation disguised by religious and political masks, it has substituted exploitation, direct, cynical and unashamed. It has turned professions
formerly thought honourable, as being forms of service to the
community, into mere hired labour: acquisitive in its aims, it has
degraded every form of life. This was achieved by calling
immense new natural resources into existence: the feudal
framework could not contain the new development, and was split
asunder. Now the process has repeated itself. The frequent
economic crises due to over-production are a symptom of the fact
that capitalism can in its turn no longer control its own resources.
When a social order is forced to destroy its own products to
prevent its own facilities from expanding too rapidly and too far,
that is a certain sign of its approaching bankruptcy and doom. The

bourgeois order has created the proletariat which is at once its heir and its executioner. It has succeeded in destroying the power of all other rival forms of organisation—the aristocracy, the small artisans and leaders—but the proletariat it cannot destroy, for it is necessary to its own existence, an organic part of its system, and constitutes the great army of the dispossessed, whom, in the very act of exploiting, it inevitably disciplines and organises. The more international capitalism becomes—and as it expands, it inevitably grows more so—the wider and more international the scale on which it automatically organises the workers, whose union and solidarity will eventually overthrow it. The international of capitalism breeds inevitably, as its own necessary complement, the international of the working class. This dialectical process is inexorable, and no power can arrest it or control it. Hence it is futile to attempt to restore the old medieval idyll, to build Utopian schemes on a nostalgic desire to return to the past, for which the ideologists of peasants, artisans, small traders so ardently long. The past is gone, the classes which belonged to it have long been decisively defeated by the march of history; their hostility toward the bourgeoisie, often falsely called socialism, is a reactionary attitude, a futile attempt to reverse the advance of human evolution. Their only hope of triumph over the enemy lies in abandonment of their independent existence and fusion with the proletariat, whose growth corrodes the bourgeoisie from within; for the increases of crises and of unemployment forces the bourgeoisie to exhaust itself in feeding its servants instead of feeding on them, which is its natural function.

From attack the Manifesto passes to defence. The enemies of socialism declare that the abolition of private property will destroy liberty and subvert the foundations of religion, morality and culture. This is admitted. But the values which it will thus destroy will be only those which are bound up with the old order—bourgeois liberty and bourgeois culture, whose appearance of absolute validity for all times and places is an illusion due solely to their function as a weapon in the class struggle. True personal freedom is possession of the power of independent action, of which the artisan, the small trader, the peasant, have long been deprived by capitalism. As for culture, 'the culture the loss of which is lamented is, for the enormous majority, a mere training to act as a machine'. With the total abolition of the class struggle these illusory ideals will necessarily vanish and be succeeded by the new and wider form of life founded upon a classless society. To mourn their loss is to lament the disappearance of an old familiar ailment.

The revolution must differ in differing circumstances, but its first measures everywhere must be the nationalisation of land, credit, transport, the abolition of rights of inheritance, the increase of taxation, the intensification of production, the destruction of the barriers between town and country, the introduction of compulsory work and of free education for all. Only then can serious social reconstruction begin. The rest of the Manifesto exposes and refutes various forms of pseudo-socialism—the attempts of various enemies of the bourgeoisie, the aristocracy, or the Church, to gain the proletariat to its cause by specious pretence of common interest. Into this category enters the ruined *petite bourgeoisie*, whose writers, adept as they are at exposing the chaos of capitalist production, the pauperisation and degradation caused by the introduction of machinery, the monstrous inequalities of wealth, offer remedies which, being conceived in obsolete terms, are Utopian. Even this cannot be said of the German 'True Socialists',[1] who, by translating French platitudes into the language of Hegelianism, produce a collection of nonsense phrases which cannot long deceive the world. As for Proudhon, Fourier or Owen, their followers draw up schemes to save the bourgeoisie, as if the proletariat did not exist, or else could be drawn upwards into capitalist ranks, leaving only exploiters and no exploited. This endless variety of views represents the desperate plight of the bourgeoisie, unable or unwilling to face its own impending death, concentrating upon vain efforts to survive under the guise of a vague and opportunist socialism. The communists are not a party or a sect, but the self-conscious vanguard of the proletariat itself, obsessed by no mere theoretical ends, but seeking to fulfil their historical destiny. They do not conceal their aims. They openly declare that these can be gained only when the entire social order is overthrown by force of arms, and they themselves seize all political and economic power. The Manifesto ends with the celebrated words: 'The workers have nothing to lose but their chains. They have a world to win. Workers of all lands, unite!'

Later scholars have convincingly shown how much familiar

[1] i.e. Hess, Grün and the rest, whose error is to advocate socialism not because it is historically due, but because it is just and demanded by human nature conceived as a permanent essence, an entity not radically transformed by history or class war.

material from earlier programmes—especially Babouvist—has been incorporated in the Manifesto; nevertheless it has been fused into an unbroken unity. No summary can convey the quality of its opening or its closing pages. As an instrument of destructive propaganda it has no equal anywhere; its effect upon succeeding generations is unparalleled outside religious history; had its author written nothing else, it would have ensured his lasting fame. Its most immediate effect, however, was upon his own fortunes. The Belgian Government, which behaved with considerable tolerance to political exiles, could not overlook this formidable publication, and brusquely expelled him and his family from its territory. On the next day the long-expected revolution broke out in Paris. Flocon, a radical member of the new French Government, in a flattering letter, invited Marx to return to the revolutionary city. He set off immediately and arrived a day later.

He found the city in a state of universal and uncritical enthusiasm. The barriers had fallen once more, this time, it seemed, for ever. The king had fled, declaring that 'he had been driven out by moral forces', a new Government had been appointed containing representatives of all the friends of humanity and progress: the great physicist Arago and the poet Lamartine received portfolios, the workers were represented by Louis Blanc and Albert. Lamartine composed an eloquent manifesto which was read, quoted, declaimed everywhere. The streets were filled with an immense singing, cheering throng of democrats of all hues and nationalities. The opposition showed little sign of life. The Church published a manifesto in which it asserted that Christianity was not inimical to individual liberty, that, on the contrary, it was its natural ally and defender; its kingdom was not of this world, and consequently such support as it had been accused of giving to the reaction sprang neither from its principles nor from its historical position in European society, and could be radically modified without doing violence to the essence of its teaching. These announcements were received with enthusiasm and credulity. The German exiles vied with the Poles and the Italians in their predictions of the imminent and universal collapse of the reaction, and of the immediate appearance on its ruins of a new moral world. News presently arrived that Naples had revolted; and after it Milan, Rome, Venice and other Italian cities. Berlin, Vienna and Budapest had risen in arms. Europe was ablaze at last. Excitement among the Germans in Paris rose to fever pitch. To support the insurgent republicans, a German Legion was formed, which the poet Georg Herwegh and a Prussian communist ex-soldier named Willich were to lead. It was to start at once. The French Government, not unwilling, perhaps, to see so many foreign agitators leave its soil, encouraged the project. Engels was greatly attracted by the scheme and would almost certainly have enlisted, but was dissuaded by Marx, who viewed the proceeding with mistrust and hostility. He saw no sign of any large-scale revolt of the German masses; here and there autocratic governments were overthrown, and the princes were forced to promise constitutions and appoint mildly liberal governments, but the Prussian army was still largely loyal to the king, while the democrats were scattered, badly led, and unable to reach agreement among themselves on vital points. The elected popular congress which met in Frankfurt to decide the future government of Germany was a failure from the first, and the sudden appearance of a legion of untrained *émigré* intellectuals on German soil appeared to Marx a needless waste of revolutionary energy, likely to have a ludicrous or a pitiful end, and to be followed by a paralysing mood of shame and disillusionment. Consequently, Marx opposed the formation of the legion, took no interest in it after it had left Paris for its inevitable defeat by the royal army, and went to Cologne to see what could be done by propaganda in his native Rhineland, where he was largely instrumental in persuading a group of liberal industrialists and communist sympathisers to found a new *Rheinische Zeitung*, in succession to the journal of that name which had been suppressed five years before, and to appoint him its editor. Cologne was then the scene of an uneasy balance of power between the local democrats, who controlled the local militia, and a garrison under orders from Berlin. Acting in the name of the Communist League, Marx sent his agents to agitate among the German industrial masses, and used their reports as the material for his leading articles. There was at this time no formal censorship in the Rhineland, and his inflammatory words reached an ever-widening public. The *Neue Rheinische Zeitung* was well informed, and alone in the left-wing press possessed a clear policy of its own. Its circulation increased rapidly and it began to be widely read in other German provinces.

Marx had come armed with a complete political and economic plan of action founded on the solid theoretical basis which he had built carefully during the preceding years. He advocated a conditional alliance between the workers and the radical bourgeoisie for the immediate purpose of overthrowing a reactionary government, declaring that, whereas the French had freed themselves from the yoke of feudalism in 1789, and were by this enabled to take the next step forward in 1848, the Germans had so far achieved their revolutions in the region of pure thought alone; as thinkers they had far outstripped the French in the radicalism of their sentiments: politically they still inhabited the eighteenth century. The most backward of western nations, they thus had two stages to achieve before they could hope to attain to that of developed industrialism, thenceforth to march in step with the neighbouring democracies. The dialectical movement of history permits no leaps, and the representatives of the proletariat did ill to overlook the claims of the bourgeoisie, which, in working for its own emancipation, was furthering the general cause, and which was economically and politically far better organised and capable of ruling than the ignorant, scattered, badly-organised masses of the working class. Hence the proper step for the workers was to conclude an alliance with their fellow victims among the middle and lower middle class, and then, after the victory, to seek to control, and if necessary obstruct, the work of their new allies (who by this time would doubtless be anxious to end their compromising association) by the sheer weight of their numbers and economic power. He opposed the extreme Cologne democrats, Anneke and Gottschalk, who advocated total abstention from such opportunism, and indeed from all political action, as likely to compromise and weaken the pure proletarian cause. This seemed to him a typically German blindness to the true balance of forces. He demanded direct intervention and the sending of delegates to Frankfurt, as the only effective practical course. Political aloofness seemed to him the height of tactical folly, since it was likely to leave the workers isolated, and at the mercy of the victorious class. In foreign policy he was something of a pan-German and a rabid Russophobe. Russia had for many years occupied the same position in relation to the forces of democracy and progress and evoked the same emotional reaction as the Fascist powers in the twentieth century. It was hated and feared by democrats of all persuasions as the great champion of reaction, able and willing to crush all attempts at liberty within and without its borders.

As in 1842, Marx demanded an immediate war with Russia, because no attempt at democratic revolution could succeed in Germany in view of the certainty of Russian intervention, and as a

means of welding the German principalities into a united democratic whole in opposition to a power whose entire influence was
ranged on the side of the dynastic element in European politics;
perhaps also in order to aid those scattered revolutionary forces
within Russia itself to the existence of which Bakunin used to
make constant mysterious references. Marx was prepared to sac-
rifice many other considerations to the ends of German unity,
since in its disunion he, no less than Hegel and Bismarck, saw the
cause at once of its weakness, its inefficiency and its political
backwardness. He was neither a romantic, nor a nationalist, and
regarded small nations as so many obsolete survivals impeding
social and economic progress. He therefore acted quite consistently in later publicly approving the cold-blooded German
invasion of the Danish province of Schleswig-Holstein; an act the
open support of which by most of the leading German democrats
caused considerable embarrassment to their allies among the liberals and constitutionalists of other lands.

He denounced the succession of short-lived liberal Prussian
governments which, easily and, it seemed to him, almost with
relief, allowed power to slip from their grasp back into that of the
king and his party. There were furious outbursts against 'empty
chatter' and 'parliamentary cretinism' in Frankfurt, which ended
in a storm of indignation hardly paralleled in Das Kapital itself. He
did not either then or later despair of the ultimate outcome of the
conflict, but his conception of revolutionary tactics, and his view
of the intelligence and reliability of the masses and their leaders,
changed radically: he declared their own incurable stupidity to be
a greater obstacle to their progress than capitalism itself. His own
policy, as it turned out, proved as impracticable as that of the
intransigent radicals whom he denounced. In his subsequent
analysis he attributed the disastrous result of the revolution to the
weakness of the bourgeoisie, the ineffectiveness of the parliamentary liberals, but principally to the political blindness of the
gullible masses, obstinately loyal to the agents of their own worst
enemy who deceived and flattered them and led them only too
easily to their destruction. If the rest of his life was spent as much
over purely tactical problems and consideration of what method
it was best for revolutionary leaders to adopt in the interests of
their uncomprehending flock, as in the analysis of actual conditions, this was largely due to the lesson of the German revolution. In 1849, after the failure of the risings in Vienna and in
Dresden, he wrote violent diatribes against liberals of all per-

suasions as being cowards and *saboteurs*, still hypnotised by the king and his drill sergeants, frightened by the thought of too definite a victory, prepared to betray the revolution for fear of the dangerous forces which it might unleash, and so virtually defeated before they began. He declared that, even if the bourgeoisie succeeded in making its corrupt deal with the enemy at the expense of its allies among the *petite bourgeoisie* and the workers, at best it would not gain more than had been won by French liberals under the July monarchy in France, while at worst the bargain would be repudiated by the king and become the prelude to a new monarchist terror. No other journal in Germany dared to go as far in denouncing the government. The uncompromising directness of these analyses, and the audacity of the conclusions which Marx drew from them, fascinated his readers against their will, although unmistakable signs of panic began to show themselves among the shareholders.

By June 1848 the heroic phase of the Paris revolution had spent itself, and the conservative forces began to rally their strength. The socialist and radical members of the Government, Louis Blanc, Albert, Flocon, were forced to resign. The workers rebelled against the right-wing republicans who remained in power, threw up barricades, and after three days' hand-to-hand fighting in the streets were dispersed and routed by the National Guard and troops which remained loyal to the Government. The June *émeute* may be considered as the first purely socialist rising in Europe, consciously directed against liberals no less than against legitimists. The followers of Blanqui (who was in prison) called upon the people to seize power and establish an armed dictatorship: the spectre of the Communist Manifesto acquired substance at last; for the first time revolutionary socialism revealed itself in that savage and menacing aspect in which it has appeared ever since to its opponents in every land.

Marx reacted at once. Against the frantic protests of the owners of his newspaper, who looked upon all forms of bloodshed and violence with profound horror, he published a long and fiery leading article, taking as his subject the funeral accorded by the state to the soldiers killed during the riots in Paris:

'The fraternity of the two opposing classes (one of which exploits the other) which in February was inscribed in huge letters upon all the façades of Paris, upon all the prisons and all the barracks ... this fraternity lasted just so long as the interests of the bourgeoisie could fraternise with the interests of the proletariat.

Pedants of the old revolutionary tradition of 1793, socialist systematisers who begged the bourgeoisie to grant favours to the people, and were allowed to preach long sermons . . . needed to lull the proletarian lion to sleep, republicans who wanted the whole of the old bourgeois system, minus the crowned figurehead, legitimists who did not wish to doff their livery but merely to change its cut—these had been the people's allies in the February revolution! Yet what the people hated was not Louis-Philippe, but the crowned dominion of a class, capital enthroned. Nevertheless, magnanimous as ever, it fancied it had destroyed its own enemies when it had merely overthrown the enemy of its enemies, the common enemy of them all.

'The clashes that spontaneously arise out of the conditions of bourgeois society must be fought to the bitter end; they cannot be conjured out of existence. The best form of state is the one in which opposed social tendencies are not slurred over . . . but secure free expression, and are thus resolved. But we shall be asked: "Have you then no tears, no sighs, no words of sympathy for the victims of popular frenzy?"

'The state will take due care of the widows and orphans of these men. They will be honoured in decrees: they will be given a splendid public funeral: the official press will proclaim their memories immortal . . . but the plebeians, tormented by hunger, reviled in the newspapers, abandoned by even the surgeons, stigmatised by all "decent" people as thieves, incendiaries, convicts, their wives and their children plunged in greater misery than ever, the best among the survivors transported—surely the democratic press may claim the right to crown with laurel their grim and sombre brow?'

This article (not dissimilar to his tribute to the Paris Commune more than twenty years later) caused alarm among the subscribers and the paper began to lose money. Presently the Prussian Government, by this time convinced it had little to fear from popular sentiment, ordered the dissolution of the democratic assembly. The latter replied by declaring all taxes imposed by the Government illegal. Marx vehemently supported this decision and called upon the people to resist attempts to collect the tax. This time the Government acted promptly and ordered the immediate suppression of the *Neue Rheinische Zeitung*. The last issue was printed in a red type, containing an inflammatory article by Marx and an eloquent and fiery poem by Freiligrath, and was bought up as a collector's curiosity. Marx was arrested for incitement to sedition and tried before a Cologne jury. He turned the occasion into the opportunity of delivering a speech of great length and erudition in which he analysed in detail the social and political situation in Germany and abroad. The result was unexpected: the foreman of the jury, in announcing the acquittal of the accused, said that he wished to thank him in his own name and that of the jury for an unusually instructive and interesting lecture, by which they had all greatly profited. The Prussian Government, which had annulled his Prussian citizenship four years previously, unable to reverse the verdict itself, in July 1849 expelled him from the Rhineland. He went to Paris, where the Bonapartist agitation in favour of the first Napoleon's nephew had made the political situation even more confused than before, and it looked as if something of importance might occur at any moment. His collaborators scattered in various directions: Engels, who disliked inactivity, and declared he had nothing to lose, joined the Paris legion commanded by Willich, a single-minded communist and capable commander, whom Marx detested as a romantic adventurer, and Engels admired for his sincerity, coolness and personal courage. The legion was defeated in Baden by the royal forces without difficulty, and retired in good order to the frontier of the Swiss Confederation, where it dispersed. The majority of the survivors crossed into Switzerland, among them Engels, who preserved the pleasantest memories of his experiences on this occasion, and in later life used to enjoy telling the history of the campaign, which he represented as a gay and agreeable episode of no particular importance. Marx, whose capacity for enjoyment was more limited, found Paris a melancholy place. The revolution had patently failed. Legitimist, Orleanist and Bonapartist intrigue were undermining whatever remained of the democratic structure: such socialists and radicals as had not fled were either in prison or liable to find themselves there at any moment. The appearance of Marx, who was by this time a figure of European notoriety, was highly unwelcome to the Government. Soon after his arrival he was presented with the alternative of leaving France or retiring to the Morbihan in Brittany. Of free countries, Belgium was closed to him; Switzerland, which had expelled Weitling and showed little friendliness to Bakunin, was unlikely to permit him to stay: only one European country was likely to place no obstacle in his path. Marx arrived in Paris from the Rhineland in July; a month later a subscription among his friends, among whom Lassalle's name occurs for the first time, enabled him to pay his fare to England. He arrived in London on 24 August 1849; his family followed a month later, and Engels, after dallying in Switzerland, and making a long and enjoyable sea voyage from Genoa, came in the beginning of November. He found Marx convinced that the revolution might at any moment break out once more, and engaged on a pamphlet against the conservative French republic.

8

Exile in London: The First Phase

There is only one antidote to mental suffering, and that is physical pain.

KARL MARX, *Herr Vogt*

MARX arrived in London in 1849 expecting to stay in England for a few weeks, perhaps months: and in the event lived there uninterruptedly until his death in 1883. The isolation of England intellectually and socially from the main currents of continental life had always been great, and the middle years of the nineteenth century offered no exception. The issues which shook the Continent took many years to cross the English Channel, and when they did, tended to do so in some new and peculiar shape, transformed and anglicised in the process of transition. Foreign revolutionaries were on the whole left unmolested, provided they behaved themselves in an orderly and inconspicuous manner; but neither was any kind of contact established with them. Their hosts treated them with correctness and civility, mingled with a mild indifference to their affairs which at once irritated and amused them. Revolutionaries and men of letters, who for many years had lived in a ferment of intellectual and political activity, found the London atmosphere inhumanly cold. The sense of isolation and exile was brought home to them even more sharply by the benevolent, distant, often slightly patronising manner in which they were treated by the few Englishmen with whom they came into contact; and while this tolerant and civilised attitude did indeed create a vacuum, in which it was possible to recover physically and morally after the nightmare of 1849, the very distance from events which created this feeling of tranquillity, the immense stability which the capitalist regime appeared to possess in England, the complete absence of any symptom of revolution, at times tended to induce a sense of hopeless stagnation which demoralised and embittered all but very few of the men dedicated to it. In the case of Marx desperate poverty and squalor were added factors in desiccating his never unduly romantic or pliant character. While these years of exile benefited him as a thinker and a revolutionary, they caused him to retire almost entirely into the narrow circle composed of his family, Engels, and a few intimate friends, such as Liebknecht, Wolff and Freiligrath. As a public personality his natural harshness, aggressiveness, and jealousy, his desire to crush all rivals, increased with the years; his dislike of the society in which he lived became more and more acute and his personal contact with individual members of it more and more difficult; he was more amiable to 'bourgeois' strangers than to socialists outside his orbit; he quarrelled easily and disliked reconciliation. While he had Engels to lean on he required no other help, and towards the end of his life, when the respect and admiration which he received were at their highest, no one else dared to approach him too closely for fear of some particularly humiliating rebuff. Like many great men he liked flattery, and, even more, total submission: in his last years he obtained both in full measure, and died in greater honour and material comfort than he had enjoyed during any previous period of his life.

These were the years in which romantic patriots, like Kossuth or Garibaldi, were fêted and publicly cheered in the streets of London; they were regarded as picturesque figures from whom heroic behaviour and noble words were to be expected, rather than as interesting or distinguished men with whom human relations could be established. The majority of their followers were looked upon as harmless eccentrics, as indeed many of them were. Marx, who did not possess sufficient fame or charm to attract such attention, found himself with few friends, and practically penniless, in a country which, although he had visited it less than three years previously, remained strange to him. Living as he did in the midst of an immensely variegated and thriving society, then in the very heyday of the phenomenal growth of its economic and political power, he remained all his life personally insulated from it, treating it solely as an object of scientific observation. The collapse of militant radicalism abroad left him no choice, at any rate for a time, but that of a life of observation and scholarship. The important consequence of this was that, since the material upon which he drew was largely English, he relied for the evidence for his hypotheses and generalisations almost entirely on English authors and experience. Those pieces of detailed social and historical research which form the best and most original chapters in *Das Kapital* are chiefly occupied with periods for which most of the evidence could be obtained from the financial columns of *The Economist* newspaper, from economic histories, from statistical material to be found in government Blue Books (which he was the first scholar to put to serious scientific use) and other sources to which access could be had without leaving the confines of London, or indeed of the reading-room of the British Museum. It was done in the midst of a life spent in sporadic agitation and practical organising activity, but with an air of extreme aloofness, as if the writer were situated many miles from the scene of his discussion: a fact which sometimes causes an entirely false impression of Marx as having grown, during the years of exile, into a remote and detached man of learning who at the age of thirty-two had left the life of action behind him to engage in purely theoretical inquiries.

The moment at which Marx arrived in England was singularly unfavourable to any prospects of the revolution. The mass movement to which continental socialists looked as a model of organised proletarian action among the most highly industrialised and therefore the most socially advanced European nation—Chartism—had lately suffered an overwhelming defeat: foreign observers, including Engels, had seriously over-estimated its strength. It was a loose congeries of heterogeneous interests and persons, and included romantic Tories, advanced radicals influenced by continental models, evangelical reformers, philosophical radicals, dispossessed farmers and artisans, apocalyptic visionaries. They were united by a common horror of the growing pauperisation and social degradation of the lower middle class which marked every advance of the industrial revolution; many of them recoiled from all thought of violence, and belonged to the class so contemptuously referred to in the Communist Manifesto as 'economists, philanthropists, humanitarian improvers of the conditions of the working class, organisers of charity, members of societies for the prevention of cruelty to animals, temperance fanatics, hole-and-corner reformers of every imaginable kind'.

The movement was badly organised. Its leaders neither agreed among themselves nor possessed individually, and still less collectively, clear beliefs as to the ends to be set before their followers, or the means to be adopted for their realisation. The most steadfast members of the movement were those trade unionists of the future who were principally anxious to improve the conditions and wages of labour, and were interested in wider questions only so far as they concerned their particular cause. It is doubtful whether a serious revolutionary movement could under any circumstances have been created out of this peculiar amalgam. As it was, nothing happened. It may have been the specious relief afforded by the great Reform Act, or the power of Nonconformity which originally stemmed the tide. At any rate, by 1850 the great crisis which had begun in 1847 was over. It was succeeded by the first consciously recognised economic boom in European history, which enormously increased the rate of development of industry and commerce, and extinguished the last embers of the Chartist conflagration. Organisers and agitators remained to fight against the workers' wrongs, but the exasperated years of Peterloo and the Tolpuddle martyrs, which, in the grim and moving pamphlets of Hodgskin and Bray, and the savage irony of William Cobbett, have left a bitter record of stupid oppression and widespread social ruin, were insensibly giving way to the milder age of John Stuart Mill and the English positivists with their socialist sympathies, the Christian Socialism of the sixties, and the essentially non-political trade-unionism of such prudent and cautious opportunists as Cremer or Lucraft, who distrusted the attempts of foreign doctrinaires to teach them their own business.

Marx naturally began by establishing contact with the German exiles. London at this time contained a conflux of German *émigrés*, members of the dissolved revolutionary committees, exiled poets and intellectuals, vaguely radical German artisans who had settled in England long before the revolution, and active communists lately expelled from France or Switzerland, who attempted to reconstitute the Communist League and to renew relations with sympathetic English radicals. Marx followed his usual tactics and kept rigidly to the society of the Germans: he believed firmly that the revolution was not over; indeed he remained convinced of this until the *coup d'état* which placed Louis Napoleon on the throne of France. Meanwhile he spent what he regarded as a mere lull during the battle in pursuing the normal activities of political exile, attending meetings of refugees, and quarrelling with those who incurred his supicion. The cultured and fastidious Herzen, who was in London at this time, conceived a deep dislike for him, and in his memoirs gave a malicious and brilliant description of the position occupied by Marx and his followers, then and later, among the other political *émigrés*. The Germans in general were notoriously incapable of co-operating with the other exiles—Italians, Russians, Poles, Hungarians—whose lack of method and passion for intense personal relations shocked and digusted them. The latter, for their part, found the Germans equally unattractive; they disliked their woodenness, their coarse manners, their colossal vanity, above all their sordid and unceasing internecine feuds, in the course of which it was not unusual for intimate details of private life to be dragged into the open and brutally caricatured in the public Press.

The disasters of 1848 did not indeed shake Marx's theoretical beliefs, but they forced him seriously to revise his political programme. In the years 1847–8 he was so far influenced by the propaganda of Weitling and Blanqui as to begin to believe, against his natural, Hegelian inclination, that a successful revolution could be made by means of a *coup d'état*, carried out by a small and resolute body of trained revolutionaries, who, having seized power, would hold it, constituting themselves the executive committee of the masses in whose name they acted. This body would function as the spearhead of the proletarian attack. The broad masses of the working class, after years of bondage and darkness, could not be expected to be ripe either for self-government, or for the control and liquidation of the forces they had displaced. A party must therefore be formed to function as a political, intellectual, and legislative élite of the people, enjoying its confidence in virtue of its disinterestedness, its superior training and its practical insight into the needs of the immediate situation; able to guide the people's uncertain steps during the first period of its new freedom. This necessary interlude he termed the state of permanent revolution, guided by the class dictatorship of the revolutionary proletariat over the rest 'as a necessary intermediate step to the abolition of all class distinctions, to the abolition of all the existing productive relations upon which these distinctions rest, to the abolition of all social relations which correspond to these productive relations, and to the complete reversal of all ideas which derive from these social relations'. But here, although the end was clear, the means were left comparatively vague. The 'permanent revolution' was to be dominated by the dictatorship of the proletariat: but how was this stage to be effected, and what form was it to take? There is no doubt that by 1848 Marx thought of it as brought about by a self-appointed élite: not indeed working in secret, as Blanqui insisted, or headed by a single dictatorial figure, as occasionally advocated by Bakunin, but as, perhaps, Babeuf had conceived it in 1796, a small body of convinced and ruthless individuals, who were to wield dictatorial power and educate the proletariat until it reached a level at which it comprehended its proper task. It was as a means to this that he advocated in Cologne in 1848–9 a temporary alliance with the leaders of the radical bourgeoisie. The *petite bourgeoisie*, struggling against the pressure of the classes immediately above it, was the workers' natural ally at this stage: but being unable to rule by its own strength, it would become more and more dependent on the workers' support, until the moment when the workers, already economic masters of the situation, acquired the official forms of political power, whether by a violent *coup*, or by gradual pressure. This doctrine (the clearest formulation of which is to be found in Marx's Address to the Communist League in 1850) is familiar to the world because (revived by the Russian agitator Parvus) it was urged by Trotsky in 1905, adopted by Lenin, and put into practice by them with the most literal fidelity in Russia in 1917. Marx himself, however, in the light of the events of 1848, abandoned it, at any rate in practice, in vital respects. He gradually discarded the whole conception of the seizure of power by an élite, which seemed to him powerless to effect anything in the face of a hostile regular army and a supine and untrained proletariat. The leaders of the workers were devoid neither of courage nor of practical sense, yet it would plainly have been quite impossible for them to remain in power in 1848 against the combined force of the royalists, the army and the upper middle class. Unless the proletariat as a whole was made conscious of its historic part, its leaders must remain helpless. They might provoke an armed rising, but could not hope to retain its fruits without conscious and intelligent support from the majority of the working class. Consequently, the vital lesson of the events of 1848 is, according to Marx, that the first duty of a revolutionary leader is to disseminate among the masses the consciousness of their destiny and their task. This may prove a lengthy and laborious process, but unless it is performed, nothing will be achieved, save the squandering of revolutionary energy in sporadic outbursts led by adventurers and hotheads, which, having no real basis in the popular will, must inevitably be defeated after a short period of triumph by the recovered forces of reaction, and be followed by brutal repression which cripples the proletariat for many years to come. On this ground he refused to support, on the eve of its occurrence, the revolution which resulted in the Paris Commune of 1871: although later, and largely for tactical motives, he wrote it a moving and eloquent epitaph.

The second point on which he changed his views was the possibility of collaboration with the bourgeoisie. Theoretically, he still believed that the dialectic of history necessitated a *bourgeois* regime as a prelude to complete communism; but the strength of this class in Germany and France, and its open determination to protect itself against its proletarian ally, convinced him that a compact with it would militate against the workers as the weaker power: the plan to govern from behind the scenes could not be realised yet. This had been the chief point of difference between him and the Cologne communists who had opposed alliance with the liberals as suicidal opportunism. He now embraced their point of view himself, although not for their reasons: not, that is to say, because opportunism as such was morally degrading or necessarily self-defeating, but because it was in this particular case bound to be unsuccessful, to confuse issues in a party not too securely organised, and so lead to internal weakness and defeat. Hence his continued insistence in later years on preserving the purity of the party, and its freedom from any compromising entanglements. The policy of gradual expansion and the slow conquest of political power through recognised parliamentary institutions, accompanied by systematic pressure on an international scale upon employers through trade unions and similar organisations, as a means of securing improved economic conditions for the workers, which characterises the tactics of socialist parties in the late nineteenth and early twentieth centuries, was the legitimate product of Marx's analysis of the causes of the catastrophe of the revolutionary year 1848.

His main objective—the creation of conditions in which the dictatorship of the proletariat, 'the permanent revolution', might be realised—was left unaffected: the bourgeoisie and all its institutions were inevitably doomed to extinction. The process might take longer than he had originally supposed; if so, the proletariat must be taught patience; not until the situation itself is ripe for intervention must the leaders call for action: in the meanwhile it must devote itself to husbanding, organising and disciplining its forces into readiness for the decisive crisis. History has offered an ironical commentary on this conclusion: the makers of the communist revolution in Russia (to which, it may be added, Marx did not think his theory to be applicable), by acting in accordance with the earlier and discarded view of 1850, and striking while the popular masses were palpably unripe for their task, did, at any rate, succeed in averting the consequences of 1848 and 1871: while the orthodox German and Austrian social democrats, faithful to the master's later doctrine, by moving with deliberate caution, and expending their energy upon the education of the masses to a sense of their mission, were duly overwhelmed by the reorganised reactionary forces, whose strength the march of history, and constant sapping on the part of the proletariat, should long before have fatally undermined.

Meanwhile no sign of revolution could be detected anywhere, and the mood of irrational optimism was succeeded by one of profound depression. 'One cannot recollect those days without acute pain', wrote Herzen in his memoirs. '... France was moving with the velocity of a falling star towards the inevitable *coup d'état*. Germany lay prostrate at the feet of Tsar Nicholas, dragged down by wretched, betrayed Hungary... The revolutionaries carried on empty agitation. Even the most serious persons are sometimes overcome by the fascination of mere forms, and manage to convince themselves that they are in fact doing something if they hold meetings with a mass of documents and protocols, conferences at which facts are recorded, decisions are taken, proclamations are printed, and so forth. The bureaucracy of the revolution is capable of losing itself in this sort of thing just as much as real officialdom; England teems with hundreds of associations of this sort; solemn meetings take place which dukes and peers of the realm, clergymen and secretaries, ceremoniously attend; treasurers collect funds, journalists write articles, all are busily engaged in doing nothing at all. These philanthropic or religious gatherings fulfil the double function of serving as a form of amusement and acting as a sop to the troubled consciences of these somewhat worldly Christians ... The whole thing was a contradiction in terms: an open conspiracy, a plot concocted behind open doors.'

In the sultry atmosphere of continual intrigue, suspicion and recrimination which fills the early years of any large political emigration whose members are bound to each other by circumstances rather than by any clearly conceived common cause, Marx spent his first two years in London. He resolutely declined to have any dealings with Herzen, Mazzini and their associates, but he was not inactive. He transformed the *Neue Rheinische Zeitung* into a review, organised committees to help refugees, published a denunciation of the methods of the police in the Cologne trials of his associates, tracking down and exposing the gross forgeries and perjury perpetrated by its agents; which, if it did not free his comrades, made trials of the same kind more difficult in the future; carried on a vendetta against Willich within the Communist League, and, believing that an institution which promotes half-truths is more dangerous than total inactivity and is better dead, by remorseless intrigue brought about its dissolution. Having thus successfully torpedoed his own former associates, and feeling nothing but contempt for the rest of the emigration as a collection of ineffective and harmless chatterers, he constituted himself and Engels as an independent centre of propaganda, a personal union round which the broken and scattered remnants of German communism would gradually be gathered into a force once more. The plan was completely successful.

His most important writings of this period are concerned with the recent events in France: his style, often opaque and obscure when dealing with abstract issues, is luminous when dealing with facts. The essays on *The Class Struggles in France*, and the articles reprinted under the title *The Eighteenth Brumaire of Louis Bonaparte*, are models of penetrating and cruel pamphleteering. The two essays cover much of the same ground and give a brilliant, polemical description of the revolution and the second republic, analysing in detail the relations and interplay of the political, economic and personal factors in terms of the alignment of classes whose needs they embody. There is a brilliant analysis of the role of the French state which functions less as the committee of the ruling class (the formula of *Communist Manifesto*) than as an independent source of power supported by, but at times overriding the wishes of, the bourgeoisie, in order to preserve the social and political *status quo*. In a series of sharp, epigrammatic sketches the leading representatives of the various parties are classified and assigned to the classes on whose support they depend. The evolution of the political situation from vague liberalism to the conservative republic, and thence to the open class-struggle, ending in naked despotism, is represented as a travesty of the events of 1789: then every successive phase was more violent and revolutionary than the last; in 1848 the exact reverse occurred: in June the proletariat was deserted and betrayed by its *petit-bourgeois* allies; later those were in their turn abandoned by the middle class; finally they too were outmanoeuvred by the great landowners and financiers and delivered into the hands of the army and Louis Napoleon. Nor could this have been prevented by a different policy on the part of individual politicians since it was determined by the stage of historical development reached by French society at this time.

Marx's other activities at this period included popular lectures on political economy to the German Workers' Educational Association, and finally a considerable correspondence with the German revolutionaries now scattered everywhere, and notably with Engels, who reluctantly and unhappily, having no other means of supporting himself, made his peace with his parents and settled down in Manchester to work in the office of his father's firm of cotton-spinners. The comparative security which he obtained by this means he used to support Marx, materially and intellectually, during the remainer of his life. Marx's own financial position was for many years desperate: he had no regular source of income, a growing family, and a reputation which precluded the possibility of employment by any respectable concern. The squalid poverty in which he and his family lived during the next twenty years, and the unspeakable humiliations which this entailed, have often been described: at first the family wandered from one hovel to another, from Chelsea to Leicester Square and thence to the disease-ridden slums of Soho; often there was no money to pay the tradesmen and the family would literally starve until a loan or the arrival of a pound note from Engels temporarily eased the situation; sometimes the entire clothing of the family was in pawn, and they were forced to sit for hours without light or food, interrupted only by the visits of dunning creditors, who were met on the doorstep by one or other of the children with the unvarying and automatic answer, 'Mr Marx ain't upstairs.'

A lively description of the conditions in which he lived during the first seven years of exile survives in the report of a Prussian spy who contrived to worm his way into the Dean Street establishment: '. . . He lives in one of the worst and cheapest neighbourhoods in London. He occupies two rooms. There is not one clean or decent piece of furniture in either room, everything is broken, tattered and torn, with thick dust over everything . . . manuscripts, books and newspapers lie beside the children's toys, bits and pieces from his wife's sewing basket, cups with broken rims, dirty spoons, knives, forks, lamps, an inkpot, tumblers, pipes, tobacco ash—all piled up on the same table. On entering the room smoke and tobacco fumes make your eyes water to such an extent that at first you seem to be groping about in a cavern—until you get used to it, and manage to make out certain objects in the haze. Sitting down is a dangerous business. Here is a chair with only three legs, there another which happens to be whole, on which the children are playing at cooking. That is the one that is offered to the visitor, but the children's cooking is not removed, and if you sit down you risk a pair of trousers. But all these things do not in the least embarrass Marx or his wife. You are received in the most friendly way and are cordially offered pipes, tobacco, and whatever else there may happen to be. Presently a clever and interesting conversation arises which repays for all the domestic deficiencies and this makes the discomfort bearable. . . .'[1]

A man of genius forced to live in a garret, to go into hiding when his creditors grow importunate, or to lie in bed because his clothes are pawned, is a conventional subject of gay and sentimental comedy. Marx was not a bohemian, and his misfortunes affected him tragically. He was proud, excessively thin-skinned, and made great demands upon the world: the petty humiliations and insults to which his condition exposed him, the frustration of his desire for the commanding position to which he thought himself entitled, the repression of his colossal natural vitality, made him turn in upon himself in paroxysms of hatred and of rage. His bitter feeling often found outlet in his writings and in long and savage personal vendettas. He saw plots, persecution, and conspiracies everywhere; the more his victims protested their innocence, the more convinced he became of their duplicity and their guilt.

His mode of living consisted of daily visits to the British Museum reading-room, where he normally remained from nine in the morning until it closed at seven; this was followed by long hours of work at night, accompanied by ceaseless smoking, which from a luxury had become an indispensable anodyne; this affected his health permanently and he became liable to frequent attacks of a disease of the liver sometimes accompanied by boils and an inflammation of the eyes, which interfered with his work, exhausted and irritated him, and interrupted his never certain means of livelihood. 'I am plagued like Job, though not so God-fearing', he wrote in 1858. 'Everything that these gentlemen [the doctors] say boils down to the fact that one ought to be a prosperous *rentier* and not a poor devil like me, as poor as a church

---

[1] Quoted from *Karl Marx: Man and Fighter*, by B. Nicolaievsky and O. Maenchen-Helfen (Penguin Books, 1976), pp. 256–7.

mouse.' In other moods he would swear that the bourgeoisie would one day pay dearly for every one of his carbuncles. Engels, whose annual income during those years does not appear to have exceeded one hundred pounds, with which, as his father's representative, he had to keep up a respectable establishment in Manchester, could not, with all his generosity, afford much systematic help at first: occasionally, friends in Cologne, or generous German socialists like Liebknecht or Freiligrath, managed to collect small sums for him, which, together with fees for occasional journalism, and occasional 'loans' from his rich uncle Philips in Holland and small legacies from relatives, enabled him to continue on the very brink of subsistence. It is not therefore difficult to understand that he hated poverty and the vicious slavery and degradation which it entails at least as passionately as servility. The descriptions scattered in his works of life in industrial slums, in mining villages or plantations, and of the attitude of civilised opinion towards them, are given with a combination of violent indignation and frigid, wholly unhysterical bitterness which, particularly when his account grows detailed and his tone grows unnaturally quiet and flat, possess a frightening quality and induce anger and shame in readers left unmoved by the fiery rhetoric of Carlyle, the dignified and humane pleading of J. S. Mill, or the sweeping eloquence of William Morris and the Christian Socialists. During these years three of his children, his two sons Guido and Edgar and his daughter Franziska, died, largely as a result of the conditions in which they lived. When Franziska died he had no money to pay for a coffin, and was rescued only by the generosity of a French refugee. The incident is described in harrowing details in a letter written by Frau Marx to a fellow exile. She was herself often ill, and the children were looked after by their family servant, Helene Demuth, who remained with them until the end.

'I could not and cannot fetch the doctor', he wrote to Engels on one of these occasions, 'because I have no money for the medicine. For the last eight or ten days I have fed my family on bread and potatoes, and today it is still doubtful whether I shall be able to obtain even these.'

He was uncommunicative by nature, and less than anyone who has ever lived given to self-pity; indeed, in his letters to Engels he sometimes satirised his own misfortunes with a grim irony which may conceal from the casual reader the desperate condition in which he frequently found himself. But when in 1856 his son

Edgar, of whom he was very fond, died at the age of six, it broke through even his iron reserve: 'I have suffered every kind of misfortune,' he wrote to his friend, 'but I have only just learnt what real unhappiness is . . . in the midst of all the suffering which I have gone through in these days the thought of you, and your friendship, and the hope that we may still have something reasonable to do in this world, has kept me upright. . .

'Bacon says that really important people have so many contacts with nature and the world, have so much to interest them, that they easily get over any loss. I am not of those important people. My child's death has affected me so greatly that I feel the loss as bitterly as on the first day. My wife is also completely broken down.'

The only form of pleasure which the family could allow itself was an occasional picnic on Hampstead Heath during the summer months. They used to set out on Sunday morning from the house in Dean Street, and, accompanied by Lenchen Demuth (to whom Marx became attached[1]) and one or two friends, carrying a basket of food and newspapers bought on the way, walked to Hampstead. There they would sit under the trees, and while the children played or picked flowers, their elders would talk or read or sleep. As the afternoon wore on, the mood grew gayer and gayer, particularly when the jovial Engels was present. They made jokes, sang, ran races. Marx recited poetry, which he was fond of doing, took the children for rides on his back, entertained everyone, and as a final turn, would solemnly mount and ride a donkey up and down in front of the party: a sight which never failed to give general pleasure. At nightfall they would walk back, often singing patriotic German or English songs on their way home to Soho. These agreeable occasions were, however, few and rare, and did little to lighten what Marx himself in one of his letters to Engels called the sleepless night of exile.

To this condition some slight relief was brought by the sudden invitation to write regular articles on affairs in Europe for the New York *Tribune*. The offer was made by Charles Augustus Dana, its foreign editor, who had been introduced to Marx by

[1] In 1851 she bore him a son, known as Frederick (Freddy) Demuth, whom Marx did not appear to like, and so far as is known never acknowledged. He was looked after by the faithful Engels, and, later, by his half-sister Eleanor, to whom Engels, on his death-bed, revealed the truth. Frederick Demuth was a manual worker, and appears to have died at the age of eighty in England.

Freiligrath in Cologne in 1849, and was greatly impressed by his political shrewdness. The New York *Tribune* was a radical newspaper, founded by a group of American followers of Fourier, which at this period had a circulation of over 200,000 copies, then probably the greatest of any newspaper in the world; its outlook was broadly progressive: in internal affairs it pursued an anti-slavery, free trade policy, while in foreign affairs it attacked the principle of autocracy, and so found itself in opposition to virtually every government in Europe. Marx, who stubbornly refused offers of collaboration with continental journals whose tendency he thought reactionary, accepted this offer with alacrity. The new correspondent was to be paid one pound sterling per article. For nearly ten years he wrote weekly dispatches for it roaming over a wide field of subjects, which are of some interest even now. Dana's first request to him was to write a series of articles on the strategy and tactics of both armies during the civil war in Germany and Austria, together with general comments on the art of modern warfare. As Marx was entirely ignorant of the latter subject and had at this period very little English, he found the request far from easy to fulfil: but to refuse anything which offered a steady if meagre source of income was unthinkable. In his perplexity he turned to Engels, who, as on so many occasions in later life, readily and obligingly wrote the articles and signed them with Marx's name. Henceforward, whenever the subject was unknown or uncongenial to him, or he was prevented from working by absence or ill-health, Engels was called upon, and performed his task with such efficiency that the *Tribune*'s London correspondent soon acquired a considerable popularity in America as an exceptionally versatile and well-informed journalist, with a definite public of his own.

Engels's articles on the German revolution were reprinted as a pamphlet by Marx called *Revolution and Counter-Revolution in Germany*, and end with the assurance that the revolution is about to break out with even greater violence in the near future. Later the friends admitted they were over-optimistic. Marx formulated the celebrated generalisation that only an economic slump could lead to a successful revolution; thus the revolution of 1848 was nurtured in the economic collapse of 1847, and the boom of 1851 removed all hope of imminent political conflagration.

Henceforth the attention of both is concentrated upon detecting symptoms of a major economic crisis. Engels from his office in Manchester filled his letters with information about the state of world markets; gold losses by the Bank of England, the bank-ruptcy of a Hamburg bank, a bad harvest in France or America, are noted exultantly as indicating that the great crisis cannot be far off. In 1857 a genuine slump did at last occur on the required scale. It was not, however, except in agricultural Italy, followed by any revolutionary developments. After this there is less mention of inevitable crises, and more discussion of the organisation of a revolutionary party. The acute disappointment had left its effect.

While Engels dealt with the military intelligence required by the American public, Marx published a rapid succession of articles on English politics, internal and external, on foreign policy, on Chartism, and the character of the various English ministries, which he became expert at summing up in a few malicious sentences, usually at the expense of *The Times*, which always remained his bugbear. He wrote a good deal about the English rule in India and in Ireland. India was, he declared, bound in any case to have been conquered by a stronger power:

'The question is not whether the English had any right to conquer India, but whether we should have preferred her to have been conquered by Turks or Persians, or Russians . . . Of course it is impossible to compel the English bourgeoisie to want the emancipation or improvement of the social condition of the Indian masses, which depends not only on the development of the forces of production, but on the ownership of them by the people. But what it can do is to create the material conditions for the realisation of this double need.'

And again: 'However melancholy we may find', he wrote in 1853, 'the spectacle of the ruin and desolation of these tens of thousands of industrious, peaceful, patriarchal, social groups . . . suddenly cut off from their ancient civilisation and their tradi-tional means of existence, we must not forget that these idyllic village communities . . . always provided a firm basis to oriental despotism, confining the human intelligence within the nar-rowest limits, making of it the obedient traditional instrument of superstition, stunting its growth, robbing it . . . of all capacity of historical activity; let us not forget the egoism of barbarians who, concentrated on an insignificant portion of earth's surface, watched unmoved while immense empires crumbled, unspeak-able cruelties were committed, the populations of entire cities were butchered—observed this as if they were events in nature, and so themselves became the helpless victims of every invader who happened to turn his attention to them . . . In causing social revolution in India, England was, it is true, guided by the lowest motives, and conducted it dully and woodenly. But that is not the point. The question is whether humanity can fulfil its purpose without a complete social revolution in Asia. If not, then England, in spite of all her crimes, was the unconscious instrument of history in bringing about this revolution.'

Of Ireland he said that the cause of English labour was inextricably bound up with the liberation of Ireland, whose cheap labour was a continual threat to the English unions; her economic subjection, as in the analogous cases of serfdom in Russia and slavery in the United States, must be abolished before Ireland's English masters, among whom the English working class (who treated the Irish much as the 'poor whites' of the Southern states of America treated the Negroes) must be included, could hope to emancipate themselves and create a free society. In both cases he consistently underestimated the force of rising nationalism: his hatred of all separatism, as of all institutions founded on some purely traditional or emotional basis, blinded him to their actual influence. In a similar spirit Engels, writing of the Czechs, observed that the nationalism of the Western Slavs was an artificially preserved, unreal phenomenon, which could not long resist the advance of the superior German culture. Such absorption was a fate inevitably in store for all small and local civilisations, in virtue of the force of historical gravitation which causes the smaller to be merged in the greater: a tendency which all progressive parties should actively encourage. Both Marx and Engels believed that nationalism, together with religion and militarism, were so many anachronisms, at once the by-products and the bulwarks of the capitalist order, irrational, counter-revolutionary forces which, with the passing of their material foundation, would automatically disappear. Marx's own tactical policy with regard to them was to consider whether in a given case they operated for or against the proletarian cause, and to decide in accordance with this criterion alone whether they were to be supported or attacked. Thus he favoured it in India and in Ireland, because it was a weapon in the fight against imperialism, and attacked the democratic nationalism of Mazzini or Kossuth because in such countries as Italy, Hungary or Poland, it seemed to him to work merely for the replacement of a foreign by a native system of capitalist exploitation, and so to obstruct the social revolution. Among English politicians he attacked Russell as a pseudo-radical who betrayed his cause at every step, but his *bête noire* was undoubtedly Palmerston, whom he accused of being a disguised Russian agent, and mocked for his sentimental support of small nationalities in Europe. He was, however, a connoisseur of political skill in all its forms, and confessed to a certain admiration of the *élan* and adroitness with which that cynical and light-hearted statesman carried off his most unscrupulous strokes.

His attacks on Palmerston brought him into contact with an exceedingly odd and remarkable figure. David Urquhart had in his youth been in the diplomatic service, and after becoming a warm Philhellene in Athens had been transferred to Constantinople, where he conceived an ardent and life-long passion for Islam and the Turks. He celebrated the 'purity' of the Turkish constitution, and the spiritual and physical effects of Turkish steam baths, to which he introduced his countrymen. He equally admired the Church of Rome, with which he remained on excellent terms, although he was born and died a Calvinist; with this he combined an equally violent hatred for Whigs, free trade, the Church of England, industrialism, and, in particular, the Russian Empire, whose malevolent and omnipotent influence he regarded as responsible for all the evils in Europe. This eccentric figure, a picturesque survival from a more spacious age, sat in Parliament as an Independent for many years, and published a newspaper and numerous tracts almost entirely devoted to the single purpose of exposing Palmerston, whom he accused of being a hired agent of the Tsar, engaged in a life-long attempt to subvert the moral order of Western Europe in his master's interest. Even Palmerston's attitude during the Crimean War did not shake him: he explained it as a cunning ruse to cloak the nature of his real activities; hence his deliberate sabotage of the entire campaign, which was clearly designed to do Russia as little damage as possible. Marx, who had somehow arrived at the same curious conclusion, seemed to be no less genuinely convinced of Palmerston's venality. The two men met and formed an alliance; Urquhart published anti-Palmerstonian pamphlets by Marx while Marx became an offical Urquhartite, contributed to Urquhart's paper and appeared on the platforms of his meetings. His articles were later published as pamphlets. The most peculiar are *The Story of the Life of Lord Palmerston* and *The Secret Diplomatic History of the Eighteenth Century*, both of which were devoted to exposing the hidden hand of Russia in all major European disasters. Each was under the impression that he was skilfully using the other for his own ends:

Marx thought Urquhart a harmless monomaniac of whom use might be made; Urquhart, for his part, thought highly of Marx's abilities as a propagandist, and on one occasion congratulated him on possessing an intelligence worthy of a Turk. This bizarre association continued harmoniously, if intermittently, for a number of years. After the deaths of Palmerston and Tsar Nicholas, the alliance was gradually dissolved. Marx obtained a good deal of amusement, and as much financial help as he could extract, from his relationship with his strange patron, of whom he soon grew quite fond; indeed, the latter was unique among his political allies in that their relation continued to be entirely friendly until Urquhart's death.

Marx found few sympathisers among the trade union leaders. The ablest of them either held views not very dissimilar to those of Owen, who by the shining example of his own achievements sought to prove the wicked baselessness of the doctrine of class war: or else were busy local labour leaders working for the immediate needs of this or that trade or industry, dead to wider issues, prepared to welcome all radicals equally in a federation called 'The Fraternal Democrats', the very name of which revolted Marx. He tolerated radicals like the voluble and energetic George Harney whom he and Engels called 'Citizen Hip Hip Hurrah'. The only Englishman who stood at all close to him in those days was Ernest Jones, a revolutionary Chartist, who made a vain attempt to revive that dying movement. Jones was born and brought up in Hanover and resembled more closely than anyone else in England the type of continental socialist familiar to Marx; his views were, especially in later years, too similar to those of the 'True Socialists' Hess and Grün to please Marx entirely, but he needed allies, the choice was limited, and he accepted Jones as the best and most advanced that England had to offer. Jones, who conceived a great admiration and affection for Marx and his household, supplied him with a great deal of information about English conditions; it was he who turned Marx's attention to the land enclosures which still went on in Scotland where many hundreds of small tenants and crofters had been evicted to make room for deer parks and pasture. The result was a vitriolic article by Marx in the New York *Tribune* on the private affairs of the Duchess of Sutherland, who had expressed sympathy for the cause of the Negro slaves in America. The article, which is a sketch for the longer passage in *Das Kapital*, is a masterpiece of bitter and vehement eloquence, directly descended from the philippics of Voltaire and Marat, and a model for many later pieces of socialist invective. The attack is not so much personal as directed at the system under which a capricious old woman, no more deranged, heartless, and vindictive than the majority of her immediate society, has it in her absolute power, with the full approval of her class and of public opinion, to humiliate, uproot and ruin an entire population of honest and industrious men and women, rendered destitute overnight in a land which was rightfully theirs, since all that was man-made in it they and their ancestors had created by their labour.

Such pieces of social analysis and polemic pleased the American public no less than Marx's dry and ironical articles on foreign affairs. The articles were well-informed, shrewd and detached in tone: they showed no particular power of prescience, nor were there any attempts to give a comprehensive survey of contemporary affairs as a whole: as a commentary on events they were less candid and less interesting than the letters which their author wrote to Engels at this period, but as journalism they were in advance of their time. Marx's method was to present his readers with a brief sketch of events or characters, emphasising hidden interests and the sinister activities likely to result from them, rather than the explicit motives furnished by the actors themselves, or the social value of this or that measure or policy. His journalism exhibits more vividly than his theoretical writings the difference between his naturalistic, acid, distrustful, ethically sceptical attitude, and that of the great majority of the more or less humanitarian and idealistic social historians and critics of his time. At the same time he was engaged in gathering material for the economic treatise which should serve as a weapon against the vague idealism of the loosely connected radical groups, which, in his view, led to confusion both of thought and of action, and paralysed the efforts of such few clear-headed leaders as the workers possessed. He applied himself to the task of establishing, in the place of this, an unambiguously worded doctrine, adherence to which, whether he intended this or not, became at once the test, the reason and the guarantee of a united, and, above all, active body of social revolutionaries. Their strength would derive from their unity, and their unity from the coherence of the practical beliefs which they had in common.

The foundations of his doctrine were embodied in his previous writings, notably in the *Communist Manifesto*. In a letter written in 1852 he carefully stated what he regarded as original in it: 'What I did that was new was to prove (1) that the *existence of classes* is only bound up with particular, historic phases in the development of production; (2) that the class struggle necessarily leads to the *dictatorship of the proletariat*; (3) that this dictatorship itself only constitutes the transition to the *abolition of all classes* and to a classless society.' On these foundations the new movement was to be built.

In a sense he succeeded more rapidly than he could have hoped: the rise and swift growth upon the ruins of 1848 of a new and militant party of socialist workers in Germany created for him a sphere of new practical activity in which the latter half of his life was spent. This party was not indeed created by him, but his ideas, and above all a belief in the political programme which he had elaborated, inspired its leaders. He was consulted and approached at every turn; everyone knew that he, and he alone, had inspired the movement and created its basis; to him all questions of theory and practice were instinctively referred; he was admired, feared, suspected and obeyed. Yet the German workers did not look to him as their foremost representative and champion: the man who had organised them into a party and ruled it with absolute power was Marx's junior by several years, born and brought up under similar conditions, but in temper and in outlook more unlike, and even opposed to, him than at the time either explicitly admitted.

Ferdinand Lassalle, who created German Social Democracy and led it during its first heroic years, was one of the most ardent public personalities of the nineteenth century. By birth a Silesian Jew, by profession a lawyer, by temperament a romantic revolutionary, he was a man whose outstanding characteristics were his acute intelligence, his gifts as an organiser, his vanity, his boundless energy and self-confidence. Since most of the normal avenues of advancement were barred to him on account of his race and his religion, he threw himself with immense passion into the revolutionary movement, where his exceptional ability, his enthusiasm, but most of all his genius as an agitator and a popular orator swiftly raised him to leadership. During the German revolution he delivered inflammatory speeches against the Government, for which he was tried and imprisoned. During the years which followed the period of recantations and dishonour, when Marx and Engels were in exile, and Liebknecht alone among the original leaders who were still in Germany remained faithful to the cause of socialism, Lassalle took upon himself the task of creating a new and better organised proletarian party upon the ruins of 1848. He conceived himself in the part of its sole leader and inspirer, its intellectual, moral and political dictator. He accomplished this task with brilliant success. His beliefs were derived in equal parts from Hegel and from Marx: from the latter he derived the doctrines of economic determinism, of the class struggle, of the inevitability of exploitation in capitalist society. But he rejected the condemnation of the state in the name of society, refusing to follow Proudhon and Marx in regarding the former as a mere coercive instrument of the ruling class, and accepting the Hegelian thesis, according to which the state, even in its present condition, constitutes the most progressive and dynamic function of a collection of human beings assembled to lead a common life. He strongly believed in centralisation and, up to a point, in internal national unity: in later years he began to believe in the possibility of an anti-bourgeois coalition between the king, the aristocracy, the army, and the workers, culminating in an authoritarian collectivist state, headed by the monarch, and organised in the interests of the only true productive, that is the labouring, class.

His relations with Marx and Engels had never been wholly easy: he declared that Marx was in theoretical matters his master, and treated him with nervous respect. He heralded him everywhere as a man of genius, arranged for the German publication of his books, and otherwise strove to be of service to him in many ways. Marx grudgingly recognised the value of Lassalle's energy, and his organising ability, but was repelled by him personally, and was deeply suspicious of him politically. He disliked his ostentation, his extravagance, his vanity, his histrionic manners, his loud public profession of his tastes, his opinions and his ambitions, he detested the very brilliance of his impressionistic surveys of social and political facts, which seemed to him flimsy, superficial, and fallacious by comparison with his own painful and laborious thoroughness: he disliked and distrusted the temperamental and capricious control which Lassalle exercised over the workers, and, even more, his absorbed flirtation with the enemy. Finally, he felt jealous and possessive about a movement which owed to him both its practical policy and its intellectual foundations, and now seemed to have deserted him, infatuated by a political *femme fatale,* a specious, glittering adventurer, an avowed opportunist both in private life and in public policy, guided by no fixed plan, attached to no principle, moving towards no clear goal. Nevertheless, a certain intimacy of relations existed between them, or if not intimacy, a mutual appreciation. Lassalle was born and brought up under intellectual influences similar to his own, they fought against the same enemy, and on all fundamental issues spoke the same language, which Proudhon, Bakunin, and the English trade unionists had never done, and the former Young Hegelians had long ceased to do. Moreover, he was a man of action, a genuine revolutionary, and absolutely fearless. Each recognised that (although Marx might have excepted Engels) the other possessed a higher degree of political intelligence, penetration, and practical courage than any other member of their party. They understood each other instinctively, and found communication both easy and exhilarating: when Marx went to Berlin, he stayed quite naturally with Lassalle. When Lassalle came to London, he stayed with Marx, and maddened his proud and sensitive host, then in the last stage of penury, by the mere fact of being a witness of his condition, and even more by his gay patter and easy extravagance, spending more on cigars and button-holes than Marx and his family spent on a week's livelihood. There was some difficulty, too, about a sum of money which Marx had borrowed from him. Of all this Lassalle, it seemed, was totally unaware, being exceptionally insensitive to his surroundings, as vigorous and flamboyant natures often are. Marx never forgot his humiliation, and after Lassalle's London visit their relations deteriorated rapidly.

Lassalle created the new party by a method still novel in his day, and employed only sporadically by the English Chartists, although familiar enough later: he undertook a series of highly publicised political tours through the industrial areas of Germany, making fiery and seditious speeches which overwhelmed his proletarian audiences and roused them to immense enthusiasm. There and then he formed them into sections of the new workers' movement, organised as an official, legally constituted party, thus breaking openly with the old method of small revolutionary cells which met in secret and carried on underground propaganda. His last journey among his followers was a triumphal tour over conquered territory: it strengthened his already unique influence upon German workers of all types, ages and professions.

The theoretical foundations of the programme were borrowed, largely from Marx, and perhaps to some extent from the radical Prussian economist Rodbertus-Jagetzow, but the party had many strongly non-Marxist characteristics: it was not specifically organised for a revolution; it was prepared for alliance with other anti-bourgeois parties; it seemed to aim at a kind of state capitalism; it was nationalistic and largely confined to German conditions and needs. One of its foremost ends was the development of a workers' co-operative system, not indeed as an alternative to, but as an intrinsic element in, political action, to be organised or financed by the state, yet still sufficiently similar to Proudhon's anti-political mutualism, and the politically sluggish English trade unionism, to incur open hostility from Marx. Moreover, it had been created by means of the personal ascendancy of one individual. There was a strong emotional element in the unquestioned dictatorship which Lassalle exercised in his last years, a form of hero-worship which Marx, who disliked every form of unreason, and distrusted spell-binders in politics, instinctively abhorred. Lassalle introduced into German socialism the theory that circumstances might occur in which something like a geniuine alliance might be formed with the absolutist Prussian government against the industrial bourgeoisie. This was the kind of opportunism which Marx must have considered the most ruinous of all possible defects; the experience of 1848, if it taught no other lesson, had conclusively demonstrated the fatal consequence to a young, and as yet comparatively defenceless, party of an alliance with a well-established older party, fundamentally hostile to its demands, in which each attempts to exploit the other, and the better armed force inevitably wins. Marx, as was made evident from his address to the Central Communist Committee in 1850, considered himself to have erred seriously in supposing that an alliance with the radical bourgeoisie was possible and even necessary before the final victory of the proletariat. But even he had never dreamed of an alliance with the feudal nobility for the purpose of delivering an attack on individualism as such, merely for the sake of attaining some kind of state control. Such a move he regarded as a typical Bakuninist caricature of his own policy and aspirations.

Both Marx and Engels were fundamentally solid German democrats in their attitude to the masses, and instinctively reacted against the seeds of romantic élitism which can now be so clearly discerned in Lassalle's beliefs and acts and speeches, particularly in his passionate patriotism, his self-dramatisation as the dedicated leader, his belief in a state-planned economy controlled, at any rate for a time, by the military aristocracy, his advocacy of armed intervention by Germany on the side of the French Emperor in the Italian campaign (which he defended against Marx and Engels on the ground that only a war would precipitate a German revolution), his unconcealed sympathy with Mazzini and the Polish nationalists, finally his belief, on which the economic policies of the fascist regimes of our century offer a curious commentary, that the existing machinery of the Prussian state can be used to aid the *petite bourgeoisie* as well as the proletariat of Germany against the growing encroachment of merchants, industrialists and bankers. He actually went to the length of negotiating with Bismarck on these lines, each being under the impression that, when the time came, he could use the other as a cat's-paw for his own ends: each recognised and admired the other's audacity, intelligence, and freedom from petty scruple; they vied with each other in the candour of their political realism, in their open contempt for their mediocre followers, and in their admiration for power and success as such. Bismarck liked vivid personalities, and in later years used to refer to these conversations with pleasure, saying that he never hoped to meet so interesting a man again. How far Lassalle had in fact gone in this direction was subsequently revealed by the discovery in 1928 of Bismarck's private record of the negotiations. They were cut short by Lassalle's early death in a duel, which arose out of a casual love-affair. If he had lived, and Bismarck had chosen to continue to play on his almost megalomaniac vanity, Lassalle would in the end almost certainly have lost, and the newly created party might have foundered long before it did; indeed, as a theorist of state supremacy and as a demagogue, Lassalle should be counted among the founders not only of European socialism, but equally of the doctrine of leadership and romantic authoritarianism; it may have been this Fascist streak that had attracted Bismarck.

In the subsequent conflict between the Marxists and the Lassalleans, Marx won a formal victory which saved the purity of his own doctrine and political method, not, oddly enough, for Germany, for which it was primarily intended, but for application in far more primitive countries which scarcely entered his thoughts, Russia, China, and, up to a point, Spain, Mexico and Cuba. The report of Lassalle's death in the spring of 1864 roused little sympathy in either Marx or Engels. To both it seemed a typically foolish end to a career of absurd vanity and ostentation. Lassalle, had he lived, might well have proved an obstacle of the first magnitude. Yet the relief, at least in the case of Marx, was not unmixed with a certain sentimental regret for the passing of so familiar a figure, one of the very few on whom he looked, in spite of his failings, with something not wholly unlike affection. Lassalle was a German and a Hegelian, inextricably connected with the events of 1848, and his own revolutionary past: a man who, in spite of all his colossal defects, stood head and shoulders above the pygmies among whom he moved, creatures into whom he had for a brief hour infused his own vitality, and who would soon sink exhausted into their old apathy, appearing even smaller, pettier, meaner than before.

'He was, after all, one of the old stock,' he wrote, 'the enemy of our enemies . . . it is difficult to believe that so noisy, stirring, pushing a man is now as dead as a mouse, and must hold his tongue altogether . . . the devil knows, the crowd is getting smaller and no new blood is coming forward.'

The news of Lassalle's death sent him into one of his rare moods of personal melancholy, almost of despair, very different from the cloud of anger and resentment in which he normally lived. He suddenly became overwhelmed by the sense of his own total isolation, and the hopelessness of all individual endeavour in the face of the triumphant European reaction, a feeling which the tranquillity and monotony of life in England sooner or later induced in all the exiled revolutionaries. Indeed the very respect, and even admiration, with which many of them spoke of English life and English institutions were an implicit acknowledgement of their own personal failure, their loss of faith in the power of mankind to achieve its own emancipation. They saw themselves gradually sinking into a cautious, almost cynical quietism which they themselves knew to be an admission of defeat and a complete stultification of a life spent in warfare, the final collapse of the ideal world in which they had invested beyond recovery everything that they themselves possessed, and much that belonged to others. This mood, with which Herzen, Mazzini, Kossuth were intimately acquainted, was with Marx uncommon: he was genuinely convinced that the process of history was both inevitable and, despite setbacks, progressive, and this intense belief excluded all possibility of doubt or disillusionment on fundamental issues; he had never relied on the sagacity or idealism of individuals or of the masses as decisive factors in social evolution, and having staked nothing, lost nothing in the great intellectual and moral bankruptcy of the sixties and seventies. All his life he strove to destroy or diminish the influence of popular leaders and demagogues who believed in the power of the individual to alter the destinies of nations. His savage attacks on Proudhon and Lassalle, his later duel with Bakunin, were not mere moves in the struggle for personal supremacy on the part of an ambitious and despotic man resolved to destroy all possible rivals. It is true that he was by nature almost insanely jealous: nevertheless, mingled with his personal feelings there was genuine indignation with the gross errors of judgement of which these men seemed to him too often guilty: and, even more strongly felt, ironical as it may seem when his own position is remembered, a violent disapproval of the influence of dominant individuals as such, of the element of personal power, which, by creating a false relation between the leader and his followers, is sooner or later bound to blind both to the demands of the objective situation.

Yet it remains the case that the unique position of authority which he himself occupied in international socialism during the last decade of his life did more to consolidate and ensure the adoption of his system than mere attention to his works, or the consideration of history in the light of them, could ever have achieved. Some of his writings published during his final years in London make depressing reading: apart from journalism in German and American papers, and literary hackwork forced on him by his poverty, he confined himself almost entirely to polemical tracts, the longest of which, *Herr Vogt*, written in 1860, was designed to clear his own name from the imputation of having brought his friends into unnecessary danger during the Cologne trials, and to counter-attack his accuser, a well-known Swiss naturalist and radical politician, Karl Vogt, by alleging that he was in the pay of the French Emperor. It is of interest only for the melancholy light which it throws on ten years of frustration, filled with squabbles and intrigues, which succeeded the heroic age. In 1859 he finally published his *A Contribution to the Critique of Political Economy*; yet despite the fact that its introductory pages contain the clearest statement of his theory of history, it was little read: its main theses were much more impressively stated eight years later, in the first volume of *Das Kapital*.

His faith in the ultimate victory of his cause remained unaffected even during the darkest years of the reaction. Speaking in the early fifties at a dinner given to the compositors and staff of *The People's Paper*, in answer to the toast 'The proletarians of Europe' he declared: 'In our days everything seems pregnant with its contradiction. Machinery gifted with the wonderful power of shortening and fructifying human labour we behold starving and overworking it. The victories of art seem bought by the loss of character. Even the pure light of science seems able to shine only against the dark background of ignorance . . . This antagonism between modern industry and science on the one hand, and modern misery and dissolution on the other, this antagonism between the productive forces and the social relations of our epoch is a fact, palpable and overwhelming. Some may bewail it, others may wish to get rid of modern arts in order to get rid of modern conflicts . . . For our part we do not mistake the shape of the shrewd spirit that continues to mark these contradictions . . . we recognise our old friend, Robin Goodfellow, the old mole that can work in the earth so fast . . . the Revolution.' This thesis must have sounded singularly unplausible to the majority of his listeners: certainly the events of the years which followed did little to bear out his prophecy.

In 1860 Marx's fame and influence were confined to a narrow circle: interest in communism had died down since the Cologne trials in 1851; with the phenomenal development of industry and commerce, faith in liberalism, in science, in peaceful progress, began to mount once more. Marx himself was almost beginning to acquire the interest of a historical figure, to be regarded as the formidable theorist and agitator of a former generation, now exiled and destitute and supporting himself by casual journalism in an obscure corner of London. Fifteen years later all this had altered. Still comparatively unknown in England, he had grown abroad into a figure of vast fame and notoriety, regarded by some as the instigator of every revolutionary movement in Europe, the fanatical dictator of a world movement pledged to subvert the moral order, the peace, happiness and prosperity of mankind. By these he was represented as the evil genius of the working class, plotting to sap and destroy the peace and morality of civilised society, systematically exploiting the worst passions of the mob, creating grievances where none existed, pouring vinegar in the malcontents' wounds, exacerbating their relations with their employers in order to create the universal chaos in which everyone would lose, and so finally all would be made level at last, the rich and the poor, the bad and the good, the industrious and the idle, the just and the unjust. Others saw in him the most indefatigable and devoted strategist and tactician of labouring classes everywhere, the infallible authority on all theoretical questions, the creator of an irresistible movement designed to overthrow the prevailing rule of injustice and inequality by persuasion or by violence. To them he appeared as an angry and indomitable modern Moses, the leader and saviour of all the insulted and the oppressed, with the milder and more conventional Engels at his side, an Aaron ready to expound his words to the benighted, half-comprehending masses of the proletariat. The event which more than any other was responsible for this transformation was the creation of the first Workers' International in 1864, which radically altered the character and history of European socialism.

9

The International

The French Revolution is the precursor of another, more magnificent revolution which will be the last.
GRACCHUS BABEUF, *Manifeste des Egaux*, 1796

THE First International came into being in the most casual possible fashion. In spite of the efforts of various organisations and committees to co-ordinate the activities of the workers of various countries, no genuine ties between them had been established. This was due to several causes. Since the general character of such bodies was conspiratorial, only a small minority of radically minded, fearless and 'advanced' workers were attracted to them; moreover, it was generally the case that before anything concrete could be achieved, a foreign war, or repressive measures by governments, put an end to the existence of the secret committees. To this must be added the lack of acquaintance and sympathy between the workers of different nations, working under totally different conditions. And finally the increased economic prosperity which succeeded the years of hunger and revolt, by raising the general standard of living, automatically made for greater individualism, and stimulated the personal ambition of the bolder and more politically minded workers towards local self-improvement and the pursuit of immediate ends, and away from the comparatively nebulous ideal of an international alliance against the bourgeoisie. The development of the German workers, led by Lassalle, is a typical example of such a purely internal movement, rigorously centralised but confined to a single land, spurred on by an optimistic hope of gradually forcing the capitalist enemy to terms by the sheer weight of numbers, without having recourse to a revolutionary upheaval or violent seizure of power. This hope was encouraged by Bismarck's anti-bourgeois policy which appeared to weight the scales in favour of the workers. In France the fearful defeat of 1848–9 left the city proletariat broken and for many years incapable of action on a large scale, healing its wounds by forming small local associations more or less Proudhonist in inspiration. Nor were they entirely discouraged in this by the government of Napoleon III. The Emperor himself had in his youth posed as a friend of the peasants, artisans and factory workers against capitalist bureaucracy, and wished to represent his monarchy as a novel and exceedingly subtle form of government, an original blend of monarchism, republicanism and Tory democracy, a kind of new order in which political absolutism was tempered by economic liberalism; while the government, although centralised and responsible to the Emperor alone, in theory rested ultimately on the confidence of the people, and was therefore to be an entirely new and thoroughly modern institution, sensitive to novel needs, responsive to every nuance of social change.

Part of Napoleon's elaborate policy of social conciliation was the preservation of a delicate balance of power between the classes by playing them off against each other. The workers were therefore permitted to form themselves into unions under strict police supervision, in order to offset the dangerously growing power of the financial aristocracy with its suspected Orleanist loyalties. The workers, with no alternative choice before them, accepted this cautiously outstretched official hand, and began constituting trade associations, a process half encouraged, half hampered, by the authorities.

When the great Exhibition of Modern Industry was opened in London in 1863, French workers were given facilities for visiting it, and a selected deputation duly came to England, half tourists, half representatives of the French proletariat, theoretically sent to the Exhibition in order to study the latest industrial developments. A meeting was arranged between them and the representatives of English unions. At this meeting, which to begin with was probably as vague in intention as other gatherings of its kind, and seemed to be mainly stimulated by the desire to help Polish democrats exiled as a result of the abortive Polish uprising in that year, there arose such questions as comparative hours and wages in France and England, and the necessity of preventing employers from importing cheap blackleg labour from abroad with which to break strikes organised by local unions. Another meeting was called in order to form an association which should not be confined merely to holding discussions and comparing notes, but for the purpose of beginning active economic and political co-operation, and perhaps for the promotion of an international democratic revolution. The initiative on this occasion came not from Marx, but from the English and French labour leaders themselves. On their fringe were radicals of various kinds, Polish democrats, Italian Mazzinists, Proudhonists, Blanquists and neo-Jacobins from France and Belgium: anyone, indeed, who desired the fall of the existing order was at first freely welcomed.

This meeting was held in St Martin's Hall in London, and was presided over by Edward Beesly, a charming and benevolent figure, then professor of ancient history in the University of London, a radical and a positivist, who belonged to the small but notable group that included Frederic Harrison and Crompton, which had been deeply influenced by Comte and the early French socialists. Its members could be counted on to support every enlightened measure, and, for many years almost alone among the educated men of their time were aligned with Mill in defending the unpopular cause of trade unionism at a period when it was being denounced in the House of Commons as an instrument deliberately invented to foment ill will between the classes. The meeting resolved to constitute an international federation of working men, pledged not to reform but to destroy the prevalent system of economic relations, and to substitute in its place one in which the workers would themselves acquire the ownership of the means of production, which would put an end to their economic exploitation and cause the fruit of their labour to be communally shared—an end that entailed the ultimate abolition of private property in all its forms. Marx, who had previously held himself coldly aloof from other gatherings of democrats, perceived the solid character of this latest attempt at combination, organised as it was by genuine workers' representatives and advertising definite and concrete purposes in which his own influence was clearly traceable. He rarely took part in any movement which he had not initiated himself. This was to be the exception. The German artisans in London appointed him their representative on the executive committee, and by the time the second meeting was held to vote the constitution, he took entire charge of the proceedings. After the French and Italian delegates, to whom the task of drafting the statutes was entrusted, had failed to produce anything but the usual faded democratic commonplaces, Marx drew them up himself, adding an inaugural address which he composed for the occasion. The constitution which, as framed by the International Committee, was vague, humanitarian, and tinged with liberalism, emerged from his hands a boldly drawn, militant document designed to constitute a rigorously disciplined body whose members were pledged to assist each other not merely in improving their common condition, but in systematically subverting, and whenever possible overthrowing, the existing capitalist regime by open political action. In particular they were to try to enter democratic parliaments, as the followers of Lassalle were beginning to attempt to do in German countries. Upon a request being made to include some expressions of respect for 'right and duty, truth, justice and freedom' the words were inserted, but in a context in which, Marx wrote to Engels, 'they could do no possible harm'. The new constitution was passed, and Marx began to work with his customary feverish rapidity, emerging into the limelight of international activity after fifteen years, if not of obscurity, of intermittent light and darkness.

The Inaugural Address of the International is, after the Communist Manifesto, the most remarkable document of the Socialist Movement. It occupies little over a dozen octavo pages and opens with the declaration '. . . That the emancipation of the working class must be conquered by the working class themselves . . . that the economic subjection of the man of labour to the monopoliser of the means of labour . . . lies at the bottom of servitude in all its forms of social misery, mental degradation and political dependence. That the economic emancipation of the working class is therefore the great end to which every political movement ought to be subordinate as a means. That all efforts aiming at this great end have hitherto failed from want of solidarity between the manifold divisions of labour in each country, and from the absence of a fraternal bond of union between the working classes of different countries . . . for these means the undersigned . . . have taken the steps necessary for founding the International Working Men's Association.'

It contains a survey of the economic and social conditions of the working class from 1848, and contrasts the rapidly growing prosperity of the propertied classes with the depressed condition of the workers. 1848 is recognised as a crushing defeat for them, yet even so not wholly without benefit to them: as a result of it, the feeling of international solidarity among workers had awoken. This development had made agitation for the legal limitation of the working day not entirely unsuccessful—the first definite victory over a policy of extreme *laissez-faire*. The cooperative movement had proved that high industrial efficiency was compatible with, and even increased by, the elimination of the capitalist slave-driver: wage labour had thus been demonstrated to be not a necessary but a transient and eradicable evil. The workers were at last beginning to grasp that they had nothing to gain and everything to lose by listening to their capitalist advisers who, whenever they could not use force, sought to play on national and religious prejudices, on personal or local interests, on the profound political ignorance of the masses. Whoever might gain by national or dynastic wars, it was the workers on both sides who always lost. Yet their strength was such that by common action they could prevent this exploitation in peace as in war: as, indeed, their success in intervening in England against the sending of help to the Southern states in the American civil war had proved. Against the formidable and in appearance overwhelming power of their enemy they had only one weapon—their numbers, 'but numbers weigh in the scales only when they are united and organised and led consciously towards a single aim'. It was in the political field that their slavery was most manifest. To hold aloof from politics in the name of economic organisation, as Proudhon and Bakunin taught, was criminal short-sightedness; they would obtain justice only if they upheld it, if necessary by force, wherever they saw it trampled upon. Even if they could not intervene with armed force, they could at least protest and demonstrate and harass their governments, until the supreme standards of morality and justice, by which relations between individuals were conventionally judged, became the laws governing relations between nations. But this could not be done without altering the existing economic structure of society which, in spite of minor improvements, necessarily worked for the degradation and enslavement of the working class. There was only one class in whose real interest it was to arrest this downward trend and remove the possibility of its occurrence: that was the class which, possessing nothing, was bound by no ties of interest or sentiment to the old world of injustice or misery—the class which was as much the invention of the new age as machinery itself. The Address ended, like the *Communist Manifesto*, with the words, 'Workers of the world unite!'

The tasks of the new organisation, as embodied in this document, were: to establish close relations between the workers of various countries and trades; to collect relevant statistics; to inform the workers of one country of the conditions, needs and the plans of the workers of another; to discuss questions of common interest; to secure co-ordinated simultaneous action in all countries in the event of international crises; to publish regular reports on the work of the associations, and the like. It was to meet in annual congresses and would be convened by a demo-cratically elected general council in which all affiliated countries would be represented. Marx left the constitution as elastic as he could, in order to be able to include as many active workers' organisations as possible, however disparate their methods and character. At first he resolved to act cautiously and with mod-eration, to bind and unify, and eliminate dissidents gradually, as a greater measure of agreement was progressively reached. He carried out his policy precisely as he had planned it. Its con-sequences proved self-destructive, although it is difficult to see what other tactics Marx could have adopted consistently with his principles.

The International grew rapidly. Union after union of workers in the principal countries of Europe was converted by the pros-pect of united warfare for higher wages, shorter hours and pol-itical representation: it was far better organised than either Chart-ism or the earlier communist leagues had ever been, partly because tactical lessons had been learnt. Independent activity on the part of individuals was suppressed, popular oratory was dis-couraged, and rigid discipline in all departments was introduced, mainly because it was led and dominated by a single personality. The only man who might have attempted to rival Marx in the early years was Lassalle, and he was dead; even so, the spell of his legend was strong enough to insulate the Germans against full support of the London centre. Liebknecht, a man of mediocre talent, boundlessly devoted to Marx, preached the new creed with enthusiasm and skill, but the continuation of Bismarck's anti-socialist policy, and the tradition of nationalism derived from Lassalle, kept the German workers' activity within the frontiers of their country, pre-occupied with problems of internal organ-isation. As for Bakunin, that great disturber of men's spirits had lately returned to Western Europe after a romantic escape from Siberia, but while his personal prestige, both in the International and outside it, was immense, he had no organised following: he had drifted away from Herzen and the liberal agrarian party among the Russian émigrés, and no one knew whither he was tending, least of all he himself. In common with the great major-ity of Proudhonists he and his followers became members of the International, but since it was openly committed to political action, they did so in defiance of their somewhat vaguely formulated anarchist principles. The most enthusiastic members at this time were English and French trade unionists, who were temporarily under the spell of the new experiment with its vast promise of prosperity and power; they were no theorists, nor wished to be, and left all such questions to the General Council of the International. While this mood lasted, Marx had no serious rivals in the organisation, being altogether superior in intellect, revolutionary experience, and strength of will, to the odd amalgam of professional men, factory workers and stray ideologists who, with the addition of one or two dubious adventurers, composed the First International Working Men's Association.

Marx was now forty-six years of age and in appearance and habits prematurely old. Of his seven children three were dead, largely as a result of the material conditions of the life led by the family in their rooms in Soho: they had contrived to move to a more spacious house in Kentish Town, although they were still almost destitute. The great economic crisis, the severest yet experienced in Europe, which began in 1857, was warmly welcomed both by him and by Engels as likely to breed discontent and rebellion, but it also curtailed Engels's income, and so struck a blow at Marx himself at a moment when he could least afford it. The New York *Tribune* and occasional contributions to radical German newspapers saved him from literal starvation; but the margin by which the family survived was for twenty years perilously thin. By 1860 even the American source began to fail; the editor of the New York *Tribune*, Horace Greeley, a fervent supporter of democratic nationalism, found himself in growing disagreement with his European correspondent's sharply worded views. The economic crisis, and the added effect of the civil war, led to the dismissal of many of the *Tribune*'s European correspondents: Dana pleaded to be allowed to retain Marx, but in vain. He was gradually edged out of his post during the beginning of 1861; the association finally ended a year later. As for the International, it added to his duties and enlivened his existence, but did not add to his income. In despair he applied for a post of booking clerk in a railway office, but his tattered clothes and his menacing appearance were unlikely to produce a favourable impression on a potential employer of clerical labour, and his application was finally rejected on account of his illegible handwriting. It is difficult to see how, without the support of Engels, he and his family could have survived at all during these fearful years.

Meanwhile branches of the International had been established in Italy and Spain; by the mid-sixties governments began to grow frightened; there was talk of arrests and proscriptions; the French Emperor made a half-hearted attempt to suppress it. This only served to heighten the fame and the prestige of the new body among the workers. For Marx, after the dark tunnel of the fifties, this was once more life and activity. The work of the International consumed his nights and days. With the customary devoted help of Engels he took personal possession of the central office, and acted not only as its semi-dictatorial adviser, but as the central drafting office and clearing-house of all correspondence. Everything passed through his hands and moved in the direction which he gave it. The French, a portion of the Swiss, to some degree the Belgian, and later the Italian sections, bred on the anti-authoritarianism of Proudhon and Bakunin, made vague but unavailing protests. Marx, who enjoyed complete ascendancy over the Council, tightened his hold still further: he insisted on rigid conformity to every point of the original programme. His old energy seemed to return. He wrote spirited, almost gay letters to Engels; even his theoretical works bear the imprint of this newly found vigour, and as often happens, intense work in one field stimulated dormant activity in another. A sketch of his economic theory had appeared in 1859: but his major work, which poverty and ill-health had interrupted, now at last began to near its end.

Marx made few personal appearances at the meetings of the congress of the International: he preferred to control its activities from London, where he regularly attended the meetings of the General Council and issued detailed instructions to his followers on it. As always he trusted and relied almost entirely on Germans: he found a faithful mouthpiece in an elderly tailor named Eccarius, long resident in England, a man not burdened with excess of intelligence or imagination, but one who seemed to him dependable and thorough. Eccarius, like the majority of Marx's underlings, eventually revolted, and joined the secessionists, but for eight years, as secretary to the Council of the International, he carried out Marx's instructions to the letter. Annual congresses were held in London, Geneva, Lausanne, Brussels, Basle, at which general problems were discussed and definite measures voted upon; common decisions were adopted with regard to hours and wages; such questions as the position of women and children, the type of political and economic pressure most suitable to differing conditions in various European countries, the possibility of collaboration with other bodies, were considered. Marx's chief concern was to arrive at a clear formulation of a concrete international policy in terms of specific demands co-ordinated with each other, and the creation of a rigorous discipline which guaranteed undeviating adhesion to this policy. He therefore successfully resisted all offers of alliance with such purely humanitarian bodies as the League of Peace and Freedom, then newly founded under the aegis of Mazzini, Bakunin and John Stuart Mill. This dictatorial policy was bound, sooner or later, to lead to discontent and rebellion; it crystallised round Bakunin, whose conception of a loose federation of semi-independent local bodies began to gain adherents in the Swiss and Italian sections of the International, and to a lesser extent in France. Finally they resolved to constitute themselves, under Bakunin's leadership, into a body to be called the Democratic Alliance, affiliated to the International, but with an internal organisation of its own pledged to resist centralisation and to support federal autonomy. This was a heresy which even a more tolerant man than Marx could not afford to overlook: the International was not intended to be a mere correspondence society between a loose association of radical committees, but a unified political party pressing for a single end in all the centres of its dispersion. He believed firmly that any connection with Bakunin—or indeed any Russian—was bound to end by badly betraying the working class, a view which he had acquired after his brief and enjoyable flirtation, and subsequent disillusionment, with the aristocratic Russian radicals of the forties. As for Bakunin, while he professed sincerely enough to admire Marx's personal genius, he never concealed either his personal antipathy for him, or his rooted loathing of Marx's belief in authoritarian methods, expressed both in his theories and in his practical organisation of the revolutionary party.

'We, revolutionary anarchists,' Bakunin declared, 'are the enemies of all forms of state and state organisation . . . we think that all state rule, all governments, being by their very nature placed outside the mass of the people, must necessarily seek to subject it to customs and purposes entirely foreign to it. We therefore declare ourselves to be foes . . . of all state organisations as such, and believe that the people can only be happy and free, when, organised from below by means of its own autonomous completely free associations, without the supervision of any guardians, it will create its own life.

'We believe power corrupts those who wield it as much as those who are forced to obey it. Under its corrosive influence, some become greedy and ambitious tyrants, exploiting society in their own interest, or in that of their class, while others are turned into abject slaves. Intellectuals, positivists, doctrinaires, all those who put science before life . . . defend the idea of the state and its authority as being the only possible salvation of society—quite logically, since from their false premise that thought comes before life, that only abstract theory can form the starting-point of social practice . . . they draw the inevitable conclusion that since such theoretical knowledge is at present possessed by very few, these few must be put in control of social life, not only to inspire, but to direct all popular movements, and that no sooner is the revolution over than a new social organisation must at once be set up; not a free association of popular bodies . . . working in accordance with the needs and instincts of the people, but a centralised dictatorial power concentrated in the hands of this academic minority, as if they really expressed the popular will . . . The difference between such revolutionary dictatorship and the modern state is only one of external trappings. In substance both are a tyranny of the minority over the majority in the name of the people—in the name of the stupidity of the many and the superior wisdom of the few—and so they are equally reactionary, devising to secure political and economic privilege to the ruling minority, and the . . . enslavement of the masses, to destroy the present order only to erect their own rigid dictatorship on its ruins.'

Bakunin's attacks on Marx and Lassalle could not pass unnoticed, the more so because they were tinged by anti-semitism, for which his friend Herzen more than once had occasion to reproach him. And yet, when in 1869 Herzen begged him to leave the International, he wrote, with a characteristic burst of magnanimity, that he could not join the opponents of a man 'who has served [the cause of socialism] for twenty-five years with insight, energy, and disinterestedness in which he undoubtedly excelled us all'.

Marx's dislike of Bakunin did not blind him to the need for conceding a certain measure of regional independence for motives of sheer expediency. Thus he successfully foiled the plan to create international trade unions because he believed that this was premature and would lead to an immediate rift with the existing, nationally organised, trade unions from which, at any rate in England, the chief support of the International was drawn. But if he made this concession, he did so not for love of federalism as such, but solely not to endanger what had already been built up, an organisation without which he could not create a body the existence of which would make the workers conscious that there stood behind their demands, not, as in 1848, merely sympathisers here and there, prepared to offer moral support or at best occasional contributions—but a well-disciplined, militant force pledged to resist, and when necessary, intimidate and coerce their own governments unless justice were done to their brothers everywhere.

In order to create the permanent possibility of such active solidarity in theory and in practice, a central body in undisputed authority, a kind of general staff responsible for strategy and tactics, seemed to him indispensable. Bakunin, by his attempts to loosen the structure of the International and to encourage varieties of opinion in the local sections, appeared to him to be deliberately aiming to destroy this possibility. If he were successful, it would mean the loss of what had been won, a return to Utopianism, the disappearance of the new sober outlook, of the realisation that the sole strength of the workers lay in unity, that what delivered them into the hands of their enemies in 1848 was the fact that they were engaged in scattered risings, sporadic emotional outbursts of violence, instead of a single carefully concerted revolution, organised to begin at a moment chosen for its historical appropriateness, directed from a common source and to a common end by men who had accurately studied the situation and their own and their enemy's strength. Bakuninism led to the dissipation of the revolutionary impulse, to the old romantic, noble, futile heroism, rich in saints and martyrs, but crushed only too easily by the more realistic enemy, and necessarily followed by a period of weakness and disillusionment likely to set the movement back for many decades. Marx did not underestimate Bakunin's revolutionary energy and power to stir men's imaginations: indeed, it was for this reason that he regarded him as a dangerously disruptive force likely to breed chaos wherever he went. The workers' cause would rest on volcanic soil if he and his followers were allowed to irrupt into the ranks of its defenders. Hence after some years of desultory skirmishing, he decided upon an open attack. It ended with the excommunication of Bakunin and his followers from the ranks of the International.

10

'The Red Terror Doctor'

We are what we are because of him: without him we should still
be sunk in a slough of confusion.

FRIEDRICH ENGELS, 1883

THE first volume of *Das Kapital* was finally published in 1867. The
appearance of this book was an epoch-making event in the history
of international socialism and in Marx's own life. The complete
work was conceived as a comprehensive treatise on the laws and
morphology of the economic organisation of modern society,
seeking to describe the processes of production, exchange and
distribution as they actually occur, to explain their present state as
a particular stage in the development constituted by the movement of the class struggle, in Marx's own words, 'to discover the
economic law of motion of modern society' by establishing the
natural laws that govern the history of classes. The result[1] was an
original amalgam of economic theory, history, sociology and
propaganda which fits none of the accepted categories. Marx
certainly regarded it as primarily a treatise on economic science.
The earlier economists, according to Marx, misunderstood the
nature of economic laws when they compared them with the laws
of physics and chemistry, and assumed that, although social conditions may change, the laws that govern them do not; with the
result that their systems either apply to imaginary worlds, peopled
by idealised economic men, modelled upon the writer's own
contemporaries, and therefore usually compounded of selected
characteristics which came into prominence only in the
eighteenth and nineteenth centuries; or else describe societies
which, if they were ever real, have long since vanished. He
therefore conceived it as his task to create a new system of

---

[1] Especially if the first volume is taken in conjunction with the posthumously published volumes which Engels, and later Kautsky, prepared
for publication out of Marx's economic manuscripts, some in the form of
notes.

concepts and definitions which should have definite application to the contemporary world, and be so constructed as to reflect the changing structure of economic life in relation not only to its past, but also to its future. In the first volume Marx made an attempt at once to provide a systematic exposition of certain basic theorems of economic science, and more specifically to describe the rise of the new industrial system, as a consequence of the new relations between employers and labour created by the effect of technological progress on the methods of production.

The first volume therefore deals with the productive process; that is, on the one hand, the relations between machinery and labour, and on the other those between the actual producers, that is the workers and those who employ and direct them. The remaining volumes, published after his death by his executors, deal largely with the impact on the theory of value of the circulation of the finished product, which must obtain before its value can be realised, that is the system of exchange and the financial machinery which it involves, and with relations between producers and consumers, which determine prices, the rate of interest and profit.

The general thesis which runs through the entire work is that adumbrated in the *Communist Manifesto* and Marx's earlier economic writings.[1] It rests on three fundamental assumptions: (a) that political economy seeks to explain who obtains what goods or services or status and why; (b) that it is therefore a science not of inanimate objects—commodities—but of persons and their activities, to be interpreted in terms of the rules which govern the capitalist market economy, and not pseudo-objective laws beyond human control, such as those of supply and demand, which govern the world of natural objects—objects whose behaviour is, as it were, external to the lives of men, who look upon this process as part of an eternal, natural order before which men must bow down, since they are impotent to alter it. This illusion, or 'false consciousness', is what he calls 'fetishism of commodities'; (c) that the decisive factor in social behaviour in modern times is that of industrialisation; with the rider that the earliest and fullest form of it—the industrial revolution in England—offers the student the best example of a process that will, in due course, take place everywhere. Marx traces the rise of the

[1] For detailed accounts of Marx's economic doctrine see Guide to Further Reading, p. 219.

modern proletariat by correlating it with the general development of the technical means of production When, in the course of their gradual evolution, these means can no longer be created by each man for his own use, and division of labour is born, certain individuals (as Saint-Simon had taught), owing to their superior skill, power and enterprise, acquire sole control of such instruments and tools, and thus find themselves in a position in which they can hire the labour of others by a combination of threats to withhold necessities of life from them and of offering them more in the form of a regular remuneration than they would receive as independent producers, vainly attempting to achieve the same results with the old and obsolete tools which alone they have in their possession. As a result of selling their labour to others, these men themselves become so many commodities in the economic market, and their labour power acquires a definite price which fluctuates precisely like that of other commodities.

A commodity is any object in a market economy embodying human labour for which there is a social demand. It is thus a concept which, Marx is careful to point out, can be applied only at a relatively late stage of social development: and is no more eternal than any other economic category. The commercial value of a commodity is asserted—this is the conclusion of his argument—to be directly constituted by the number of hours of socially necessary human labour, that is, how long it takes an average producer to create an average specimen of its kind (a view derived from a somewhat similar doctrine held by Ricardo and the classical economists). A day's work by a labourer may well produce an object possessing a value greater than the value of the minimum quantity of commodities which he needs for his own support; he thus produces something worth more in the market than he consumes; indeed, unless he did so, his master would have no economic reason for employing him. As a commodity in the market, a man's labour power may itself be acquired for $£x$, which represents the minimum sum needed to maintain him in sufficient health to enable him to do his work efficiently, and to reproduce and bring up his kind; the goods he produces will sell for $£y$; $£y\text{-}x$ represents the extent by which he has increased the total wealth of society, and this is the residue which his employer pockets. Even after the reasonable reward of the employer's own work in his capacity as the organiser and manager of the processes of production and distribution is deducted, a definite residue of the social income remains, which in the form of rent, interest on investments, or commercial profit, is shared, according to Marx, not by society as a whole, but solely by those members of it who are called the capitalist or bourgeois class, distinguished from the rest by the fact that they alone, in their capacity as sole owners of the means of production, obtain and accumulate such unearned increment.

Whether Marx's concept of value be interpreted as meaning an average norm, round which the actual prices of commodities oscillate, or an ideal limit towards which they tend, or that which in some unspecified sense prices 'ought' to be, or an element in the sociological explanation of what constitutes and satisfies the material interests of men in society, or something more metaphysical—an impalpable essence, infused into brute matter by the creativeness of human labour, or, as unsympathetic critics have maintained, a confusion of all these; and again whether the notion of a uniform entity called undifferentiated human labour (which according to the theory constitutes economic value), different manifestations of which can be compared in respect of quantity alone, is, or is not, valid—and it is not easy to defend Marx's use of either concept—the theory of exploitation based on them remains comparatively unaffected. The central thesis which made so powerful an appeal to workers, who did not for the most part begin to comprehend the intricacies of Marx's general argument about the relation of exchange value and actual prices, is that there is only one social class, their own, which produces more wealth than it consumes, and that this residue is appropriated by other men simply by virtue of their strategic position as the sole possessors of the means of production, that is, natural resources, machinery, means of transport, financial credit, and so forth, without which the workers cannot create, while control over them gives those who have it the power of starving the rest of mankind into capitulation on their own terms.

Political, social, religious and legal institutions of the capitalist era are represented as being so many moral and intellectual weapons designed to organise the world in the interest of the employers. These last employ, over and above the producers of commodities, that is, the proletariat, a whole army of ideologists: propagandists, interpreters and apologists, who defend the capitalist system, embellish it, and create literary and artistic monuments to it, likely to increase the confidence and optimism of those who benefit under it, and make it appear more palatable to its victims—in Rousseau's phrase, 'cover their chains with garlands of flowers'. But if the development of technology, as Saint-Simon correctly discovered, has for a period given this unique power to landowners, industrialists and financiers, its uncontrollable advance will no less inevitably destroy them.

Already Fourier, and after him Proudhon, had declaimed against the processes by which the great bankers and manufacturers, by means of their superior resources, tend to eliminate small traders and craftsmen from the economic market, creating a mass of discontented, *déclassé* individuals, who are automatically forced into the ranks of the proletariat. But the capitalist is, in his day, a historical necessity. He extracts surplus value and accumulates; this is indispensable to industrialisation and is history's agency of progress. 'Fanatically bent on increasing value, he ruthlessly forces the human race to produce for the sake of production.' He may do so brutally and for purely selfish motives; but in the course of this 'he creates those material conditions which alone can form the real foundations of a higher form of society, of which the full and free development of every man is the dominant principle'. He had already paid his tribute to the progressive role of industrialisation in the *Communist Manifesto*. 'The bourgeoisie', he wrote, 'cannot exist without constantly revolutionising the instruments of production, and thereby the relations of production and with them the entire relations of society . . . During its rule of scarcely one hundred years, it has created more massive and colossal productive forces than all the earlier generations taken together. Subjection of the forces of nature to man, application of chemistry and industry to agriculture, steam navigation, railways, the electric telegraph, clearing entire continents for cultivation, canalisation of rivers, whole populations conjured up out of the earth—what earlier age had even a presentiment of such gigantic social forces slumbering in the lap of socialised labour?' But the capitalist will have played his part, and will then be superseded. He will be 'liquidated' by his own essential characteristics as an accumulator. Ruthless competition between individual capitalists, seeking to increase the quantity of surplus value, and the natural necessity arising from this of lowering the cost of production and finding new markets, is bound to lead to greater and greater fusion of rival firms, that is to a ceaseless process of amalgamation, until only the largest and most powerful groups are left in existence, all others being forced into a position of dependence or semi-dependence, in the new centralised industrial hierarchy, ruling over a concentration of productive and distributive machinery, which grows, and will continue to grow, faster and faster. Centralisation is a direct product of rationalisation: of increased efficiency in production and transport secured by the pooling of resources, of the formation of great monopolistic trusts and combines which are capable of planned co-ordination. The workers previously scattered among many small enterprises, reinforced by continual influx of the sons and daughters of the ruined small traders and manufacturers, automatically become united into a single, evergrowing, proletarian army by the very processes of integration at work among their masters. Their power as a political and economic body, increasingly conscious of its historical role and resources, grows correspondingly greater. Already trade unions, developing in the shadow of the factory system, represent a far more powerful weapon in the hands of the proletariat than any that existed before. The process of industrial expansion will tend to organise society more and more into the shape of an immense pyramid, with fewer and increasingly powerful capitalists at its summit and a vast, discontented mass of exploited workers and colonial slaves forming its base. The more machinery replaces human labour, the lower the rate of profit is bound to fall, since the rate of 'surplus value' is determined solely by the latter. The struggle between competing capitalists and their countries, which are in effect controlled by them, will grow more deadly, being wedded to a system of unhampered competition, under which each can only survive by overreaching and destroying his rivals.[1]

Within the framework of capitalism and unchecked private enterprise, these processes cannot be made rational, since the vested interests on which capitalist society rests depend for their survival on freedom of competition, if not between individual producers, then between combines and monopolies. The inexorable tendency of technological progress to increasingly collective forms of production will conflict more and more violently

[1] If this is really so, why should not the capitalist dispense with machines and increase surplus value by returning to slave labour? In the posthumous volumes of *Das Kapital* edited by Engels from Marx's manuscripts, it is maintained that machinery does not indeed increase profits, relatively or absolutely: but in the short run it does increase them for the individual capitalist, and competition therefore compels him to introduce it. Moreover, it helps to eliminate inefficient competitors; the rate of profit continues to fall, but it is divided among increasingly fewer capitalists—the 'fittest' in this jungle warfare. The reader can tell for himself whether, or how far, this has occurred.

with individual forms of distribution, that is, private control, private property. Big Business, which Marx was among the few to foresee, with its military allies, will destroy *laissez-faire* and individualism. Marx did not, however, allow for the consequences of the growth of state control or democratic resistance, nor the development of political nationalism as a force cutting across and transforming the development of capitalism itself, either as an obstacle to unchecked exploitation or as a bulwark to the gradually impoverished section of the *bourgeoisie*, which would form an alliance with the reaction in its desperate anxiety to avoid its Marxist destiny of falling into the proletariat below it. In other words, he foresees neither Fascism nor the welfare state.

His classification of social strata into the obsolescent military-feudal aristocracy, the industrial *bourgeoisie*, the *petite bourgeoisie*, the proletariat, and that casual riff-raff on the edge of society which he called the *Lumpenproletariat*—a fruitful and original classification for its time—over-simplifies issues when it is too mechanically applied to the twentieth century. A more elaborate instrument is required, if only to deal with the independent behaviour of classes, like the semi-ruined *petite bourgeoisie*, the growing salaried lower middle class, and above all the vast agricultural population, classes which Marx regarded as naturally reactionary, but forced by their growing pauperisation either to sink to the level of the proletariat, or to offer their sevices as mercenaries to its protagonist, the industrial *bourgeoisie*. The history of post-war Europe, at any rate in the west, requires to be considerably distorted before it can be made to fit this hypothesis.

Marx prophesied that the periodic crises due to the absence of planned economies, and unchecked industrial strife, would necessarily grow more frequent and acute. Wars, on a hitherto unprecedented scale, would ravage the civilised world, until finally the Hegelian contradictions of a system whose continuance depends upon more and more destructive conflicts between its constituent parts would obtain a violent solution. The ever-increasing group of capitalists in power would be overthrown by the workers whom they themselves would have so efficiently drilled into a compact, disciplined body. With the disappearance of the last possessing class, the final end would be reached of the war between the classes, and with it of the last obstacle to the overcoming of economic scarcity, and consequently of social strife and human misery and degradation.

In a celebrated passage in the twenty-second chapter of the first volume of *Das Kapital* he declared: 'While there is a progressive diminution in the number of capitalist magnates, there is of course a corresponding increase in the mass of poverty, enslavement, degeneration and exploitation, but at the same time there is a steady intensification of the role of the working class—a class which grows ever more numerous, and is disciplined, unified and organised by the very mechanism of the capitalist method of production which has flourished with it and under it. The centralisation of the means of production and the socialisation of labour reach a point where they prove incompatible with their capitalist husk. This bursts asunder. The knell of private property sounds. The expropriators are expropriated.' The state, the instrument whereby the authority of the ruling class is artificially enforced, having lost its function, will disappear. He had, in the *Communist Manifesto* of 1847–8, and again in 1850 and 1852, made it clear that the state will not vanish immediately: there must occur a period of revolutionary transformation from capitalism to communism. In this transitional period the authority of the state must be preserved, and indeed enforced, but it will now be controlled entirely by the workers, once they have become the dominant class; indeed (to use the formula of one of his later writings), in this first phase of the revolution the state will be 'the revolutionary dictatorship of the proletariat'. In this period, before economic scarcity has been overcome, the reward of the workers must be proportional to the labour they supply. But once the 'all-round development of the individual' has created a society in which 'springs of co-operative wealth flow more abundantly', the communist goal will be reached. Then, and not before, the whole community, painted in colours at once too simple and too fantastic by the Utopians of the past, will at last be realised—a community in which there will be neither master nor slave, neither rich nor poor, in which the world's goods, being produced in accordance with social demand unhampered by the caprice of individuals, will be distributed not indeed equally—a notion so lamely borrowed by the workers from the liberal ideologists with their utilitarian concept of justice as arithmetical equality—but rationally, that is unequally: for, as a man's capacities and needs are unequal, his reward, if it is to be just, must, in the later formula of the *Critique of the Gotha Programme* of 1875, accrue 'from every one according to his ability, to every one according to his need'. Men, emancipated at last from the tyranny both of nature and of their own ill-adapted and ill-controlled and therefore oppressive institutions, will be enabled to realise their potentialities to the fullest extent. History will cease to be the succession of one exploiting class after another. Subordination to the division of labour will cease. Real freedom, so obscurely adumbrated by Hegel, will be realised. Human history in the true sense will only then begin.

The publication of *Das Kapital* had at last provided a definite intellectual foundation for international socialism in the place of a scattered mass of vaguely defined and conflicting ideas. The interdependence of the historical, economic and political theses preached by Marx and Engels was revealed in this monumental compilation. It became the central objective of attack and defence. All subsequent forms of socialism hereafter defined themselves in terms of their attitude to the position taken in it, and were understood and classified by their resemblance to it. After a brief period of obscurity, its fame began to grow and reached an extraordinary height. It acquired a symbolic significance beyond anything written since the age of faith. It has been blindly worshipped, and blindly hated, by millions who have not read a line of it, or have read without understanding its, at times, obscure and tortuous prose. In its name revolutions were made (and are); counter-revolutions concentrated (and concentrate) upon its suppression as the most potent and insidious of the enemy's weapons. A new social order has been established which professes its principles and sees in it the final and unalterable expression of its faith. It has called into existence an army of interpreters and casuists, whose unceasing labours for nearly a century have buried it beneath a mountain of commentary which has outgrown in influence the sacred text itself.

In Marx's own life it marked a decisive moment. He intended it to be his greatest contribution to the emancipation of humanity, and had sacrificed to it fifteen years of his life and much of his public ambition. The labour which had gone towards it was truly prodigious. For its sake he endured poverty, illness and persecution both public and personal, suffering these not gladly indeed, but with a single-minded stoicism whose strength and harshness both moved and frightened those who came in contact with it.

He dedicated his book to the memory of Wilhelm Wolff, a Silesian communist, who had been his devoted follower since 1848, and had recently died in Manchester. The published volume was the first part of the projected work; the rest was still a confused mass of notes, references and sketches. He sent copies of it to his old associates, to Freiligrath, who congratulated him on having produced a useful work of reference, and to Feuerbach, who said that he found it 'rich in undeniable facts of the most interesting, but at the same time most horrible nature'. Ruge gave it more discriminating praise; it obtained at least one critical notice in England, in the *Saturday Review*, which quaintly observed that 'the presentation of the subject invests the driest economic questions with certain peculiar charm'. It was more widely noticed in Germany where Marx's friends Liebknecht and Kugelmann, a Hanover physician who had conceived an immense admiration for him, made vigorous propaganda for it. In particular Joseph Dietzgen, a self-taught German cobbler in St Petersburg, who became one of Marx's most ardent disciples, did much to popularise it with the German masses.

Marx's scientific appetite had not diminished since his Paris days.[1] He believed in exact scholarship and sternly drove his reluctant followers into the reading-room of the British Museum. Liebknecht, in his memoirs, describes how day after day the 'scum of international communism' might be seen meekly seated at the desks in the reading-room, under the eye of the master himself. Indeed no social or political movement has laid such emphasis on research and erudition. The extent of Marx's own reading is to some degree indicated by the references in his works alone, which explore exceedingly obscure by-ways in ancient, medieval, and modern literature. The text is liberally sprinkled with footnotes, long, mordant and annihilating, which recall Gibbon's classical employment of this weapon. The adversaries at whom they are directed are for the most part forgotten names today, but occasionally his shafts are aimed at well-known figures; Macaulay, Gladstone, and one or two well-known academic economists of the time, are attacked with a savage concentration which inaugurated a new epoch in the technique of public vituperation, and created the school of socialist polemical writing which has altered the general character of political controversy. There is conspicuously little praise in the book. The warmest tribute is earned by the British factory inspectors, whose fearless

[1] He was deeply impressed by Darwin's achievement, and sent him a copy of the first volume of *Das Kapital*. But the story (which virtually every twentieth-century biographer, including the present one, has reproduced) that he offered to dedicate the second edition to him appears to be apocryphal and to rest on a mistaken identification of a letter sent by Darwin to Marx's son-in-law, Edward Aveling.

and unbiased reports, both of the appalling conditions which they witnessed, and of the means adopted by factory owners to circumvent the law, are declared to be a uniquely honourable phenomenon in the history of bourgeois society. The technique of social research was revolutionised by the example set by Marx in the use of Blue Books and official reports: he claimed to base the greater part of his detailed indictment of modern industrialism largely upon them.

After his death, Engels, who edited the second and third volumes of *Das Kapital*, found the manuscript in a far more chaotic condition than he had expected. The year in which the first volume appeared marks not a turning but a breaking-point in Marx's life. His views during the remaining sixteen years of his life altered little; he added, revised, corrected, wrote pamphlets and letters, but published nothing that was new; he reiterated the old position tirelessly, but the tone is milder; a faint note almost of querulous self-pity, totally absent before, is now discernible. His belief in the proximity, even in the ultimate inevitability of a world revolution, diminished. His prophecies had been disappointed too often: he had confidently predicted a great upheaval in 1842, during a weavers' rising in Silesia, and even inspired Heine to write the famous poem upon it which he published in his Paris journal; again in 1851, 1857 and 1872 he expected revolutionary outbreaks which failed to materialise. His prophecies of falling rates of profit, concentration of ownership of industry and land in private hands, decline in the standard of living of the proletariat, the intimate connection of capitalism and nationalism, have not, on the whole, been borne out, at least in the form in which he anticipated these developments, in this century. On the other hand he saw much that others did not: the concentration and centralisation of control of economic resources; the increasing incompatibility between Big Business methods of production and older methods of distribution, and the social and political impact of this fact; the effect of industrialisation—and science—on the methods of war; and the swift and radical transformation of ways of living that all this would cause. And he remained one of the acutest of political observers: after the annexation of Alsace-Lorraine by Prussia, he foretold that this would throw France into the arms of Russia and so bring about the first great world war. In his later years he allowed that the revolution might be longer in arriving than he and Engels had once estimated, and in some countries, notably in England, where in his day there was no real army and no real bureaucracy, it was not inevitable, only 'possible': it might actually not occur at all, for communism may be attained by evolutionary means, 'although', he enigmatically added, 'history indicates otherwise'. He was not fifty when he began to subside into conscious old age. The heroic period was over.

Das Kapital created a new reputation for its author. His previous books had been passed over in silence even in German-speaking countries: his new work was reviewed and discussed as far afield as Russia and Spain. In the next ten years it was translated into French, English, Russian, Italian; indeed, Bakunin himself gallantly offered to translate it into Russian. But this project, if it was ever begun, collapsed in circumstances of sordid personal and financial scandal which were partly responsible for the demise of the International five years later. The sudden rise to fame of this organisation was due to a major event which two years earlier altered the history of Europe and completely changed the direction in which the working-class movement had hitherto developed.

If Marx and Engels sometimes predicted events which failed to happen, they more than once failed to foresee events which did. Thus Marx denied that the Crimean War would occur, and backed the wrong side in the Austro-Prussian War. The Franco-Prussian War of 1870 came to them as something wholly unexpected. For years they had underestimated Prussian strength; the true alliance of cynicism and brute force was in their eyes represented by the Emperor of the French. Bismarck was an able Junker, who served his King and his class; even his victory over Austria did not convince them of his real quality or aims. Marx may have been to some extent genuinely deceived by Bismarck's representation of the war as being on his part purely defensive, for he signed the protest which the Council of the International immediately published only after it had been altered to make this clear—a step for which many socialists in Latin countries never forgave him, insisting in later years that it was inspired by pure German patriotism to which both he and Engels were always conspicuously prone. The International in general, and in particular its German members, behaved irreproachably throughout the brief campaign. The Council in its proclamation, issued in the middle of the war, warned the German workers against supporting the policy of annexation which Bismarck might well pursue; it explained in clear terms that the interests of the French and German proletariat were identical, being menaced only by the common enemy the capitalist bourgeoisie of both countries, which had brought about the war for its own ends, wasting for their sakes the lives and substance of the working class equally of Germany and of France. In due course it exhorted the French workers to support the formation of a republic on a broadly democratic basis. During the wild wave of war chauvinism which swept over Germany, and engulfed even the left wing of the Lassallians, only the Marxists, Liebknecht and Bebel, preserved their sanity. To the indignation of the entire country they abstained from voting for war credits and spoke vigorously in the Reichstag against the war, and in particular against the annexation of Alsace-Lorraine. For this they were charged with treason and imprisoned. In a celebrated letter to Engels, Marx pointed out that the defeat of Germany, which would have strengthened Bonapartism and crippled the German workers for many years to come, might have been even more disastrous than Germany's victory. By transferring the centre of gravity from Paris to Berlin, Bismarck was doing their work for them, however unintentionally; for the German workers, being better organised and better disciplined than the French, were consequently a stronger citadel of social democracy than Frenchmen could have been; while the defeat of Bonapartism would remove a nightmare from Europe.

In the autumn the French army was defeated at Sedan, the Emperor taken prisoner, and Paris besieged. The King of Prussia, who had solemnly sworn that the war was defensive and directed not against France but against Napoleon, changed his tactics, and, armed with an enthusiastic plebiscite from his people, demanded the cession of Alsace-Lorraine and the payment of an indemnity of five billion francs. The tide of English opinion, hitherto anti-Bonapartist and pro-German, under the influence of continual reports of Prussian atrocities in France, veered round sharply. The International issued a second Manifesto violently protesting against the annexation, denouncing the dynastic ambitions of the Prussian King, and calling upon the French workers to unite with all defenders of democracy against the common Prussian foe. 'If frontiers are to be fixed by military interests,' wrote Marx in 1870, 'there will be no end of claims, because every military line is necessarily faulty and may be improved by annexing some more outlying territory: they can never be fixed fairly or finally because they always must be improved by the conqueror or the conquered, and consequently carry within them the seeds of fresh wars. History will measure its retribution, not by the extent of square miles conquered from France, but by the intensity of the crime of reviving, in the second half of the nineteenth century, *the policy of conquest.*' This time war credits were voted against, not by Liebknecht and Bebel alone, but also by the Lassalleans, shamed out of their recent patriotism. Marx jubilantly wrote to Engels that for the first time the principles and policy of the International had obtained public expression in a European legislative assembly: the International had become a force to be officially reckoned with: the dream of a united proletarian party with identical ends in all countries was beginning to be realised. Paris was presently starved into submission, and capitulated; a national assembly was elected; Thiers was made President of the new republic, and appointed a provisional government of conservative views. In March the government made an attempt to disarm the Paris National Guard, a volunteer citizen force which showed signs of radical sympathies. It refused to give up its arms, declared its autonomy, deposed the officials of the provisional government, and elected a revolutionary committee of the people as the true government of France. The regular troops were brought to Versailles and invested the rebellious city. It was the first campaign of what both sides immediately recognised to be an open class war.

The Commune, as the new government described itself, was neither created nor inspired by the International: it was not even, in a strict sense, socialist in its doctrines, unless a dictatorship of any popularly elected committee in itself constitutes a socialist phenomenon. It consisted of a highly heterogeneous collection of individuals, for the most part followers of Blanqui, Proudhon and Bakunin, with an admixture of neo-Jacobin rhetoricians, like Félix Pyat, who knew only that they were fighting for France, the people, and the revolution, and proclaimed death to all tyrants, priests and Prussians. Workmen, soldiers, writers, painters like Courbet, scholars like the geographer Élisée Réclus and the critic Vallès, ambivalent politicians like Rochefort, foreign exiles of mildly liberal views, bohemians and adventurers of every description were swept up in a common revolutionary wave. It rose at a moment of national hysteria after the moral and material misery of a siege and a capitulation, at a moment when the national revolution which promised to do away finally with the last relics of Bonapartist and Orleanist reaction, abandoned by the middle classes, denounced by Thiers and his ministers, uncertain of support among the peasantry, seemed suddenly threatened with the return of all that it most feared and loathed, the generals, the financiers, the priests. By a great effort the people had shaken off the nightmare first of the Empire, then of the siege; they had hardly awoken yet when the spectres seemed to advance upon them once again: terrified, they revolted. This common sense of horror before the resurgence of the past was almost the sole bond which united the Communards. Their views on political organisation (beyond common hatred of the centralised government dear to Marx) were vague to a degree: they announced that the state in its old form was abolished, and called upon the people in arms to govern itself.

Presently, as supplies began to give out, and the condition of the besieged grew more desperate, terror developed: proscriptions began, men and women were condemned and executed, many of them certainly guiltless, and few deserving of death. Among those executed was the archbishop of Paris, who had been held as a hostage against the army at Versailles. The rest of Europe watched the monstrous events with growing indignation and disgust. The Communards seemed even to enlightened opinion, even to old and tried friends of the people like Louis Blanc and Mazzini, to be a band of criminal lunatics dead to the appeal of humanity, social incendiaries pledged to destroy all religion and all morality, men driven out of their minds by real and imaginary wrongs, scarcely responsible for their enormities. Practically the entire European Press, reactionary and liberal alike, combined to give the same impression. Here and there a radical journal condemned less roundly than the others, and timidly pleaded extenuating circumstances. The atrocities of the Commune did not long remain unavenged. The retribution which the victorious army exacted took the form of mass executions; the white terror, as is common in such cases, far outdid in acts of bestial cruelty the worst excesses of the regime whose misdeeds it had come to end.

The International vacillated; composed as it largely was of opponents of the Proudhonists, the Blanquists and neo-Jacobins who formed the majority of the Commune, opposed to the loosely federal Communard programme, and in particular to acts of terrorism, it had, moreover, formally advised against the revolt, declaring that 'any attempt at upsetting the new government in the present crisis . . . would be desperate folly'. The English members were particularly anxious not to compromise themselves by open association with a body which, in the opinion of the majority of their countrymen, was little better than a gang of common murderers. Marx solved their doubts by a very characteristic act. In the name of the International he published an address in which he proclaimed that the moment for analysis and criticism had passed. After giving a swift and vivid account of the events which led to the creation of the Commune, of its rise and fall, he acclaimed it as the first open and defiant manifestation in history of the strength and idealism of the working class—the first pitched battle which it had fought against its oppressors before the eyes of the whole world, an act forcing all its false friends, the radical bourgeoisie, the democrats and humanitarians, to show themselves in their true colours, as enemies to the ultimate ends for which it was prepared to live and die. He went further than this: he recognised the replacement of the *bourgeois* state by the Commune as that transitional form of social structure by passing through which alone the workers could gain their ultimate emancipation. The state is revealed as the embodiment of 'the civilisation and justice of the *bourgeois* order', legalising parliamentarism which, once challenged by its victims, 'stands forth as undisguised savagery and lawless revenge'. The state must therefore be destroyed root and branch. To this extent he once more, as in 1850 and 1852, retracted the doctrine of the *Communist Manifesto*, which had asserted, as against the French Utopians and early anarchists, that the immediate end of the revolution was not to destroy, but to seize the state ('the proletariat will . . . centralise all instruments of production in the hands of the state') and make use of it to liquidate the enemy.

While he approved many of the measures of the Commune, he blamed it for not being ruthless and radical enough: nor did he believe in its aim of creating immediate social and economic equality. 'Right can never be higher', he wrote some years afterwards, 'than the economic structure of society and the cultural development thereby determined.' These cannot be transformed overnight.

His pamphlet, later entitled *The Civil War in France*, was not primarily intended as a historical study: it was a tactical move, and one of typical audacity and intransigence. Marx was sometimes blamed by his own followers for allowing the International to be linked in the popular mind with a band of law-breakers and assassins, an association which earned for it an unnecessarily sinister reputation. This was not the kind of consideration which could have influenced him in the slightest degree. He was, all his life, a convinced and uncompromising believer in a violent working-class revolution. The Commune was the first spontaneous rising of the workers in their capacity as workers: the June *émeute* of 1848 was, in his view, an attack on, and not by, them. The Commune was not directly inspired by Marx. He regarded it, indeed, as a political blunder: his adversaries the Blanquists and Proudhonists predominated in it to the end; and yet its significance in his eyes was immense. Before it there had indeed been many scattered streams of socialist thought and action; but this rising, with its world repercussions, the great effect which it was bound to have upon the workers of all lands, was the first event of the new era. The men who had died in it and for it were the first martyrs of international socialism; their blood would be the seed of the new proletarian faith: whatever the tragic faults and shortcomings of the Communards, they were as nothing before the magnitude of the historical role which these men had played, the position which they were destined to occupy in the tradition of proletarian revolution.

By coming forward to pay them open homage he achieved what he intended to achieve: he helped to create a heroic legend of socialism. Engels, when asked to define the 'dictatorship of the proletariat', had pointed to the Commune as the closest realisation to date of this conception. More than thirty years later Lenin defended the Moscow rising, which occurred during the abortive Russian revolution of 1905, against the criticisms of Plekhanov, by quoting the attitude of Marx towards the Commune: by pointing out that the emotional and symbolic value of the memory of a great heroic outburst, however ill conceived, however damaging in its immediate results, was an infinitely greater and more permanent asset to a revolutionary movement than the realisation of its futility at a moment when what matters most is not to write accurate history, or even to learn its lessons, but to make it.

The publication of the address embarrassed and shocked many members of the International and hastened its ultimate dissolution. Marx attempted to forestall reproaches by revealing his name as the sole author of the work. 'The Red Terror Doctor', as he was now popularly known, became overnight the object of public odium: anonymous letters began to arrive, his life was several times threatened. Jubilantly he wrote to Engels: 'It is doing me good after twenty long and boring years of idyllic isolation like a frog in a swamp. The government organ—the

Observer—is even threatening me with prosecution. Let them try it. I snap my fingers at the *canaille*!' The hubbub died down, but the damage done to the International was permanent: it became indissolubly connected in the minds both of the police and of the general public with the outrages of the Commune. A blow was dealt to the alliance of the English trade-union leaders with the International, which was, in any case, from their point of view entirely opportunist, based on its usefulness in promoting specific union interests. The unions were at this time being strongly wooed by the Liberal Party with promises of support upon these very issues. The prospect of a peaceful and respectable conquest of power made them less than ever anxious to be associated with a notorious revolutionary conspiracy; their sole end was to raise the standard of living and the social and political status of the skilled workers whom they represented. They did not look upon themselves as a political party, and if they subscribed to the programme of the International, this was due partly to a degree of elasticity in its statutes, which skilfully avoided committing its members to openly revolutionary ends, but most of all to their haziness on political issues. This fact was well appreciated by the Government, which, in reply to a circular from the Spanish Government demanding the suppression of the International, replied in the person of the Foreign Secretary, Lord Granville, that in England they felt no danger of armed insurrection: the English members were peaceful men, solely occupied in labour negotiations, and gave the Government no ground for apprehension. Marx himself was bitterly aware of the truth of this: even Harney and Jones were in his eyes preferable to the men he now had to deal with, solid trade-union officials like Odger, or Cremer or Applegarth, who distrusted foreigners, cared little for events outside their country, and took little interest in ideas.

No meetings of the International having been held in 1870–1, a meeting was convened in London in 1872. The most important proposal brought up by this Congress, that the working class henceforth cease to rely in the political struggle upon the assistance of bourgeois parties, and form a party of their own, was, after a stormy debate, carried by the votes of the English delegates. The new political party was not set up during Marx's lifetime, but, in idea at least, the Labour party was born at this meeting, and may be regarded as Marx's greatest single contribution to the internal history of his adopted land. At the same congress the English delegates insisted on, and won, the right to form a separate local organisation instead of, as before, being represented by the General Council. This displeased and frightened Marx: it was a gesture of distrust, almost of rebellion; at once he suspected the machinations of Bakunin, whom the recent events in France had put in a proud and ecstatic mood, since he felt that they were overwhelmingly due to his personal influence. A large part of Paris was destroyed by fire during the Commune: this fire seemed to him a symbol of his own life, and a magnificent realisation of his favourite paradox: 'The passion for destruction, too, is a creative passion.'

Marx neither understood nor wished to understand the emotional basis of Bakunin's acts and declarations: the influence of this 'Mahomet without a Koran' was a menace to the movement, and must consequently be destroyed.

'The International was founded', he wrote in 1871, 'in order to replace the socialist and semi-socialist sects with a genuine organisation of the working class for its struggle . . . Socialist sectarianism and a real working-class movement are in inverse ratio to each other. Sects have a right to exist only so long as the working class is not mature enough to have an independent movement of its own: as soon as that moment arrives sectarianism becomes reactionary . . . The history of the International is a ceaseless battle of the General Council against dilettantist experiments and sects . . . Towards the end of 1868 the International was joined by Bakunin whose purpose it was to create an International within the International, and to place himself at its head. For M. Bakunin, his doctrine (an absurd patchwork composed of bits and pieces of views taken from Proudhon, Saint-Simon, etc.) was, and still is, something of secondary importance, serving him only as a means of acquiring personal influence and power. But if Bakunin, as a theorist, is nothing, Bakunin, the intriguer, has attained to the highest peak of his profession . . . As for his political non-participation, every movement in which the working class as such is opposed to the ruling classes, and exercises pressure upon it from without, is *eo ipso* a political movement . . . but when the workers' organisation is not so highly developed that it can afford to risk decisive engagement with the dominant political power—then it must be prepared for this by ceaseless agitation against the crimes and follies of the ruling class. Otherwise it becomes a plaything in its hands, as was demonstrated by the September revolution in France, and, to some extent, by the recent successes in England of Gladstone & Co.'

Bakunin at this period had entered upon the last and strangest phase of his bizarre existence. He had fallen under the spell of a young Russian terrorist, Nechaev, whose audacity and freedom from scruple he found irresistible. Nechaev, who believed in blackmail and intimidation as essential revolutionary methods justified by their end, had written an anonymous letter to the agent of the prospective publisher of Bakunin's Russian version of *Das Kapital*, threatening him in general but violent terms if he should continue to force his wretched hackwork upon men of genius, or pester Bakunin for the return of the advance which had been paid him. The frightened and infuriated agent sent the letter to Marx. It is doubtful whether the evidence of the intrigues conducted by Bakunin's organisation, the Democratic Alliance, would in itself have been sufficient to secure his expulsion, since he numbered many personal supporters at the Congress; but the report of the committee instructed to look into this scandal, and the dramatic production of the Nechaev letter, turned the scale. After long and stormy sessions, in the course of which even the Proudhonists had finally been persuaded that no party could preserve its unity while Bakunin was in its ranks, he and his closest associates were expelled by a small majority.

Marx's next proposal also came as a bombshell to the uninitiated members of the Congress: it was to transfer the seat of the Council to the United States. Everyone realised that this was tantamount to the dissolution of the International. America was not merely infinitely distant from European affairs, but insignificant in the affairs of the International. The French delegates declared that one might as well remove it to the moon. Marx gave no explicit reason for this proposal, which was formally moved by Engels, but its purpose must have been clear enough to all those present. He could not operate without the loyal and unquestioned obedience of at least some sections of the body over which he ruled: England had seceded; he had thought of moving the Council to Belgium, but there, too, the anti-Marxist element was becoming formidable; in Germany the government would suppress it; France, Switzerland and Holland were far from reliable; Italy and Spain were definitely Bakuninist strongholds. Sooner than face a bitter struggle which could end at best in a Pyrrhic victory and destroy all hope of a proletarian unity for many generations, Marx decided, after ensuring that it did not fall into Bakuninists' hands, to allow the International to die in peace.

His critics claim that he judged the merit of all socialist

assemblies solely by the degree to which he was himself permitted to control them: this equation was certainly made both by him and by Engels, and made quite automatically; neither ever showed any sign of understanding the bewildered indignation which this attitude excited among broad sections of their followers. Marx attended the Hague congress in person, and his prestige was such that, in spite of violent opposition, the Congress finally by a narrow majority voted its own virtual extinction. Its later meetings were travesties: it finally expired in Philadelphia in 1876. The International was, indeed, reconstituted thirteen years later, but by that time—a period of rapidly increasing socialist activity in all countries—its character was very different. Despite its explicitly revolutionary aims, it was more parliamentary, more respectable, more optimistic, essentially conciliatory in temper, more than half committed to the belief in the inevitability of the gradual evolution of capitalist society into moderate socialism under persistent but peaceful pressure from below.

11

Last Years

I remarked [to Marx] that as I grew older I became more tolerant.
'Do you,' he said, '*do* you?'

H. M. HYNDMAN, *Record of an Adventurous Life*

THE duel with Bakunin is the last public episode in Marx's life.
The revolution seemed dead everywhere, although its embers
glowed faintly in Russia and Spain. The reaction was once more
triumphant, in a milder form, indeed, than in the days of his
youth, prepared to make definite concessions to its adversary, but
appearing to possess all the more stability for that reason. The
peaceful conquest of political and economic control seemed the
workers' best hope of emancipation. The prestige of Lassalle's
followers in Germany rose steadily, and Liebknecht, who represented the Marxist opposition, now that the International was
dead, was inclined to come to terms with them, in order to form a
single united party. He was persuaded that, placed as he was inside
Germany, he had a better grasp of the tactical exigencies than
Marx and Engels, who continued to live in England and would
not listen to any suggestion of compromise. The two parties
finally held a conference at Gotha in 1875 and formed an alliance,
issuing a common programme composed by the leaders of both
factions. It was naturally submitted to Marx for approval. He left
no doubt as to the impression which it made on him.

A violently worded attack was instantly dispatched to
Liebknecht in Berlin and Engels was commanded to write in a
similar strain. Marx accused his disciples of straying into the use
of the misleading, half-meaningless terminology inherited from
Lassalle and the True Socialists, interspersed with vague liberal
phrases which he had spent half his life in exposing and eliminating. The programme itself seemed to him to be permeated by the
spirit of compromise—especially in accepting the permanent
compatibility with socialism of their worst enemy, the state—and
to rest on a belief in the possibility of attaining social justice by

peacefully agitating for such trivial ends as a 'just' remuneration for labour, and the abolition of the law of inheritance—Proudhonist and Saint-Simonian remedies for this or that abuse, calculated to prop up the state and the capitalist system rather than hasten their collapse. In the form of angry marginal notes he conveyed for the last time his own conception of what the programme of a militant socialist party ought to be. The loyal Liebknecht received this, as everything else which came from London, meekly, and even reverently, but made no use of it. The alliance continued and grew in strength. Two years later Liebknecht was again sharply criticised by Engels, who took an even lower view than Marx of his political capacity. On this occasion the cause was the appearance in the pages of the official organ of the German Social Democratic party of articles by, and in support of, a certain Eugen Dühring, a radical lecturer on economics in the University of Berlin, a man of violently anti-capitalist but hardly socialist views, who was acquiring growing influence in the ranks of the German party. Against him Engels published his longest and most comprehensive work, the last written in collaboration with Marx; it contained an authoritative version of the materialist view of history, expounded in the blunt, vigorous, lucid prose which Engels wrote with great facility. *Anti-Dühring*, as it came to be called, is an attack on the undialectical, positivistic materialism, then increasingly popular among scientific writers and journalists, which maintained that all natural phenomena could be interpreted in terms of the motion of matter in space, and advances against it the principle of the universal working of the dialectical principle far beyond the categories of human history, in the realms of biology, physics and mathematics. Engels was a versatile and well-read man, and had, by sheer industry, acquired some rudimentary knowledge of these subjects, but his discussions of them are not illuminating. In particular such over-ambitious attempts as the discovery of the working of the triad of the Hegelian dialectic in the mathematical rule by which the product of two negative quantities is positive, has proved a source of embarrassment to later Marxists, who have found themselves saddled with the impossible task of defending an eccentric view not entailed by anything that Marx himself had ever asserted, at any rate in his published writings. Marxist biology and mathematics of our own day are subjects which, like Cartesian physics, form a peculiar and isolated enclave in the development of a great intellectual movement, of antiquarian rather than scientific interest. More important, Engels's version of the materialist conception of history, while it faithfully develops Marx's attack on liberal or idealist historiography, is more mechanistic and crudely determinist than most of Marx's writings on the subject, especially in his early years. In this Engels, perhaps because he wrote so clearly, was followed by the overwhelming majority of Marxist writers, with Kautsky and Plekhanov at their head, for more than half a century. Perhaps when Marx, towards the end of his life, declared (he was thinking of his French disciples) that whatever else he might be, he was above all not a Marxist, he had such popularisations in view. The most readable are the chapters later reprinted as a pamphlet under the title *Socialism: Utopian and Scientific*. That is written in Engels's best vein, and gives a somewhat Darwinian account of the growth of Marxism from its origins in German idealism, French political theory and English economic science. It is the best brief autobiographical appreciation of Marxism by one of its creators, and has had a decisive influence on both Russian and German socialism.

The attack on the Gotha Programme was Marx's last violent intervention in the affairs of the party. No similar crisis occurred again in his lifetime, and he was left free to devote his remaining years to theoretical studies and vain attempts to restore his failing health. He had moved from Kentish Town first to one, then to another home in Haverstock Hill, not far from Engels, who had sold his share in the family business to his partner, and had established himself in London in a large, commodious house in St John's Wood. A year or two before this he had settled a permanent annuity on Marx, which, modest though it was, enabled him to pursue his work in peace. They saw each other nearly every day, and together carried on an immense correspondence with socialists in every land, by many of whom they had come to be regarded with increasing respect and veneration. Marx was now without question the supreme moral and intellectual authority of international socialism; Lassalle and Proudhon had died in the sixties, Bakunin in 1876. The death of his last great enemy evoked no public comment from Marx: perhaps because his harsh obituary notice of Proudhon in a German newspaper had caused a wave of indignation among the French socialists, and he thought it more tactful to remain silent. His sentiments towards his adversaries, living and dead, had not altered, but he was physically less capable of the active campaigns of his youth and middle years;

overwork and a life of poverty had finally undermined his strength; he was tired, and often ill, and began to be preoccupied by his health. Every year, generally accompanied by his younger daughter Eleanor, he would visit the English seaside, or a German or Bohemian spa, where he would occasionally meet old friends and followers, who sometimes brought with them young historians or economists anxious to meet the celebrated revolutionary.

He rarely spoke of himself or of his life, and never about his origin. The fact that he was a Jew neither he nor Engels ever directly mentioned; there are, at most, two oblique indications of this fact in Marx's writings. His references to individual Jews, particularly in his letters to Engels, were virulent to a degree: his origin was evidently a personal stigma which he was unable to avoid pointing out in others; his denial of the importance of national or religious applications, his emphasis upon the international character of the proletariat, takes on a peculiar sharpness of tone. His impatience and irritability increased with old age, and he took care to avoid the society of men who bored him or disagreed with his views. He became more and more difficult in his personal relations; he broke off all connection with one of his oldest friends, the poet Freiligrath, after his patriotic odes in 1870; he deliberately insulted his devoted adherent Kugelmann, a German physician, to whom some of his most interesting letters were written, because the latter insisted on joining him in Karlsbad after he had made it clear that he wished for no company. On the other hand, when he was tactfully approached, his behaviour could be friendly and even gracious, particularly to the young revolutionaries and radical journalists who came to London in growing numbers to pay homage to the two old men. Such pilgrims were agreeably received at his house, and through them he established contacts with his followers in countries with which he had had no previous relations, notably with Russia, where a vigorous and well-disciplined revolutionary movement had at last taken root. His economic writings, and in particular *Das Kapital*, had had a greater success in Russia than in any other country: the censorship—ironically enough—permitted its publication on the ground that 'although the book has a pronounced socialist tendency . . . it is not written in a popular style . . . and is unlikely to find many readers among the general public'. The reviews of it in the Russian Press were more favourable and more intelligent than any others, a fact which surprised and pleased him, and did much to change his contemptuous attitude to 'the Russian clodhoppers' into admiration for the new generation of austere and fearless revolutionaries whom his own writings had done so much to educate.

The history of Marxism in Russia is unlike its history in any other country. Whereas in Germany and in France, unlike other forms of positivism and materialism, it was primarily a proletarian movement, marking a sharp revulsion of feeling against the ineffectiveness of the liberal idealism of the bourgeoisie in the first half of the century, and represented a mood of deflationary realism, in Russia, where the proletariat was still weak and insignificant by western standards, not only the apostles of Marxism but the majority of its converts were middle-class intellectuals for whom it itself became a kind of romanticism, a belated form of democratic passion. It grew during the height of the populist movement, which preached the need for personal self-identification with the people and their material needs, in order to understand them, educate them, and raise their intellectual and social level, and was thus equally directed against the reactionary anti-western party with its mystical faith in autocracy, the Orthodox Church and the Slav genius on the one hand, and the mild agrarian liberalism or socialism of the pro-westerners, such as Turgenev and Herzen, on the other.

This was the time when well-to-do young men in Moscow and St Petersburg, notably the 'penitent' young noblemen and squires, ridden by social guilt, threw away career and position in order to immerse themselves in the study of the condition of peasants and factory workers, and went to live amongst them with the same noble fervour with which their fathers and grandfathers had followed Bakunin or the Decembrists. Historical and political materialism—emphasis on concrete, tangible, economic reality as the basis of social and individual life, criticism of institutions and of individual actions in terms of their relation to, and influence upon, the material welfare of the popular masses, hatred and scorn of art or life pursued for their own sake, isolated from the sufferings of the world in an ivory tower—were preached with a self-forgetful passion: 'A pair of boots is something more important than all the plays of Shakespeare,' said a celebrated radical materialist, and expressed a general mood. In these men Marxism produced a sense of liberation from doubts and confusions, by offering for the first time a systematic exposition of the nature and laws of development of society in clear, material terms: its very flatness seemed sane and lucid after the romantic nationalism of the Slavophiles and the mystery and grandeur of Hegelian idealism, and, finally, the failure in practice of revolutionary populism. This general effect resembled the feeling induced in Marx himself after reading Feuerbach forty years before: it aroused the same sense of the finality of its solution and of the limitless possibility of action on its basis. Russia had not experienced the horrors of 1849, its development lagged far behind that of the west, its problems in the seventies and eighties in many respects resembled those which had faced the rest of Europe half a century before. The Russian radicals read the *Communist Manifesto* and the declamatory passages of *Das Kapital* with the sense of exhilaration with which men had read Rousseau in the previous century; they found much which applied exceptionally well to their own condition: nowhere was it as true as in Russia that 'in agriculture as in manufacture the capitalist transformation of the process of production signifies the martyrdom of the producer; the instrument of labour becomes the means of subjugating, exploiting and impoverishing the worker; the social combination and organisation of the labour process functions as an elaborate method for crushing the worker's individual vitality, freedom and independence'. Only in Russia the method, particularly after the liberation of the serfs had enormously enlarged the labour market, was not elaborate, but simple.

To his own surprise, Marx found that the nation against which he had written and spoken for thirty years provided him with the most fearless and intelligent of his disciples. He welcomed them in his home in London, and entered into a regular correspondence with Danielson, his translator, and Sieber, one of the ablest of Russian academic economists. Marx's analyses were largely concerned with industrial societies; Russia was an agrarian state and any attempt at direct application of a doctrine designed for one set of conditions to another was bound to lead to errors in theory and practice. Letters reached him from Danielson in Russia, and from the exiles Lavrov and Vera Zasulich, begging him to apply himself to the specific problems presented by the peculiar organisation of the Russian peasants into primitive communes, holding lands in common, and in particular to state his view on propositions derived from Herzen and Bakunin and widely accepted by Russian radicals, which asserted that a direct transition was possible from such primitive communes to developed communism, without the necessity of passing through the intermediate stage of industrialism and urbanisation, as had happened in the west. Marx, who had previously treated this hypothesis with contempt as emanating from sentimental Slavophile ideal- isation of the peasants disguised as radicalism—combined with the childish belief that it was 'possible to cheat the dialectic by an audacious leap, to avoid the natural stages of evolution or shuffle them out of the world by decrees'—was by now sufficiently impressed by the intelligence, seriousness, and, above all, the fanatical and devoted socialism of the new generation of Russian revolutionaries to re-examine the issue. In order to do this he began to learn Russian; at the end of six months he had mastered it sufficiently to read sociological works[1] and government reports which his friends succeeded in smuggling to London. Engels viewed this new alliance with some distaste: he had an incurable aversion to everything east of the Elbe, and he suspected Marx of inventing a new occupation, in order to conceal from himself his reluctance, due to sheer physical weariness, to complete the writ- ing of *Das Kapital*. After duly tunnelling his way through an immense mass of statistical and historical material, Marx made considerable doctrinal concessions. He admitted[2] that if a revolu- tion in Russia should be the signal of a common rising of the entire European proletariat, it was conceivable, and even likely, that communism in Russia could be based directly upon the semi- feudal communal ownership of land by the village as it existed at the time; but this could not occur if capitalism continued among her nearest neighbours, since this would inevitably force Russia in sheer economic self-defence along the path already traversed by the more advanced countries of the west.

The Russians were not alone, however, in paying homage to the London exiles. Young leaders of the new united German social democratic party, Bebel, Bernstein, Kautsky, visited him and consulted him on all important issues. His two eldest daughters had married French socialists and kept him in touch with Latin countries. The founder of French social democracy, Jules Guesde, submitted the programme of his party to him, and had it drastically revised. Marxism began to oust Bakuninist anarchism in Italy and Switzerland. Encouraging reports came

---

[1] e.g. by Chernyshevsky, for whom he expressed his admiration, and by Flerovsky.

[2] In a letter left unpublished by Plekhanov, who evidently thought that it was a dangerous concession to populism. It saw the light only some years after the October Revolution.

from the United States. The best news of all came from Germany, where the socialist vote, in spite of Bismarck's anti-socialist laws, was mounting with prodigious speed. The only major European country which continued to stand aloof, virtually impervious to his teaching, was that in which he himself lived and of which he spoke as his second home. 'In England', he wrote, 'prolonged prosperity has demoralised the workers . . . the ultimate aim of this most bourgeois of lands would seem to be the establishment of a bourgeois aristocracy and a bourgeois proletariat side by side with the bourgeoisie . . . the revolutionary energy of the British workers has oozed away . . . it will take long before they can shake off their bourgeois infection . . . they totally lack the mettle of the old Chartists.' He had no intimate English friends—he had known Ernest Jones, he worked with a good many labour leaders, he was visited by radicals such as Belfort Bax, Crompton, Johnstone and Ray Lankester, he even accepted an invitation to his club from such a member of the ruling class as Sir Mountstuart Elphinstone Grant Duff, a member of Parliament of independent views, and his friend the publisher Leonard Montefiore. But such meetings touched the barest surface of his life. He did indeed, in the last years of his life, allow himself to be wooed for a brief period by H. M. Hyndman, the founder of the Social Democratic Federation, who did much to popularise Marxism in England. Hyndman was an agreeable, easy going, expansive individual, a genuine radical by temperament, an amusing and effective speaker, and a lively writer on political and economic subjects. A light-hearted amateur himself, he enjoyed meeting and talking to men of genius, and, being somewhat indiscriminate in his taste, presently abandoned Mazzini for Marx. He thus described him in his memoirs: 'The first impression of Marx as I saw him was that of a powerful, shaggy, untamed old man, ready, not to say eager, to enter into conflict, and rather suspicious himself of immediate attack; yet his greeting of us was cordial . . . When speaking with fierce indignation of the policy of the Liberal Party, especially in regard to Ireland, the old warrior's brows wrinkled, the broad, strong nose and face were obviously moved by passion, and he poured out a stream of vigorous denunciation which displayed alike the heat of his temperament, and the marvellous command he possessed over our language. The contrast between his manner and utterance when thus deeply stirred by anger, and his attitude when giving his views on the economic events of the period, was very marked. He turned from the role of prophet and violent denunciator to that of the calm philosopher without any apparent effort, and I felt that many a long year might pass before I ceased to be a student in the presence of a master.'

Hyndman's sincerity, his naïvety, his affable and disarming manner, and above all his whole-hearted and uncritical admiration for Marx, whom, with typical ineptitude, he called 'the Aristotle of the nineteenth century', caused the latter to treat him for some months with marked friendliness and indulgence. The inevitable breach occurred over Hyndman's book, *England for All*, a most readable, if not very accurate, account of Marxism in English. The debt to Marx was not acknowledged by name, a fact which Hyndman lamely tried to explain on the ground that 'the English don't like being taught by foreigners, and your name is so much detested here . . .'. This was sufficient. Marx held violent opinions on plagiarism: Lassalle had been made to suffer for far less; moreover, he had no wish to be associated with Hyndman's own confused ideas. He broke off the connection at once and with it his last remaining link with English socialism.

His mode of life had scarcely changed at all. He rose at seven, drank several cups of black coffee, and then retired to his study where he read and wrote until two in the afternoon. After hurrying through his meal he worked again till supper, which he ate with his family. After that he took an evening walk on Hampstead Heath, or returned to his study, where he worked until two or three in the morning. His son-in-law, Paul Lafargue, has left a description of this room:

'It was on the first floor and well lighted by a broad window looking on the park. The fireplace was opposite the window, and was flanked by bookshelves, on the top of which packets of newspapers and manuscripts were piled up to the ceiling. On one side of the window stood two tables, likewise loaded with miscellaneous papers, newspapers and books. In the middle of the room was a small plain writing-table, and a windsor chair. Between this chair and one of the bookshelves was a leather-covered sofa on which Marx would lie down and rest occasionally. On the mantelpiece were more books interspersed with cigars, boxes of matches, tobacco jars, paperweights and photographs—his daughters, his wife, Engels, Wilhelm Wolff . . . He would never allow anyone to arrange his books and papers . . . but he could put his hand on any book or manuscript he wanted. When conversing he would often stop for a moment to show the relevant passage in a book or to find a reference . . . He disdained appearances when arranging his books. Quarto and octavo volumes and pamphlets were placed higgledy-piggledy so far as size and shape were concerned. He had scant respect for their form or binding, the beauty of page or of printing: he would turn down the corners of pages, underline freely and pencil the margins. He did not actually annotate his books, but he could not refrain from a question mark or note of exclamation when the author went too far. Every year he re-read his notebooks and underlined passages to refresh his memory . . . which was vigorous and accurate: he had trained it in accordance with Hegel's plan of memorising verse in an unfamiliar tongue.'

Sundays he dedicated to his children: and when these grew up and married, to his grandchildren. The entire family had nicknames; his daughters were Qui-Qui, Quo-Quo, and Tussy; his wife was Möhme; he himself was known as the Moor or Old Nick on account of his dark complexion and sinister appearance. His relations with his family remained—even with the difficult Eleanor—warmly affectionate. The Russian sociologist Kovalevsky, who used to visit him in his last years, was pleasantly surprised by his urbanity. 'Marx is usually described', he wrote many years later, 'as a gloomy and arrogant man, who flatly rejected all bourgeois science and culture. In reality he was a well-educated, highly cultivated Anglo-German gentleman, a man whose close association with Heine had developed in him a vein of cheerful satire, and one who was full of the joy of life, thanks to the fact that his personal position was extremely comfortable.' This vignette of Marx as a gay and genial host, if not wholly convincing, at any rate conveys the contrast with the early years in Soho. His chief pleasures were reading and walking. He was fond of poetry and knew long passages of Dante, Aeschylus and Shakespeare by heart. His admiration for Shakespeare was limitless, and the whole household was brought up on him: he was read aloud, acted, discussed constantly. Whatever Marx did, he did methodically. Finding on arrival that his English was inadequate, he set himself to improve it by making a list of Shakespeare's turns of phrase: these he then learnt by heart. Similarly, having learnt Russian, he read the works of Gogol and Pushkin, carefully underlining the words whose meaning he did not know. He had a sound German literary taste, acquired early in his youth, and developed by reading and re-reading his favourite works. To distract himself he read the elder Dumas or Scott, or light French novels of the day; Balzac he admired prodigiously: he looked upon him as having provided in his novels the acutest analysis of the bourgeois society of his day; many of his characters did not, he declared, come to full maturity until after the death of their creator, in the sixties and seventies. He had intended to write a study of Balzac as a social analyst, but never began it. (In view of the quality of the only extant piece of literary criticism from his pen, that of Eugène Sue, the loss may not be one to mourn.) His taste in literature, for all his love of reading, was, on the whole, undistinguished and commonplace. There is nothing to indicate that he liked either painting or music; all was extruded by his passion for books.

He had always read enormously, but towards the end of his life his appetite increased to a degree at which it interfered with his creative work. In his last ten years he began to acquire completely new languages: thus he tried to learn Turkish, for the ostensible purpose of studying agrarian conditions in that country: it may be that as an old Urquhartite he laid his hopes on the Turkish peasantry which he expected to become a disruptive, demo-cratising force in the Near East. As his bibliomania grew, Engels's worst fears became confirmed; he wrote less and less, and aban-doned all effort to order the mountain of chaotic manuscript notes, on which the second and third volumes of *Das Kapital*, edited by Engels, and the supplementary studies which form the fourth volume, edited by Kautsky, were based. There is a great deal in them in no wise inferior to the first volume, which alone became a classic.

Physically he was declining fast. In 1881 Jenny Marx died of cancer after a long and painful illness. 'With her the Moor has died too,' Engels said to Marx's favourite daughter Eleanor. Marx lived for two more years, still carrying on an extensive cor-respondence with Italians, Spaniards, Russians, but his strength was virtually spent. In 1882, after a particularly severe winter, his doctor sent him to Algiers to recuperate. He arrived with acute pleurisy which he had caught on the journey. He spent a month in North Africa which was uncommonly cold and wet, and returned to Europe ill and exhausted. After some weeks of vain wandering from town to town on the French Riviera in search of the sun, he went to Paris, where he stayed for a time with his eldest daughter Jenny Longuet. Not long after his return to London, news came of her sudden death. He never fully recovered from this blow: he fell ill in the following year, developed an abscess in the lung, and on 14 March 1883 died in his sleep, seated in an armchair in his study. He was buried in Highgate cemetery and laid next to his wife. There were not many present: members of his family, a few personal friends, and workers' representatives from several lands. A dignified and moving funeral address was delivered by Engels, who spoke of his achievements and his character:

'His mission in life was to contribute in one way or another to the overthrow of capitalist society . . . to contribute to the liberation of the present-day proletariat which he was the first to make conscious of its own position and its needs, of the conditions under which it could win its freedom. Fighting was his element. And he fought with a passion, a tenacity and a success which few could rival . . . and consequently was the best-hated and most calumniated man of his time . . . he died, beloved, revered and mourned by millions of revolutionary fellow workers from the mines of Siberia to the coasts of California, in all points of Europe and America . . . his name and his work will endure through the ages.'

His death passed largely unnoticed among the general public; *The Times* did, indeed, print a brief and inaccurate obituary notice, but this, although he died in London, appeared as a message from its Paris correspondent, who reported what he had read in the French Socialist Press. His fame increased steadily after his death as the revolutionary effects of his teaching became more and more apparent. As an individual he never captured the imagination either of the public or of professional biographers as greatly as his more sensitive or more romantic contemporaries; and indeed Carlyle, Mill, Herzen were more tragic figures, tormented by intellectual and moral conflicts which Marx neither experienced nor understood, and far more profoundly affected by the *malaise* of their generation. They have left a bitter and minute account of it, better written and more vivid than anything to be found in the writings, public or private, of either Marx or Engels. Marx fought against the mean and cynical society of his time, which seemed to him to vulgarise and degrade every human relationship, with a hatred no less profound. But his mind was made of stronger and cruder texture; he was insensitive, self-confident, and strong-willed; the causes of his unhappiness lay outside him—they were poverty, sickness, and the triumph of the enemy. His inner life seems uncomplicated and secure. He saw the world in simple terms of black and white; those who were not with him were against him. He knew upon whose side he was, his life was spent in fighting for it, he knew that it must ultimately win. Such crises of faith as occurred in the lives of the gentler spirits among his friends—the painful self-examination of such men as Hess or Heine—received from him no sympathy. He may have looked upon them as so many signs of bourgeois degeneracy, which took the form of morbid attention to private emotional states, or still worse, the exploitation of social unrest for some personal or artistic end—frivolity and irresponsible self-indulgence, reprehensible in men before whose eyes the greatest battle in human history was being fought. This uncompromising sternness towards personal feeling and almost religious insistence on a self-sacrificing discipline, was inherited by his successors, and imitated by his enemies in every land. It distinguishes his true descendants among his followers and his adversaries from tolerant liberalism in every sphere.

Others before him had preached a war between classes, but it was he who conceived and successfully put into practice a plan designed to achieve the political organisation of a class fighting solely for its interests as a class—and in so doing transformed the entire character of political parties and political warfare. Yet in his own eyes and in those of his contemporaries he appeared as first and foremost an economic theorist. The classical premises on which his economic doctrines rest, and his own development of them, have entered subsequent discussion as one view among many, dismissed by some as superseded, to be revived and defended by others; yet they can scarcely be said to have occupied the centre of the stage of economic theory at any time. The doctrine which has had a greater and more lasting influence both on opinion and on action than any other system of ideas put forward in modern times, is his theory of the evolution and structure of capitalist society, of which he nowhere gave a detailed exposition. This theory, by asserting that the most important question to be asked with regard to any phenomenon is concerned with the relation which it bears to the economic structure, that is, the relations of economic power in the social structure of which it is an expression, has created new tools of criticism and research the development and use of which has altered the nature and direction of the social sciences in our generation. All those whose work rests on social observation are necessarily affected. Not only conflicting classes and groups and movements and their leaders in every country, but historians and sociologists, psychologists and political scientists, critics and creative artists, so far as they try to analyse the changing quality of the life of their society, owe the form of their ideas in large part to the work of Karl Marx. Almost a century has passed since its completion, and during these years it has received more than its due share of praise and blame. Exaggeration and over-simple application of its main principles have done much to obscure its meaning, and many blunders (to call them by no harsher name), both of theory and of practice, have been committed in its name. Nevertheless its effect was, and continues to be, revolutionary.

It set out to refute the proposition that ideas decisively determine the course of history, but the very extent of its own influence on human affairs has weakened the force of its thesis. For in altering the hitherto prevailing view of the relation of the individual to his environment and to his fellows, it has palpably altered that relation itself; and in consequence remains the most powerful among the intellectual forces which are today permanently transforming the ways in which men act and think.

Guide to Further Reading

by

Terrell Carver

I have compiled this Guide primarily for the English-speaking student, covering MAJOR COLLECTIONS of works by Marx and Engels, SMALL COLLECTIONS AND INDIVIDUAL WORKS, BIOGRAPHY AND REMINISCENCE, and CRITICAL STUDIES. All books listed in these sections were in print in the U.K. or U.S.A. at some time during the period 1970–7 unless otherwise noted. Where two publishers are listed, the first is British and the second American; where only one publisher is mentioned, I give place of publication if outside the British Isles. Dates are those of the most recent edition or reprint. My purpose has been to provide a guide to recent writings rather than to compile a conventional list of works, many of which would necessarily be outdated.

For the more advanced student I have appended a section on SCHOLARLY EDITIONS, BIBLIOGRAPHIES, AND JOURNALS.

MAJOR COLLECTIONS

The publication of the *Collected Works* of Karl Marx and Frederick (originally Friedrich) Engels was begun in 1975 by Lawrence & Wishart and International Publishers, with Progress Publishers of Moscow. The 7 volumes which have already appeared include English translations of published and unpublished works, letters, manuscript materials, and documents of biographical interest dating from 1835 to 1848. When the edition is complete there will be approximately 50 volumes containing 'all the extant works of Marx and Engels published in their lifetime and a considerable part of their legacy of manuscripts', together with 'all the letters of Marx and Engels that have been discovered by the time the volumes appear' (vol. 1, pp. xix–xx). At the end of each volume there are notes and then indexes of names, quoted and mentioned literature, and subjects covered. This apparatus is invaluable and makes the edition exceptionally easy to use.

The Marx Library (begun in 1973 by Allen Lane/Penguin in conjunction with *New Left Review* and by Random House/Vintage in conjunction with *Monthly Review*) offers a particularly interesting selection of Marx's works, though the arrangement is topical rather than strictly chronological. Marx's celebrated 'Economic and Philosophical Manuscripts (1844)' appear in the Marx Library volume *Early Writings*, together with various works and letters of the period 1843–4. The 1845 theses 'Concerning Feuerbach', and the 1859 'Preface (to *A Contribution to the Critique of Political Economy*)' round out the collection. The 1857–8 rough drafts for Marx's *magnum opus*, his critique of political economy, were published in 1973 in the first complete English translation as the *Grundrisse*, now uniform with the Marx Library edition of the first volume of *Capital* in a new translation. The latter includes an English translation of a manuscript chapter, 'Results of the Immediate Process of Production'. New translations of volumes 2 and 3 of *Capital* are promised by the publishers.

The Marx Library includes three volumes of political writings, translated into English or transcribed from Marx's own English text. *The Revolutions of 1848* contains the 'Manifesto of the Communist Party' and speeches and articles by Marx and Engels dating from 1847 to 1850. *Surveys from Exile* includes Marx's 'The Class Struggles in France: 1848 to 1850', 'The Eighteenth Brumaire of Louis Bonaparte', and articles on British domestic and imperial politics and the American civil war. Marx's 'The Civil War in France', his 'Conspectus' on Bakunin, and the 'Critique of the Gotha Programme' appear in *The First International and After*, as well as letters and documents of the period 1864–70.

The introductions by Lucio Colletti, David Fernbach, Ernest Mandel, and Martin Nicolaus in the Marx Library volumes are of particular interest.

SMALL COLLECTIONS AND INDIVIDUAL WORKS

Karl Marx: Selected Writings (Oxford University Press, Oxford and New York, 1977) contains a comprehensive selection of works and extracts edited by David McLellan. The one-volume

Selected Works of Marx and Engels, published by Lawrence & Wishart and International (1975), remains a useful basic collection, though new translations of corrected texts have largely superseded these selections. Some of the English translations in this collection are now of historical interest, since they were influential in the development of Marxist and anti-Marxist thought from the turn of the century to the 1960s.

Marx's 'Paris Manuscripts' of 1844, in which the concept of alienation is discussed at length, have attracted considerable attention since the late 1950s. There are English translations by Martin Milligan in *Economic and Philosophic Manuscripts of 1844* (Lawrence & Wishart, International, revised edition 1970); by T. B. Bottomore in *Early Writings* (McGraw-Hill, New York, 1963); by David McLellan in *Early Texts* (Blackwell, Barnes & Noble, 1971); and by Loyd D. Easton and Kurt H. Guddat in *Writings of the Young Marx on Philosophy and Society* (Anchor/Doubleday, Garden City, New York, 1967).

Probably the most difficult of all Marx's works is his 1843 manuscript known as *Critique of Hegel's Philosophy of Right*, which has been edited by Joseph O'Malley (Cambridge University Press, London and New York, 1972). *The Holy Family*, a satirical attack by Marx and Engels on neo-Hegelian philosophers (first published in 1845) is available from Progess, Moscow, 2nd revised edition, 1975. *The German Ideology*, Marx and Engels's manuscript work of 1845–6, is in English in a substantially complete edition (Progress, Moscow, 1972), but the first part has been newly reconstructed and published as *Feuerbach: Opposition of the Materialist and Idealist Outlooks* (Lawrence & Wishart, 1973). Marx's attack on P.-J. Proudhon, *The Poverty of Philosophy* (written in French and first published in 1847), is in English translation from Progress, Moscow (1976).

The Communist Manifesto by Marx and Engels is available from Monthly Review, New York (1968), and from Penguin, Harmondsworth and Baltimore (1969) with an introduction by A. J. P. Taylor. The classic edition by David Ryazanov (also transliterated as Riazanov, Ryazanoff, Rjazanov, and other variants), the first scholarly editor of the works of Marx and Engels, was published in English in 1936 and has been reprinted by Russell/Atheneum, New York (1963). Another influential edition is that of Harold Laski, now reprinted by Seabury, New York (1975), with an introduction by T. B. Bottomore. D. J. Struik's *The Birth of the Communist Manifesto* (International, New York,

1971) includes supplementary documents of the period 1847–8, as well as the basic text. Marx's articles *Wage-labour and Capital*, written for German-speaking workers during these revolutionary years, were subsequently edited by Engels and then published in English translation (Progress, Moscow, 1970).

What Marx called his 'general introduction' to a critique of political economy, written in rough draft in 1857 in the same series of notebooks as the *Grundrisse*, contains interesting remarks on method (Marx's own and the methods of political economists) and a discussion of aesthetics and the history of art. This text appears in David Horowitz (ed.), *Marx and Modern Economics* (MacGibbon & Kee, 1968); in a volume of selections from *The German Ideology*, edited with an introduction by C. J. Arthur (Lawrence & Wishart, 1976; International, 1970); in an English translation of Marx's published work of 1859, *A Contribution to the Critique of Political Economy*, translated by S. W. Ryazanskaya (Lawrence & Wishart, International, 1971); in *Marx's Grundrisse*, a volume of selections edited by David McLellan (2nd edition, Paladin, 1973; Harper Torchbooks, 1972); and in Karl Marx, *Texts on Method*, translated by Terrell Carver (Blackwell, Barnes & Noble, 1975), which includes a commentary on the text. *Pre-capitalist Economic Formations,* edited by E. J. Hobsbawm (Lawrence & Wishart, 1964; International, 1965) represents a self-contained section of the *Grundrisse* in which the materialist interpretation of history is applied by Marx himself.

The order of composition of the volumes of Marx's master-work *Capital: A Critique of Political Economy* differs from the numerical order of the published volumes, and is as follows. The intended fourth volume was reconstructed by Karl Kautsky from manuscripts of 1861–3 and published in three parts as *Theories of Surplus Value* (Lawrence & Wishart, 1964, 1969, 1975). The third volume was edited by Engels from manuscripts written (for the most part) between 1864 and 1865 and is available from Lawrence & Wishart (1972) and International (1967). The first volume was the next to be written and was seen through three German editions and a French translation by Marx himself. The English translation by Samuel Moore and Edward Aveling (Marx's son-in-law) was prepared from the third edition and is available from Allen & Unwin (1971). The fourth German edition, with additions and editorial changes by Engels, was the basis for the English-language version published by Lawrence & Wishart (1974), and International (1967); this edition was also used for the

Marx Library volume previously mentioned. The second volume of *Capital*, the last to be written, was reconstructed by Engels from Marx's manuscripts of 1867–79, and is also published in English by Lawrence & Wishart (1971) and International (1967). Marx's lectures *Value, Price and Profit* (also known as *Wages, Price and Profit*), written in 1867 for English-speaking workers, were edited by his daughter Eleanor Marx Aveling and published in 1898; there is a reprint from International (1969).

The *Civil War in France* by Marx appears in several centennial editions: *On the Paris Commune* (Lawrence & Wishart, 1971); *Writings of Marx and Engels on the Paris Commune*, edited by Hal Draper (Monthly Review, New York, 1972); and *The Paris Commune 1871*, edited by Christopher Hitchens (Sidgwick & Jackson, 1971).

The last recorded critical work by Marx on political economy, the *Notes on Adolph Wagner* of 1879–80, is included in *Texts on Method*, mentioned above, and in *Value: Studies by Karl Marx* (New Park, 1976). Marx's *Ethnological Notebooks* of 1880–1 have been edited by Lawrence Krader (Humanities, New York, 1972).

Certain short works by Marx and extracts from his writings are of particular interest to students of political philosophy, sociology, and economics. The most useful recent collections are: *Selected Writings in Sociology and Social Philosophy*, edited by T. B. Bottomore and Maximilien Rubel (Penguin, 1970; McGraw-Hill, 1964); *Basic Writings on Politics and Philosophy*, edited by Lewis S. Feuer (Fontana, Peter Smith, 1969); *Karl Marx on Society and Social Change*, edited by Neil J. Smelser (University of Chicago Press, London and Chicago, 1974); *Karl Marx on Economy, Class and Social Revolution*, edited by Z. A. Jordan (Nelson, 1972; Scribner, 1975); *The Economics of Marx*, edited by M. C. Howard and J. E. King (Penguin, 1976); *Marx on Economics*, edited by Robert Freedman (Penguin, 1971); *The Marx-Engels Reader*, edited by Robert C. Tucker (Norton, New York, 1972); *The Essential Writings*, edited by F. L. Bender (Peter Smith, Magnolia, Massachusetts, 1973); *Marx in his own Words*, edited by Ernst Fischer and Franz Marek (Penguin, 1973; published in the U.S.A. as *The Essential Marx* by Herder & Herder, New York, 1970); *Selected Essays*, edited by Henry Stenning (Essay Index Reprint, Plainview, New York, 1968).

The Karl Marx Library, edited by Saul K. Padover and published (beginning in 1972) by McGraw-Hill, New York, contains essays and extracts topically arranged: *On Revolution*, *On America*

and the Civil War, *On the First International*, *On Freedom of the Press
and Censorship*, *On Religion: Christianity, Judaism, and Jews*, and
On Education, Women and Children have so far appeared.

Other topical collections of Marx's writings include: *On
Colonialism and Modernization*, edited by Shlomo Avineri
(Anchor/Doubleday, Garden City, New York, 1969); *On Col-
onialism* (International, New York, 1972); *On Ireland: Ireland and
the Irish Question* (Lawrence & Wishart, 1971; International, 1972);
On China (Lawrence & Wishart, 1968); *The First Indian War of
Independence* (Progress, Moscow, 1968); *The Eastern Question*,
edited by Edward Aveling and Eleanor Marx Aveling (Frank
Cass, 1970; A. M. Kelley, 1974); *Revolution in Spain* (Greenwood,
Westport, Connecticut, 1975); *Articles on Britain* (Lawrence &
Wishart, 1971); *The Russian Menace to Europe*, edited by P. W.
Blackstock and B. F. Hoselitz (Free Press, Glencoe, Illinois, 1952);
The Civil War in the United States (International, New York,
1961); *On the Population Bomb*, edited by R. L. Meek (2nd edition,
Ramparts, Berkeley, California, 1971; formerly published as *On
Malthus*); *The Woman Question* (International, New York, 1970);
Women and Communism (Greenwood, Westport, Connecticut,
1973); *Anarchism and Anarcho-syndicalism* (Lawrence & Wishart,
International, 1972); *On Religion* (Lawrence & Wishart, 1972); *On
Literature and Art*, edited by Lee Baxandall and Stefan Morawski
(Telos, St. Louis, 1974); *On Historical Materialism* (International,
New York, 1975).

There are several interesting collections of Marx's journalism:
The Revolution of 1848–49: Articles from the Neue Rheinische Zeitung
(Lawrence & Wishart, International, 1973); *The Secret Diplomatic
History of the Eighteenth Century and The Story of the Life of Lord
Palmerston*, edited by Lester Hutchinson (Lawrence & Wishart,
International, 1969); *The Cologne Communist Trial*, edited by
Rodney Livingstone (Lawrence & Wishart, 1970).

The most useful collection of letters by Marx and Engels (to
each other and to third parties) is their *Selected Correspondence* (3rd
edition, Progress, Moscow, 1975). Marx's *Letters to Dr Kugelmann*, originally published in English in 1934, has been reprinted
by Greenwood, Westport, Connecticut (1973). *Letters to Ameri-
cans* by Marx and Engels is published by International, New York
(1969).

The major works of Friedrich Engels are available in English
translation. Two early works, the usefulness of which Marx
explicitly acknowledged, were the 1844 'Outlines of a Critique of

Political Economy', published in English as an appendix to Struik's translation of Marx's '1844 Manuscripts' mentioned above, and in *Engels: Selected Writings*, edited by W. O. Henderson (Penguin, Harmondsworth and Baltimore, 1967). Engels's first book, published in 1845, appears in English as *The Condition of the Working Class in England*, edited by W. O. Henderson and W. H. Chaloner (Blackwell, 1971; Stanford University Press, 1968). There are other editions from Panther (1969) and Lawrence & Wishart (1973). 'The Peasant War in Germany' and 'Germany: Revolution and Counter-revolution' (formerly attributed to Marx) appear in the *The German Revolutions*, edited by Leonard Krieger (Chicago University Press, London and Chicago, 1968).

Engels's two most substantial contributions to Marxist theory date from the period 1876–86. *Anti-Dühring* (usually subtitled 'Herr Eugen Dühring's Revolution in Science', a translation of the original title) is published by Progress, Moscow (1969), as is the posthumously edited *Dialectics of Nature*, translated by Clemens Dutt (1972). Three chapters of *Anti-Dühring* make up *Socialism: Utopian and Scientific*; that work, and *The Origin of the Family, Private Property and the State* (first published in 1884) and the 1886 *Ludwig Feuerbach and the End of Classical German Philosophy* appear in the *Selected Works* of Marx and Engels already mentioned. *The Role of Force in History: A Study of Bismarck's Policy of Blood and Iron* (drawn, in part, from *Anti-Dühring*) has been edited by Ernst Wangermann and published by Lawrence & Wishart and International (1968).

BIOGRAPHY AND REMINISCENCE

The most comprehensive biography of Marx is *Karl Marx: His Life and Thought* by David McLellan (Paladin, 1976; Harper & Row, 1974). Maximilien Rubel and Margaret Manale have written the informative *Marx Without Myth: A Chronological Study of his Life and Work* (Blackwell, Harper & Row, 1975). *Karl Marx: Man and Fighter*, by Boris Nicolaievsky and Otto Maenchen-Helfen (revised edition, Penguin, 1976) is especially good on Marx's political activities, as was Franz Mehring's *Karl Marx* (London, 1951; New York, 1935; out of print). Werner Blumenberg's *Karl Marx* (New Left, 1972) is a useful short biography. David Riazanov's *Karl Marx and Frederick Engels* has been reissued by Monthly Review, London and New York (1974), and an

English translation of Achille Loria's *Karl Marx* has recently been reprinted by Gordon, New York (1976).

Karl Marx: Biographical Memoirs by Wilhelm Liebknecht has been reprinted (Journeyman, 1975); and recollections of Marx and Engels by their friends and acquaintances can be found in *Reminiscences of Marx and Engels* from Progress of Moscow. *When Karl Marx Died*, edited by Philip S. Foner (International, New York, 1973), is a collection of contemporary panegyrics.

The most recent life of Engels is W. O. Henderson's two-volume *Friedrich Engels* (Frank Cass, 1976). Gustav Mayer's *Friedrich Engels: A Biography* is in English in an abridged version (H. Fertig, New York, 1969).

Marx's daughter Eleanor has been the subject of several biographies, among them Yvonne Kapp's *Eleanor Marx*, vol. 1: *Family Life 1855–83* (Lawrence & Wishart, 1972; International, 1973), vol. 2: *The Crowded Years 1884–98* (Lawrence & Wishart, 1976); and C. Tsuzuki's less detailed *The Life of Eleanor Marx 1855–98: A Socialist Tragedy* (Oxford University Press, London and New York, 1967).

CRITICAL STUDIES

There is an immense literature on Marx and Marxism, much of it interesting for what is revealed about the authors rather than the subject. The terms of debate about Marx have changed since the late 1950s; new texts, translations, and a critical reassessment have revealed that the Marx discussed by many well-known writers (both Marxist and anti-Marxist) was a figure quite unlike the original. For a list of works about Marx which includes many now out of print, see the bibliography in David McLellan's recent life, mentioned above.

The most prolific commentator on the early Marx has been David McLellan, whose *The Young Hegelians and Karl Marx* (Macmillan, Praeger, 1969) and *Marx Before Marxism* (Macmillan, Harper & Row, 1970) are standard works. The most useful textbook on Marx is McLellan's *The Thought of Karl Marx: An Introduction* (Macmillan, 1971; Harper & Row, 1974), since it combines selected texts with biography, commentary, and bibliography. McLellan's *Marx*, in the Modern Masters series (Fontana, Viking, 1975), provides a brief account of Marx's life, thought, and reputation.

The pioneering work of modern research on Marx is Shlomo Avineri's *The Social and Political Thought of Karl Marx* (Cambridge University Press, London and New York, 1970). *Karl Marx*, by Michael Evans (Allen & Unwin, Indiana University Press, 1975) provides an introduction to Marx's life and writings, with critical comment.

A study of the relationship between Marx's political ideas and his own political activities has been undertaken by Richard N. Hunt in *The Political Ideas of Marx and Engels*, vol. 1: *Marxism and Totalitarian Democracy 1818–1850* (Macmillan, 1975; University of Pittsburgh Press, 1974). Other studies include Hal Draper, *Karl Marx's Theory of Revolution*, part 1: *State and Bureaucracy* (Monthly Review, London and New York, 1977); John Sanderson, *An Interpretation of the Political Ideas of Marx and Engels* (Longmans, 1969); Henry Collins and Chimen Abramsky, *Karl Marx and the British Labour Movement* (new edition, Macmillan, 1975); Oscar J. Hammen, *The Red 48ers: Karl Marx and Friedrich Engels* (Scribner, New York, 1969); and a collection of essays edited by Shlomo Avineri, *Marx's Socialism* (Lieber–Atherton, New York, 1973).

There is much of interest in the philosophical studies of Marx's thought by Alfred Schmidt, *The Concept of Nature in Marx*, translated by Ben Fowkes (New Left, 1971; Humanities, 1972); István Mészáros, *Marx's Theory of Alienation* (Merlin, 1970; Harper & Row, 1972); Bertell Ollman, *Alienation: Marx's Conception of Man in Capitalist Society* (2nd edition, Cambridge University Press, London and New York, 1977); John Maguire, *Marx's Paris Writings: An Analysis*, with an introduction by David McLellan (Gill & Macmillan, 1972; Barnes & Noble, 1973); John Plamenatz, *Karl Marx's Philosophy of Man* (Clarendon Press, 1975); and Adolfo Sanchez Vazquez, *The Philosophy of Praxis* (Merlin, Humanities, 1977).

Three classic studies are those by G. V. Plekhanov, *Fundamental Problems of Marxism* (Lawrence & Wishart, International, 1969); George Lukács, *History and Class Consciousness*, translated by Rodney Livingstone (Merlin, M.I.T. Press, 1971), and Herbert Marcuse, *Reason and Revolution* (Routledge & Kegan Paul, 1968).

Other philosophical studies include Ernest Mandel and George Novack, *The Marxist Theory of Alienation* (2nd edition, Pathfinder, New York, 1973); Richard Schacht, *Alienation* (Allen & Unwin, 1971; Doubleday, 1970); Sebastiano Timpanaro, *On Materialism* (New Left, 1975); Agnes Heller, *The Theory of Need in Marx* (Allison & Busby, 1976); James J. O'Rourke, *The Problem of*

Freedom in Marxist Thought (D. Reidel, Dordrecht and Boston, 1974); Graeme Duncan, *Marx and Mill* (Cambridge University Press, London and New York, 1973); Dick Howard, *The Development of the Marxian Dialectic* (Southern Illinois University Press, Carbondale, Illinois, 1972); Lucio Colletti, *From Rousseau to Lenin: Studies in Ideology and Society* (New Left, 1972); Sidney Hook, *Revolution, Reform and Social Justice* (Blackwell, 1977; New York University Press, 1975); William Leon McBride, *The Philosophy of Marx* (Hutchinson, 1977); Karl Korsch, *Marxism and Philosophy* (New Left, 1972); A. R. Manser, *The End of Philosophy: Marx and Wittgenstein* (Southampton University, 1973); Arend Theodor van Leeuwen, *Critique of Heaven* (Lutterworth, 1972), and *Critique of Earth* (Lutterworth, Scribner, 1975); and a collection of essays published by the International Social Science Council: *Marx and Contemporary Scientific Thought* (Humanities, New York, 1970). Now out of print, but still of interest, are Auguste Cornu, *The Origins of Marxian Thought* (Springfield, Illinois, 1957), and Eugene Kamenka's *The Ethical Foundations of Marxism* (2nd edition, London and Boston, 1972).

Pre-eminent among commentators who have discussed Marx's works and their relationship to the Marxist tradition is George Lichtheim. His *Marxism: An Historical and Critical Study* (2nd edition, Routledge & Kegan Paul, 1968; Praeger, 1965) is still very valuable. Some of his essays are collected in *From Marx to Hegel* (Orbach & Chambers, 1971; Seabury, 1974). Other interesting studies of Marx and Marxism are *Revisionism*, edited by Leo Labedz (Essay Index Reprint, Plainview, New York, 1974); *Marx and the Western World*, edited by Nicholas Lobkowicz (University of Notre Dame Press, Notre Dame, Indiana, 1970); Iring Fetscher, *Marx and Marxism* (Herder & Herder, New York, 1971); Mihailo Marković, *The Contemporary Marx* (Spokesman, 1974); Umberto Melotti, *Marx and the Third World* (Macmillan, 1977); and Perry Anderson, *Considerations on Western Marxism* (New Left, 1976). Leszek Kolakowski's *Marxism and Beyond* (London, 1969) is unfortunately out of print.

Karl Marx, a collection of essays edited by T. B. Bottomore (Prentice-Hall, Engelwood Cliffs, New Jersey, 1973) takes up sociological aspects of Marx's work, as does Alan Swingewood's *Marx and Modern Social Theory* (Macmillan, Wiley, 1975), and Anthony Giddens's *Capitalism and Modern Social Theory* (Cambridge University Press, London and New York, 1973). Marx's contributions to anthropology and ethnology are discussed in Emmanuel Terray, *Marxism and 'Primitive' Societies* (Monthly Review, London and New York, 1972); his work on imperialism in V. G. Kiernan, *Marxism and Imperialism* (Edward Arnold, 1974); and his views on the peasantry in David Mitrany, *Marx Against the Peasant* (London and Chapel Hill, North Carolina, 1951, out of print).

Karl Marx and World Literature by S. S. Prawer (Oxford University Press, London and New York, 1976) examines Marx's use of literary materials. Terry Eagleton's *Marxism and Literary Criticism* (Methuen, 1976) treats the subject in brief.

Ben Fine has written a short, clear introduction to Marx's economic writings: *Marx's Capital* (Macmillan, 1975). *From Alienation to Surplus Value* by Andrew Gamble and Paul Walton (Sheed & Ward, 1972) and *The Political Economy of Marx* by M. C. Howard and J. E. King (Longman, 1975) are useful introductory works. Other recent studies of Marx's economic thought include: Maurice Dobb, *Marx as an Economist* (Lawrence & Wishart, 1975); Ronald L. Meek, *Studies in the Labour Theory of Value* (2nd edition, Monthly Review, New York, 1975); Paul Mattick, *Marx and Keynes* (Merlin, 1971; P. Sargent, 1969); Murray Wolfson, *Karl Marx* (Columbia University Press, London and New York, 1971); Paul C. Roberts and Matthew A. Stephenson, *Marx's Theory of Exchange, Alienation and Crisis* (Hoover Institution, Stanford, California, 1973); Michio Morishima, *Marx's Economics* (Cambridge University Press, London and New York, 1973); Pat Sloan, *Marx and the Orthodox Economists* (Blackwell, Rowman & Littlefield, 1973); Suzanne de Brunhoff, *Marx on Money* (Urizen, New York, 1976); and Paul Walton and Stuart Hall (eds.), *Situating Marx* (Chaucer, 1972).

Ernest Mandel's treatment of Marxian economics is expounded in his *Marxist Economic Theory* (Merlin, Monthly Review, 1972); *Introduction to Marxist Economic Theory* (2nd edition, Pathfinder, New York, 1973); *The Formation of the Economic Thought of Karl Marx* (Monthly Review, New York, 1971); *The Economic and Social Thought of Karl Marx* (New Left, 1971); and *Late Capitalism* (New Left, 1976).

A classic critique of Marxian economic theory has recently been reprinted: Eugen von Böhm-Bawerk, *Karl Marx and the Close of his System*. This edition includes Rudolf Hilferding's reply, and an article by Ladislaus von Bortkiewicz on the transformation of value into prices (A. M. Kelley, Clifton, New Jersey, 1973).

The works of Louis Althusser have become an object of study

in their own right, reflecting the fact that he has, for better or worse, left Marx well behind in his thinking. His essays and articles have been translated by Ben Brewster and collected in *For Marx* (Allen Lane, Random House, 1970); *Reading Capital* (New Left, 1970); and *Politics and History: Montesquieu, Rousseau, Hegel and Marx* (New Left, 1972). *Althusser's Marxism* by Alex Callinicos (Pluto, Urizen, 1976) is a recent critical study.

The only full-length study of the differences between Marx and Engels is Norman Levine's *The Tragic Deception: Marx contra Engels* (Clio, Oxford and Santa Barbara, California, 1975). David McLellan published in 1977 *Engels* for the Modern Masters series (Fontana, Viking). *Engels, Manchester and the Working Class* by Steven Marcus (Weidenfeld & Nicolson, 1974; Vintage, 1975) is a study of Engels's masterpiece.

SCHOLARLY EDITIONS, BIBLIOGRAPHIES, AND JOURNALS

The first attempt at a complete scholarly edition of the works of Marx and Engels in original languages (primarily German, French, and English) was left unfinished in the mid-1930s: Karl Marx, Friedrich Engels, *Gesamtausgabe*, edited by D. Rjazanov and V. Adoratskij (Frankfurt, Berlin, Moscow and Leningrad, 1927–35). This edition is usually known as MEGA, and a total of thirteen volumes were published. There is a reprint from Detlev Auvermann, Glashütten im Taunus (1970).

A considerable amount of manuscript material by Marx and Engels was first published in the *Marx-Engels-Archiv*, edited by D. Rjazanov (Frankfurt, 1925–7), and in Russian translation in the *Arkhiv K. Marksa i F. Engel'sa*, published in Moscow and Leningrad (5 vols., 1924–30), now reprinted by Kraus of Nendeln, Liechtenstein (1969). After Ryazanov's death in a Soviet camp, the series continued from 1933 as the *Arkhiv Marksa i Engel'sa* (5 vols.). Shorter extracts appeared in another periodical, also under Ryazanov's editorship: *Letopisi Marksizma* (Moscow and Leningrad, 13 nos, 1926–30).

The German-language edition of the works of Marx and Engels, begun in 1956, is now complete, though it fulfils a function different from that envisaged by the editors of MEGA. The Karl Marx, Friedrich Engels, *Werke* (Dietz, [East] Berlin), usually known as MEW, includes only a selection of manuscript materials, omits many textual variants, and translates French and English works into German. There are thirty-nine numbered volumes, two supplementary volumes, and a two-volume index. A finding list covering various editions of works by Marx and Engels was compiled by Gertrud Hertel: *Inhaltsvergleichsregister der Marx-Engels Gesamtausgaben* (Dietz, [East] Berlin, 1957).

The definitive edition of the complete writings of Marx and Engels (in original languages with textual variants) in approximately 100 volumes began recently with an introductory specimen: Karl Marx, Friedrich Engels, *Gesamtausgabe: Editionsgrundsätze und Probestücke* (Dietz, [East] Berlin, 1972). This new MEGA series will be in four parts, the first part or *Abteilung* to cover works, writings, and articles, with the exception of *Capital* and related manuscripts, which will appear in the second *Abteilung*. The third *Abteilung* contains all correspondence undertaken by Marx and Engels, including relevant letters from third parties; and the fourth *Abteilung* comprises notebooks kept by the two writers, chronological tables compiled by the editors, and apparatus to cover textual variants. A comprehensive index is projected, and it is thought that publication of the series will be completed around the year 2000. The following volumes were published by Dietz Verlag in 1975–6: *Abteilung* I, vol. 1, containing Marx's works to March 1843; *Abteilung* II, vol. 1.1 (i.e. first partial volume), beginning Marx's economic manuscripts of 1857–8; and *Abteilung* III, vol. 1, covering letters of Marx and Engels and their correspondents to April 1846.

The standard bibliography of Marx's writings is Maximilien Rubel's *Bibliographie des oeuvres de Karl Marx avec en appendice un répertoire des oeuvres de Friedrich Engels* (Rivière, Paris, 1956), with a *Supplément* (1960). The introductions and notes to Rubel's selection of Marx's writings, translated into French, are of the same high standard as the *Bibliographie*. Two volumes have appeared: Karl Marx, *Oeuvres: Économie* (Gallimard, Paris, 1963, 1968). Two specialist bibliographies of literature on Marx and Marxism might be useful: J. Lachs, *Marxist Philosophy: A Bibliographical Guide* (University of North Carolina Press, Chapel Hill, North Carolina, 1967), and a Russian-language guide to bibliographical works: L. A. Levin, *K. Marks, F. Engel's, V. I. Lenin, Ukazatel' bibliograficheskikh rabot 1961–72*, published in Moscow in 1973. The International Institute of Social History, Amsterdam, has published an *Inventar des Marx-Engels-Nachlasses*, and the Marx Memorial Library, London, began publication of its catalogue in 1971.

The chronology of Marx's life published in German in 1934 in Moscow is now reprinted: *Karl Marx: Chronik seines Lebens in Einzeldaten* (Makol, Frankfurt, A. M. Kelley, Clifton, New Jersey, 1971). Another chronology, compiled by Maximilien Rubel, has been published in German as *Marx-Chronik: Daten zu Leben und Werk* (Hanser, Munich, 1968). The fate of the libraries of Marx and Engels is traced in Bruno Kaiser (ed.), *Ex Libris Karl Marx und Friedrich Engels: Schicksal und Verzeichnis einer Bibliothek* (Dietz, [East] Berlin, 1967).

A number of scholarly journals have published articles and special numbers on Marx; these include: *American Economic Review, Bulletin of the Conference of Socialist Economists, Critique, Economy and Society, Encounter, History of Political Economy, Ideology and Consciousness, Inquiry, International Review of Social History, Journal of Economic Literature, Journal of Political Economy, Journal of Politics, Journal of the History of Ideas, New German Critique, New Left Review, New Literary History, New Politics, Philosophy and Public Affairs, Political Studies, Political Theory, Politics and Society, Praxis, Review of Economic Studies, Review of Politics, Socialist Register, Studies in Comparative Communism, Studies on the Left, Telos, Theoretical Practice*; in French: *Cahiers internationaux de sociologie, Études de Marxologie, L'Homme et la société, Le Mouvement social, Revue d'histoire économique et sociale, Revue française de sociologie, Revue socialiste*; in German: *Arbeit und Wirtschaft, Archiv der Sozialgeschichte, Archiv des Sozialismus und der Arbeiterbewegung, Deutsche Zeitschrift für Philosophie, Jahrbücher für Nationalökonomie, Kyklos, Marxismusstudien*.

Index